TIME TO MOVE ON

Structural Recovery from the Global Economic Crisis

Evolution toward the next economic plateau—prolonged sustainable development, prosperity, and civilization for man

Dawn of a new economic model

Virtus—The Value-Based Evolutionary Prosperity Model

A paradigm shift greater than the barter to a currency-based economy

A book for all—those who care about their future

Albert B. Fonluce

Focus on the centrality of man and how you might be able to contribute and make a difference in shaping your:

employment, job creation, generation and growth of opportunities, prospects and business, increase investment possibilities—and in the economy of the 21st century.

Order this book online at www.trafford.com
or email orders@trafford.com

Most Trafford titles are also available at major online book retailers.

Printed in the United States of America.

ISBN: 978-1-4669-7344-2 (sc)
ISBN: 978-1-4669-7343-5 (hc)
ISBN: 978-1-4669-7342-8 (e)

Library of Congress Control Number: 2013903498

Trafford rev. 05/08/2014

 www.trafford.com

North America & international
toll-free: 1 888 232 4444 (USA & Canada)
fax: 812 355 4082

To my wife, Anna Maria.
To our son, Daniele.
To current and future generations.

Disclaimer notice and release of liability

content found in such sources and or their continued availability/accessibility/updating (fully or partially). You agree that the author is not responsible for any content, associated links, resources, or products or services associated with a third parties that may appear on the sources' material or their web sites or any additional recommended reading—nor a solicitation to use these in any way. You further agree that the author is not and shall not be liable for any loss or damage of any sort associated with your use of this or third party content. Any eventual links and access to web sites are provided to credit the source and for the readers sole convenience only. The Author does not necessarily own each component of the content included in the book. The author therefore does not warrant that the use of the content contained in the work will not infringe on the rights of third parties. The risk of claims resulting from such infringement rests solely with you.

The findings, interpretations, and conclusions expressed in this book do not necessarily reflect the views of the Author. The Author does not guarantee the accuracy of the data included in this work. The boundaries, colors, denominations, and other information shown on any map in this work do not imply any judgment on the part of the Author concerning the legal status of any territory or the endorsement or acceptance of such boundaries. The Author does not suggest, promote, set preference or provide ideological, religious or political views nor the economic models these might represent of any kind shape or form. Any conclusions derived from this work is the sole responsibility of those that arrive at such conclusions.

The author also disassociates himself with and refutes and repudiates any type of thought and or idea in any way shape or form related, associated to or linked with any notion of violence, xenophobic, offensive, diminishing, etc. and in general any other form of hate related, discriminatory, sectarian or segregational, denigratory, extremist, gender cultural or origin related arguments etc. including any ideological thought processes or ideas, opinions, etc. whatsoever of any kind shape or form and/or that may lead to such things.

To the contrary a life lived internationally have made the author extremely sensitive and appreciative of different cultures and to the immense wealth each perspective added to the author—and adds to humanity.

The real intent of this book and the author is to highlight the potential risks the economic crisis and the current unsustainable global imbalances might pose to peace internationally and to provide a possible solution that might allow to step to a higher level of civilization that makes treasure of peace and diversity and promotes healthy and balanced international trade, exchange of ideas and the free movement of persons among nations.

The reader/user also agrees that this book represents a mere introduction to a possible new/evolved set of concepts, notions and perspectives among many others and that it does in no way shape or form suggest this to be the only solution, the best solution or one with all the answers. The reader/user agrees that what is being presented here is at best a baseline framework that if validated and concurred by a pool of experts in all fields necessary and ratified as a possible way forward by any organization, state or government—that this will need to receive the contribution of many before it can be completed rolled-out and implemented.

The author's central concepts, notions, models and opinions have been presented in absolute good faith and that after more than reasonable research, and hence to the authors best knowledge, were genuinely developed by the author. It is understood and agreed also that it is objectively impossible to verify all possible view-points at any given point in time hence any eventual similarities are to be considered solely and purely coincidental and in anyway only an additional perspective and opinion and hence the author does not accept any eventual claims or liability for this.

The author's hope through this work is to add a further perspective an infinitesimally small contribution to how we might wish to change ourselves and maybe through small pragmatic steps contribute to rendering the world a better place to live for as many as possible independent of citizenry.

CONTENTS

PART 1:
Structural and Systemic Blocks, Dichotomies,
New Variables, and Paradigms

PART 2:
A Possible Solution

ACKNOWLEDGMENTS

This work would have not been possible had it not been for the continued and sustained trust and motivation I received from my wife, Anna Maria, and our son, Daniele, throughout the development of this book and the many difficult moments.

Sincere gratitude to my parents, who gave me the opportunity to travel and see the world and develop an appreciation for different cultures, perspectives, windows on reality, and viewpoints. And to my sister Desirèe for her support.

Many thanks also go to the valuable contribution of the thousands of professionals internationally behind the studies, research papers, reports, data, databases, blogs, websites, and textbooks that were referenced in this book, especially to those behind the scenes.

To the valuable publicly available information provided transparently by agencies of the US government, international organizations such as the UN, the World Bank, IMF, and the European Central Bank, the many international news and information providers around the world, and the professional men and women who contributed to these but whose names might not appear in these works.

To be earnest I must also include the many teachers, professors, mentors, colleagues, and friends. This includes all those whom I was lucky to encounter, even for a brief moment, during the twenty-seven international relocations in my personal journey through this amazing experience called life. Each added personal and intellectual wealth.

THE PROBLEM

Loss of: source(s) of income, employment and jobs, business, prospects for the young, hard-earned investments and wealth, market value, pension, . . . retirement, and consequentially health, well-being, and peace of mind and ultimately loss of independence and need for dependence on others.

An economic model that might no longer be able to provide answers.

For how long can we allow this to bring this dissolution to a growing number of societies, economies, businesses, families, and individuals around the world?

Modern-day man and the economy have reached a pivotal moment in evolution: the next step-level advancement toward a new level of civilization and economic development.

THE OPPORTUNITY

No one has the right to inhibit the realization of dreams be it those of an individual or of billions of persons. The young must have the chance to realize their dreams, ambitions and future. The middle-aged have the right to finalize and crown their endeavors, honor their responsibilities to their families, and allow their children to continue their voyage toward adulthood. The young at heart among us have the right to finally reap the rewards of their hard-earned accomplishments in relative peace and serenity, allowing them to leave an honorable legacy of their life achievements.

No dream, person, enterprise, business, or employment should be sacrificed to the altar of man-made models that might have reached their maximum potential and can no longer provide answers and can be changed and allowed to evolve.

As a species that has gone to the moon and Mars, reaching the outmost corners of our solar system, and delved into the smallest particles of matter, Lord willing, we can achieve any feat. We have an obligation to make things better. An opportunity awaits us.

At the dawn of the twenty-first century—notwithstanding the unprecedented levels of advancement humanity has achieved so far —in a moment of rapidly changing paradigms (standards, models, prototypes, theories), dimensions, many new challenges, and variables (natural and man-made) in different domains of our lives, we are on the verge of either making the biggest leap in our evolution, opening an era of unprecedented opportunities and long-term prosperity, undertaking a step-level ascent toward a new plateau of a more evolved society and civilization and greater scientific and spiritual enlightenment, or potentially affronting multiple structural, systemic, and economic meltdowns of unfathomable consequences.

The global financial and economic crisis, the accelerated depletion of natural and energetic resources, population growth and mass immigration, rising levels of poverty, and exposure to seemingly more frequent geological and natural events of extraordinary destructive scales represent only a few of the trials we face and not necessarily the ones posing the most immediate and proximate threat to our evolution and continued survival as a species.

We live in a time of unprecedented turmoil and uncertainty, business closures, joblessness, and unemployment. We are potentially on the brink of defaulting economic systems and nations, escalating social unrest, etc.

This is happening at a time that seemingly had to come; a time that is exerting extreme hardships on a growing numbers of persons and other concerns; a time when existing models no longer seem to provide answers; a time of great irresolvable systemic paradoxes (inconsistencies, impossibilities, absurdities), blocks, and dichotomies (irreconcilable differences and contradictions e.g.: increasing taxes while sources of income disappear); and a time that demands evolution toward something that can provide lasting solutions.

Many man-made shackles and chains, convictions, restraints, preconceptions, and economic dogmas are impeding humanity in finding new ways of accomplishing greater endeavors, addressing new challenges, affronting countless new possibilities, and opening roads toward new frontiers.

The ability to evolve our economy, lives, and societies is quintessential to prolonged survival, success, and prosperity. This ability allows us to open new perspectives and be able to tap into opportunities that will otherwise remain invisible, uneconomical, improbable, impractical, and/or unimaginable under the existing model.

Consenting to the achievement of aspirations both as individuals and a society, finally going beyond the obvious, sets the stage for increased potential for optimism, confidence, hope, opportunity, and development.

A better future is possibly within our reach. It is up to us to seize the moment. It is up to us to evolve to a new level (plateau) of advancement, development, and civilization.

Do we—as adults and a society of free men and women from every walk of life, world leaders of policy, economy, business, and enterprise—wish to take on the challenge of leading the opening of a new era and taking responsibility for its design, development, and steering?

THE PARADOX

- Overextension of Resources;
- Shift of Economic Focus and Gravitas of Economy Toward the East;
- Increased Hoarding of Liquidity, Precious Minerals, etc.;
- Decreasing Capability in Developing Local Economies;
- Increasing Unemployment and Debt;
- Decreasing Sources of Income and Remuneration and Means of Sustenance;
- Extraordinary Implementation of Severe Austerity Measures in Different Regions;
- Increased Tax and Fiscal Pressures;
- Vortex of Business Closures;
- Decreased Availability of Liquidity, Credit, and Financing;
- Increasing Defaults;
- Increased Risk from Ideological-, Desperation-, or Famine-Led Disorders, Social Unrest, and Extremist Actions and Terrorism;
- Faulting Leadership in Absence of True Answers.

The above seem to be news headlines from recent TV and network news agencies, heated political debates, newspaper or magazine articles, websites, or simply those that spur our day-to-day discussions among colleagues, business partners, government leaders, and so on.

In reality, these "headlines" are incredibly similar to those elements that are said to have contributed to the fall, decline, or transformation of entire states, countries, governments and empires such as the Roman Empire (Greer & et al). They are reminiscent of scenarios that all too often have repeated themselves throughout history. These are also the types of headlines one would have read prior to the Great Depression and First and Second World Wars.

The contribution of each element or a different combination of these as causes of the demise of entire economic systems and civilizations is still a much debated subject among economists, scholars, and historians. But this is not the main issue, is it?

The main issue is that we are facing an economic crisis, one of formidable and immeasurable dimensions, that touches our lives. What we are going to do about it, how we are going to resolve it, in what time frames, and at what opportunity, cost, etc.—these are some of the more impelling questions that need urgent answers.

DEVELOPMENT OF
AN ECONOMY

In the absence of viable solutions, one needs to find new alternatives.

Simplifying any economic paradigm down to its most essential elements, one could generically venture to state that civilizations, countries, states, and their economies evolve and prosper when they experience economic development.

If there is no economic development or a diminution of it,

- the amount of business decreases;
- the amount of money in circulation decreases;
- the propensity toward risk taking in the real economy decreases;
- the amount of investments, credit, and financing decreases;
- the level of employment decreases;
- sources of income and sustenance decrease;
- capital, investments, and new ideas move elsewhere (where they have better chances of recompense, return, and reward);
- the level of personal, business, and government debt increases; and
- the number of austerity measures and their pressure increase.

By the same token,

- innovation capability is hindered and curtailed;
- competitiveness decreases;

- the number of business closures, bankruptcies, and sell-offs increases;
- the amount of technology, technical capability, and know-how transfer increases;
- the amount of poverty increases;
- the exposure to social unrest increases; and
- the exposure to conflict and war-based economic recovery models increases.

Ultimately, the amount of dependency on others increases.

Inexorably continuing down this path without developing an economy and creating an appeal for what it produces, your wealth as an individual, a business, a society, an economy, a nation, or a union of nations ultimately migrates toward those that develop their economies.

If others don't perceive a value added or a value proposition in what you produce and offer, they won't need to buy from you any longer. You will eventually be drained of what once constituted your leadership, resilience, and wealth.

But worst is that you might relinquish your freedom, your independence, and your way of life to those that will fill that gap, first in a suggestive modality but ultimately simply enforced.

However, is this just limited to a specific echelon or sectors of the economy (i.e., brick and mortar)? To one or more classes of society? Or could it be inherent in a more generalized scenario?

There are some, for example, that believe the solution is in financial markets, the banking industry, or strategies such as amassment, hoarding of scarce resources (i.e., gold), leveraging virtual enhancers (which will be discussed later), provoking (consciously or unconsciously) among other things scarcity in credit and liquidity, inducing price increases and speculative roller-coaster market conditions.

Historical reality and data though suggest that—at least for the majority of those that elect this stratagem—they might wish to reconsider. In the medium term, this strategy at best is functional for a limited few. Just as the nascent earth and the planets came about, attracting smaller masses of material around their growing cores, financial gravitational pull inevitably attracts smaller elements toward bigger cores.

Additional unassuming paradoxes or simply unpredictable variables could also potentially hinder or nullify the primary objectives these solutions were intended to deliver. In the example of the rush for the accumulation of gold, those wishing to pursue this strategy might wish to look at a very well-designed presentation on the US Department of Treasury website that brilliantly discloses the number of times gold hoarding was stopped by government decree and its effects nullified by simple legislation enactment, catching most off guard. The last time this sort of legislation was enacted was not too far off. We are talking about the pre-World War II period and, to some extent, the years leading up to the Nixon presidency (US Department of Treasury).

In the long run, any sustained and prolonged financial success is also dependent on the general well-being of an economy as a whole.

The development of a healthy economy is key to improving society, enhancing advancement, *prosperity*, relative *tranquility, security,* and *peace; secure the blessings of liberty* to living generations and *toward posterity, to the safekeeping of unalienable rights, such as life, freedom and the pursuit of happiness, and the exercise of democracy.* In italics are excerpts taken from the United Nations Universal Declaration of

Human Rights and the Declaration of Independence of the United States. These are not very dissimilar in their fundamental essence to the majority of modern constitutions of many nations around the world. What our forefathers had envisioned as the fundamental elements of human evolution and civilization still holds true.

Welcome to the twenty-first century! To our moment in history! The chapter our living generations will ultimately write! To the legacy we create for ourselves and will leave for our prosperity! The definition of choices is simple: Do we wish to indulge or abandon ourselves to self-defeat, or do we wish to show resilience and take action? Should we wish to do so, we just might be able to contribute to shaping a better future in shorter time frames without sacrificing more. Evolution is taking us there; it depends on whether we want to be proactive participants in leading it.

THE GAME

Anyone who has played the game of Monopoly or other similar board games knows all too well that at the end of "n" iterations of the game, one player takes over everything. This occurs in a situation where all players begin with the same amount of Monopoly money, with no one owning any property, streets, hotels, etc. With only one winner left, continuing the game becomes impossible—not only for those who have lost all their belongings but also for the winner, since there is no one left with whom to play.

Contenders at the table face the following options: 1) agree to start the same game all over, 2) start a completely different game, or 3) simply call it quits and walk away. The eagerness to play repeatedly is directly linked to a fair possibility of winning for all players.

After a while, independent of one's favorite game, any game becomes stale, and the degree to which it becomes stale is linked to its ability to provide new chances, prospects, and challenges to players.

If you add to this scenario another level of complexity—one where external events and conditions no longer enable the game to be played with the original rules and conditions—that game is bound to fail. Independent of the strategy for which the above players opt, at the end of the day the game will never be the same game.

Whatever is decided next implies an evolution from the status quo. Put into the context of today's economic environment, we are potentially at the nth iteration, only a few rounds from reaching the semifinals. Each elimination round though translates in a mounting number of businesses, enterprises, investment concerns, professionals, and individuals that fall out of the economic cycle. How far out and deep we wish to take this depends on each one of us.

CHALLENGES AND DILEMMAS

What is happening to our investments, businesses, enterprises, corporations, trade, and opportunities? What is happening to jobs, employment, remuneration possibilities, etc.? What prospects are left to young generations? What happens to their right of realizing their dreams, hopes, and goals? What happens to their natural right to form families and provide them with relative peace of mind and security?

What about those in critical age groups (i.e., forties and fifties) in terms of a family's responsibility? They are too far away from retirement and pensions, and they have increasingly less appeal in the job market.

What is happening to financial markets, banking, our savings, our pensions, and our hard-earned money? How might businesses be transformed? If there are less jobs and less businesses, on what will the economy run? How will people provide for their families and pay their bills?

How will governments address and resolve the growing challenges? Do the currently adopted solutions work? How will the numerous dichotomies and forces that pull in diametrically opposing directions (i.e., debt, unemployment, taxes, competitiveness) be addressed?

Are industrialized and developed countries destined to remain *in bilico* ("in frail balance"), walking on a thin rope in a balancing act between potential defaults and ever-increasing debts? Are they destined to be exposed to financial speculation and/or undeclared conflicts?

Will austerity measures based on dogmatic and theoretical concepts, or self-serving logics, ultimately strangle and suffocate any remaining vital signs of economic activity? Are uncontrolled speculation and austerity going to bring about an economic implosion? Will the developed world become the backyard of emerging nations? Are we sure emerging nations will not face the same crisis or remain immune to the same dilemmas advanced economies are facing in less time than is politically comfortable?

Are jobs, businesses, production, ideas, and human intellect going to move away from the developed nations to other parts of the world? Will those that lose this competitive advantage be able to recuperate in viable time frames. Will new technologies replace everything, close many businesses, and reduce even more jobs?

For how much longer will we allow businesses to vanish under the avalanche effect that stem from reduced possibilities, cause curtailed sales, and weaken margins that avalanche in cash-flow disasters, shedding wasteland and economic and employment destruction along its path only to be followed by increasing fiscal pressures on the few that continue to survive?

Will entire economies implode or the vast majority of the 7 billion souls that inhabit this minuscule and unique planet be destined to mass poverty? Will our societies be preordained to a vortex of degradation? Will we face a new prolonged neo-feudal dark age—an unpromising life in mass crime-infested stenchful slums? Real examples of these growing megacity agglomerations are already visible in many parts of the world. All we has to do is open our eyes.

How will ever-growing numbers of persons, families, and businesses that deal with declining or stagnant revenues or income cope with real price increases and inflation (not the formal inflation data)?

How much longer can this model be allowed to dominate real lives, policies, economic and national prosperity, well-being, and success?

Will the solution to all economic maladies continue to lie only in the same few variables, such as retirement age? Health care? Government spending and taxes? Austerity? The spread? Or the same model? Are these concepts being transformed into a set of "must cope with" maladies and chimeras? Are we in front of a self-consuming paradox?

What will our lives look like if we continue down this path? Have current economic models reached their limits?

Are there any answers for any of the above questions? Is there anything different from the same cures or a different mix of their ingredients? Is the current economic scenario similar to that of a patient who is no longer responding to the plethora of known treatments?

Are we sure we are looking at the problem from all perspectives —the right perspectives—or are we fixated in looking at it from known perspectives?

Is man made for the economy, or should the economy be for the prosperity and well-being of mankind? Have the solutions implemented thus far produced tangible results? How far away are we from a lasting recovery?

FUNDAMENTAL PREMISES

This book has an important set of premises. It is an introductory nonfiction book on the possible solution to the global crisis and an evolved economic model that might help in achieving this goal and beyond. In its current version, this book is intended to acquaint us with the subject matter, making it available to as many as possible. It is written in plain language in an effort to explain complicated economic terminology, matters, jargon, etc., hopefully rendering an otherwise dry subject matter for most in a more appreciable from. To reach this very objective, the book will make substantial use of analogies, similitudes, and references to everyday, readily understandable concepts in explaining the new model and protocol—in general, the possible solution.

The book has nothing to do with a choice between current or historic ideologies—be they between left, center, or right; conservative or liberal; capitalist or communist; anarchic or centralized state control; nor any other "isms" or versions in between that have come and left their mark in history or are currently being adopted.

It is not intended to be politically correct or its inverse but wishes to work as hard as humanly possible with objectivity, trying to see beyond the layers, clutter, and filters of accumulated complexity.

It does not set preferences toward, espouse, choose, promote, or judge different political views or the views of any one of the many economic schools of thought, international agencies, government and nongovernment departments or organizations, or any kind in nature.

It does though start off with the existing market-based economic model, as it is the result of thousands of years of human evolution and the place where we stand today.

It is not meant to validate or antagonize any of the above, perspectives they might represent or persons who live by these or make a living out of them.

It is not about east or west, north or south, or even the middle. Should this book ever be associated with a sense of direction or motion, it would only be that intrinsic with natural evolution and progression—the immediate and long-term future. It is not about controversy, rhetoric, speculation, or conspiracy theories.

It does not in any shape or form wish to covey arrogance in having the answer to it all. Quite differently, it seeks to provide a mere starting point, a baseline model, a framework, a transition and conversion protocol, etc., that will make available a common ground on which economists of different creeds, professionals from various walks of life, academia, business leaders, policy makers, strategists, international organizations, and specialized government agencies can contribute to and finally complete these notions, arriving at a solution through a consensus-driven approach.

It is not about promoting revolution, anarchy, chaos, fundamentalist ideas, wishful thinking, drastic change, about-turns, or elaborate complexity. Any material produced or used herewith has the intent of completing information only and in no way is to be interpreted as a basis for fueling hard feelings, offensiveness, or controversy.

This book seeks to simply take a step back from it all and look at the overall picture, go beyond the existing, the given, the accepted frameworks, paradigms, assumptions, or boxes these have been contained in and used to find a possible solution.

The current economic crisis potentially touches the majority of persons who wake up each morning and need to provide for their families, develop and grow their businesses and investments, make a living, achieve aspirations, go to school to realize their dreams, acquire independence as adults, have the opportunity to set the foundations for their families, improve their lives, generate new ideas, reach challenging new objectives, and procure a future and a deserved retirement—to live their lives.

Hence, in its current version this book cannot be limited to focusing only on quenching the justified nature of demanding, exacting, professional, and intellectual curiosity of a smaller subset of potential readers in one or two fields; it must address the varied needs of a larger audience with expertise in as many other fields as possible.

Led by a very strong intuition about an evolved model, this book is the result of a nearly five-year endeavor in analyzing data from many different authoritative sources, not only to verify the validity of the premises, but also to corroborate the applicability of this possible new model. This book is not about enforcing a single viewpoint but about providing different perspectives, allowing ample room for readers to arrive at their own conclusions.

There is, however, one element to keep in mind throughout the book: all models are the result of human intellect; in other words, they are man-made. As such, all models have a limit, an Achilles' heel—a set of weak points. Though these weak points might differ, there is one trait that seems to be common to most models—namely, their capacity to evolve and adapt to new variables, forces, and challenges. This is one trait that the proposed model seeks to address simply because any model that comes next must be able to evolve at least as rapidly as growing human and natural challenges will be placing on it.

The natural equidistance and/or independence of the solution from existing "isms" will become self-apparent.

COMING OUT OF THE FOG

Each of the known ideologically formed "isms" seem to have come about in a specific historical moment in answer to the stimuli, needs, and requirements existent in that time frame. These thrived for a while, producing the maximum results attainable, and then entered a downward spiral until they were replaced by another more evolved model. Each of these "isms" built their foundation on a set of fundamental truths or assumptions valid for their historic moment; they were implemented within the framework of rules and norms that made them work.

Today we are faced with ever-growing numbers of new paradigms, changing variables, and elements that bear down on existing economic models with new dimensions, exerting tremendous multidimensional and multidirectional strains.

The prolonged crisis and other feats testify that our models have not been devised, geared, or equipped to recognize, identify, elaborate on, and address these new variables properly and effectively. Hence, they substantially fail to address the challenges these pose and provide the necessary answers. The properties and characteristics that constitute new or evolved genomes of these new variables are so different that our models simply fail to recognize them, inhibiting them from being effective. Looking around, it is not hard to perceive that there is a mounting need for answers to the increasing new challenges.

I don't know if there has been a time similar to today, where the fate of so many across the globe is interlinked. With a few exceptions, essential questions and needs seem to coincide on a planetary scale.

It is now time to pose the very tough questions and to seek valid, workable answers that are able to withstand the test of time.

An increasing number of experts in different fields joins the multitude of persons in openly posing fundamental questions, such as: Does the current economic model still provide an effective framework to address mounting challenges? Are we sure the existing models are the only economic models possible? Are there no other alternatives? Is the only perspective from which to look at matters? Is the only way out of the current global crisis through extraordinarily tough (and desperate) austerity policies forced upon millions of people that, while surely developed in good faith, might just not work any longer? Are we sure that an alarmingly swelling number of people across the world need to lose their otherwise healthy and long-standing businesses, investments, enterprises, jobs, employment, opportunities, income, trade, homes, wealth, and pensions and, in the process, their physical, psychological, and emotional well-being?

As we walk along the streets of our towns and cities, we are forced to ask ourselves what is happening to the world around us, to our communities that seemed to function properly literally till not so long ago.

It is not hard to remain flabbergasted when realizing that only four years ago there was an economy made of real needs, real exchanges, real trade, and real jobs. Why is everything closing down? What happened to these real needs? Why are they disappearing? Is there no stopping this? Can't we reverse this onslaught?

In searching for answers that provide us temporary personal relief and peace of mind, our self-survival mechanism activates the logical and rational part of our brains. We articulate a hypothesis, reasoning, for example, that "surely someone is thinking about how to resolve the grave issues at hand." We reassure ourselves that "it will end sooner or later. It must finish. There is too much at stake." In other words, we force ourselves to acknowledge that the answer to these questions is surely one with an outcome that appeals to us.

And then we are hit (again) by the question we fear the most, one that haunts us before we go to sleep, one that we try to push aside in the remotest synapses of our cerebral cortex. Are we sure that our family will be among the few that will remain untouched by the crisis? For how much longer? For how much longer will we be among those that do not make it to the next list of bankrupt investors and entrepreneurs; closing businesses; layoffs; companies that have not won the decreasing numbers of bids; corporations that cannot pay a larger number of their suppliers; companies that need to sell off their technology, innovations, advanced machinery, trademarks, or patents; businesswomen and men who see their investments evaporate; or simply those employees, entrepreneurs, business owners, professionals, economists, policy makers, and politicians who step into oblivion?

I write these lines with the hope, drive, and passion of a father who wishes to see the best for his son and his future; a professional who witnesses current events unfolding before his eyes without being able to contribute, control, or at least effectively voice concerns to make a difference; a person among the 7 billion other inhabitants of this singular planet; and a person who is bewildered at how fast we are going toward possibly the largest precipice mankind has ever faced on a planetary scale and apprehensive as to why no one seems to be able to intervene effectively to turn the car around, stop it, or at least slow it down.

We are living in days not very dissimilar to those that preceded last century's stock market crashes, two world wars, the Depression, and the successive cyclical economic recessions that ensued. Historical data suggests that the frequency of these critical events has increased in frequency with diminishing intervals between them; both the events and their effects seem to last longer; and the scale and magnitude of the damage in absolute terms seem to be greater each time. The challenges we need to face seem to grow, each time requiring a new set of tools and frameworks on distinctly different planes (e.g., Internet bubble versus real estate bubble and the financial meltdown).

We have been dealing with the same type of malady for many years now. The cures adopted so far, however, seem to have only been useful for temporary relief from some of the symptoms. The underlying metastasis might, in reality, be growing at a faster rate than we would wish.

More and more economists seem to agree that not even hindsight and lessons learned from recent events seem to have acted as effective deterrents. Additionally many indicators seem to suggest that existing strategies, reforms and the myriad of patchwork or postponement policies simply fail in their structural effectiveness.

The logical questions that legitimately are being raised are ones such as: Are existing models to blame or faulty? Should we be balanced and objective we might need to acknowledge that existing models have brought humanity probably the longest and most prosperous period in its history, allowing an unprecedented distribution of wealth and well-being among the vast majority of persons living in the countries where these were embraced.

But is this the only question we should pose? What if the models themselves, independent of their innate flaws and shortcomings, were at the end of the day simply products of their own time, valid for the time frame and conditions for which they were developed?

What if we choose to look at the problem from a new and different perspective, stepping away from the axiom of blaming a model and concentrating on the overall picture? At a very macroscopic level, two primary variables in the equation become evident—namely, the model and context where this was applied (good or bad, the model worked adequately for the context for which it was developed). In other words, the model was built to fit the context.

So if the model was not at fault, what does that leave us with? If we look attentively, it is the world around us and our way of doing things that have dramatically changed at growing rates. Our world is currently undergoing even greater transformations and will continue doing so at increasingly higher rates in the foreseeable future.

Is it reasonably possible, hence, to expect the existing model to address increasing new challenges developing at exponentially higher rates? Objectively the logical answer we are left with is no. But is this all? Not really.

Are model and context the only two things on which we need to focus? Are these two variables enough to explain the reason the economy is not working? No, because in reality there are other variables—for example, the interaction between the model and the context that are also not working properly. As we delve into these matters, the fog starts to clear, and a light of hope emerges toward a humble initial thrust that could be useful in adding momentum to a positive evolution of the economy, our lives, and our future. It will, however, take the willingness of many to create the basis for an even better future.

CHOICES

In preparing for this book, several choices had to be made. Some were very hard, others were challenging, and still many others required a considerable will. The most arduous choice was to assure objectivity and provide different perspectives throughout. It would be tremendously easy to fall into the trap of demonizing or victimizing entire subsectors of society for the challenges we face today, which is probably the world's worst economic crisis in recorded history, at least in terms of sheer numbers.

It is too easy to judge the other. It is too easy to accuse, for example, the politicians for their inability to bring about desired outcomes, or the bankers for their greed. In reality, should each one of us look at ourselves in the mirror a bit closer, we would see that we have all—in one way, shape, or form—contributed to what we face today.

Our reality is of our making. By postulating easy judgments, we might emit our own sentence. It would be like asking humanity to step up to the bench of the accused. Probably very few could say that they are fully exempt from having consciously or not contributed in this situation directly or indirectly.

The problem doesn't stem from one person or group of persons but more likely our collective way of going about our business. He who is without sin casts the first stone! Additionally it would be too easy and banal to write a book that fills our lives with additional anger, frustration, and possibly revulsion, disgust, or animosity—all completely unessential to finding a viable solution.

This, however, is not meant to excuse or justify anyone who has acted with criminal intent and affected the life of thousands. For these individuals we must place our trust in the justice system to do its course.

At the end of the day, victimizing or finger pointing might not make an iota of difference in ending the current crisis, nor in addressing the real issues at hand or how we need to bring about reform to address the many profound problems we face today.

We also need to be reasonable. The vast majority of persons from all walks of life wake up each morning with sincere goodwill to contribute and do the best they can. This also includes the majority of those who are trying to find a solution to this very deep and serious crisis.

The other feat was going to be the effort to remain focused on the main issues and achieve the objective of identifying a new model framework and protocol toward a possible set of solutions. Equivalently, a substantial work had to be made to get rid of any preconceptions and possible biases with which we are bombarded on a daily basis or that could inadvertently permeate the source data, the material collected, analyzed, and elaborated and, hence, presented herewith.

This book looks at the many dimensions of the issues and is not limited to seeing things from one national perspective that is valid for certain geographical regions rather than others, as the problem is now planetary—it regards all of us.

It also would be easy to drift into the realm of mystic thought or conspiracy theories. It is honestly not hard to make gratuitous insinuations in describing causes and effects of the crisis. These too simply don't add anything.

No data was sought to either deny or confirm the existence of strong lobbies that push toward achieving particular interests in particular areas, common sense probably suggests that such eventualities follow one natural axiom: when money is involved, the merging of interests become reality. These relations, however, might not endure the test of time simply because they respect the nemesis of the same axiom, which states that greed and self-interest, sooner or later, lead to a conflict of interest.

Much time and many pages can be dedicated to these matters, but they cannot be part of this book. Furthermore this book is not intended to be arrogant, cynical, critical, or judgmental in demonizing existing or historical economic models by which we have lived till today. But it will try to shed light on ways to evolve from here.

This book is about the introduction of a new paradigm-, game-changing yet evolutionary concept. Any possible solution that could affect the lives of millions, if it is meant to work, must be divulged. If found reasonable, it will need to receive the contribution of many more, and only then can it be considered valid for use in part or in whole.

It is also not intended to destroy the basic principles of our current economic system made from the enormous contributions of many throughout history. At each stage in its development, the consolidated contribution was the result of hard work and, for the historical time frame in which it was produced, achieved human advancement. Additionally, as described previously, it is the world around us that has been changing.

To propose a possible solution to the current crisis, one must first understand the issues that contribute to the crisis, comprehend the underlying mechanisms, look at the boxes the current economic model is made up of and how each box interacts with others in forming the different dimensions of the problem, and only then come up with a possible answer.

The crisis has many dimensions to it and touches numerous elements that make up the current model. Given the vast number of elements involved, for the purpose of synthesis a choice had to be made in selecting those elements with possibly the most impact on the economy and the current crisis. Hence, it is important to understand that the elements and dimensions covered here are by no means the only contributing factors to the downturn.

The book will first cover each of the short-listed dimensions and elements, building up the thought process toward the possible solution. Throughout the book a set of questions will be posed, some of which might appear repetitive, but this only confirms that these question also apply to the facts being analyzed. The reason for asking questions has multiple scopes. One is to assess the adequacy and holding capacity of the existing model. The second is to find an appropriate solution. And the third is to validate the solidity and practicality of the newly evolved model and its underlying foundations.

The book will try to approach the issues and the crisis from different perspectives. Hence, the questions range from tough, provocative, inquisitive, and exacting, to those that could appear as naive and banal. But sometimes it is exactly these questions that force us to go beyond the obvious.

OBJECTIVES

The book focuses on reaching two fundamental objectives.

First, it provides explanations for why the existing model might potentially have reached its maximum systemic capability in responding to new challenges, and why new variables such as innovation and sustainability form irresolvable systemic dichotomies, adding to those already naturally forming in the major pillars of the existing models (e.g., public debt, pensions, monetary policy, business, employment, among others).

In other words, the book provides insight into the systemic dichotomies, endemic inhibitors, and newly forming paradigm-changing variables developing in and affecting the fundamental pillars of the current model. The book also provides insight into the reasons the existing model can no longer be fully effective in managing growing short- and long-term challenges or providing answers for newly developing variables.

Second, it provides a general, conceptual, and introductory description of the following:

- the "Value-Based Baseline Evolutionary Economic (Prosperity) Model (BEM^{HESD})"—its makeup, primary components, and how it evolves from the "genes" of the modern market-driven philosophy but goes much beyond creating a new level (plateau)—opening a totally new chapter in the evolution of the economy, economics, and in general our rapport with innovation advancement and the evolving ecosystems that surround us;

- the necessary governance and a balancing framework essential to providing dynamic equilibrium in the system;
- transition and conversion protocol (the Alpha-e Protocol) to facilitate evolution together with migration concepts and tools that will enable the transition from the current model toward a new open, evolutionary, and sustainable prosperity model.

In essence, this book offers a baseline framework to harness a new economic plateau for lasting, sustainable economic advancement and prosperity, one that allows us not only to addresses the plethora of new dynamically changing challenges and variables (human and nonhuman) but one that allows us to tap into, leverage, and foster new investments, business opportunities, employment, innovation, etc.—potential that would otherwise not be visible, viable, and/or available under current models.

Finally, this book highlights examples of possible areas of economic traction in different sectors where all this can be applied pragmatically to deliver near-term resilience, unblock existing dichotomies, and activate true recovery and prolonged sustainable development of investments, business, employment, new opportunities, innovation, etc., exploiting underlying potential behind the new variables (such as game-changing innovation) and allowing a new chapter to be opened in the evolution of mankind with a non-static evolutionary economic model apt to fit the feats and needs of the twenty-first century.

For the solution to be pragmatic it must have the potential to be applied in relatively short time frames to revive the economy structurally and systemically,—reasonably much less than the years that have already matured since the beginning of the crisis. This, however, is based on the willingness to bring about systemic structurally *lasting*, resilient and "future-able" evolving reforms.

If accepted as a solution the potential impact of its announcement or even a partial implementation could have positive economic resonance, potentially geometric in nature.

The paradigm shift of the proposed solution might be potentially equivalent to that faced by humanity, as it migrated in different steps from the barter- to the currency-based economic model, but exponentially higher due to the extent and numbers involved. Though this shift could potentially be perceived as an evolutionary big bang from a purely conceptual point of view, the model's rollout instead requires a step-by-step approach, benefiting, if implemented correctly, from quick wins and leveraging domino effects.

CROSSROADS

Mankind has reached an epochal moment in its history, and possibly one of the most exceptional crossroads in its evolution. We seem to have arrived at a crossroad. One of the roads in front of us is a natural continuation of the one we are currently on, one that does not imply any active decision making on our behalf. All we have to do is follow it as we go. Yet this is the road that, for the foreseeable future, will take us through the same scenery, at least as far as the eye can see from our current perspective.

In other words, should we decide to continue on this road that was consciously chosen each time, the possibility of taking a different route came along in the last decades (the Internet bubble, the housing bubbles, the near systemic crash of 2008, double-dip recession . . .). It is a road of great unnecessary economic impasse and turmoil, personal losses, pain, social unrest (as we see in different parts of the world), or, worse yet, undesirable consequences such as war (should history repeats itself).

On the other hand, there is a road distinctly different from the preceding one. We cannot appreciate the full extent of the new scenery it provides. This is somewhat like Columbus, who might have been aware he had reached a new land but had no clue as to the majesty of what lay just a few hundred nautical miles due west, northwest, or southwest of his position—a continent spanning nearly the whole longitudinal axis of our planet.

This is a road where there is a potential for advancement, an opportunity for evolution. It is the same type of route the likes of Magellan, Cook, Vasco de Gama, Adam Smith, Thomas Jefferson, etc., indicated in opening new areas of opportunity for humanity.

THE EXPERIMENT

A documentary centered on physiological experiments, carried out in the late 1950s, asked a group of volunteers from different walks of life to simply ask a set of true-or-false questions to a person in an adjacent room who they could hear, but not see, via a speaker.

For the experiment to be successful, each time they received a false answer to the list of questions with which they were provided, participants were to push a button without hesitation, knowing that it would inflict greater levels of electrical charges and pain to the person in the adjacent room. Each time the person behind the wall provided a wrong answer, the volunteers pushed the button and could hear the lamentation of increasing pain and agony from the person behind the wall. The volunteers knew they were consciously inducing this pain.

What the volunteers did not know was that the entire experiment was staged. The person behind the wall was not tied to any electrical circuit and, thus, was not being electrocuted. The person was just acting. Out of the total number of participants, only a couple refused to go beyond a certain limit, inducing increasing levels of pain, in the experiment.

The study inferred that if you provide a context, a seemingly valid purpose, a set of rules, a set of golden objectives, and a professional-looking ambiance, only a few persons will question the experiment to the point of consciously deciding to stop it and, in this case, refuse to be taken over by sheer madness. This is evident to everyone outside that context.

This is, of course, an extreme example, but given the drastic nature of the current world crisis, legitimate questions arise. Independently of what we do in life and the role each of us plays in society, are we sure we want to collectively leave our destinies and those of our children to the workings of a set of accepted norms, surely developed out of goodwill? They worked for a time but are now only inflicting greater amounts of unnecessary hardships on the vast majority for an indefinite period.

On the other hand we cannot allow for things to get out of hand for too long out of complacency and/or fear form judgment from those who staunchly remain attached to a model—let us remember that this complacency and blind reverence towards a model is at the base of scenarios where millions lost their priceless lives in wars, gulags, concentration camps in Europe and mass exterminations in Africa and southeast Asia not very long ago-yet, with the benefit of hindsight, it took the will force of relatively very few men and women in key roles to bring these horrendous genocides against humanity to an end.

Model fixation is the central theme of many advanced studies and is conducive to many real-life problems that can cause varying degrees of harmful damage to individuals, organizations, businesses, and nations.

Will the next doses of policies based on current models be able to take us out of the tunnel? Or will they only serve to take the patient to the point of no return? Are we sure that, for example, our financial systems have no alternatives other than cyclically needing to devour their shareholders, investors, customers, communities, cities, countries, and states before devouring themselves?

Are we sure the only business model left for investors, entrepreneurs, owners, management, and employees alike is one based on a never-ending paradigm of cost reduction, delocalization, a transfer of jobs, advanced technology, and production to other regions? We are not talking about protectionist stances with respect to an open business scenario.

How many more corporations, companies, businesses, shops, and professional activities need to evaporate before we realize that this model, as many that preceded it, has probably reached its maximum potential, an impending point of implosion before exploding like a dying star?

Are we sure models dogmatically applied to critical areas affecting real lives answer real-life day-to-day needs and tomorrow's challenges?

SACRED MONSTERS AND MANTRAS

Imagine today's economic model being based on the interaction between a set of well-defined dimensions, elements, and components, such as public debt, fiscal policy, employment, the banking system, and retirement. Imagine each as forming a box that is interconnected with the other boxes, which in turn produce a reference model. Any reference model allows the use of a finite set of tools effective for that reality. In theory, everything fares well until the underlying premises that gave birth to such needs remain unchanged.

Over an extended period of time, the relative success of a reference model provides the basis not only for its acceptance but also for its consolidation as a principle. The longer this axiom holds true, the greater the chance for it to become an unquestionable reality.

Once new variables are introduced and the context starts changing due to external forces, the natural tendency is to add patches to the boxes, tools, and frameworks in response to the new stimuli. This, however, can only be done up to a certain critical point. Beyond this critical point, it is not the number of tools available or the patches to the boxes that count, because the external forces substantially change the underlying paradigms on which the boxes originally relied.

When faced with such a dilemma, a natural propensity is to insist in acting on an element within each box to induce desired outcomes. The effectiveness of such a strategy is not only reduced, but due to the interconnection with other boxes, the fallout from these stimuli may produce worse effects or highly unpopular and controversial domino consequences (i.e., austerity measures, increased taxes).

Another strategy is the adoption of policies that push the problems beyond the political horizon of new legislatures for a few more years. These strategies only achieve the accumulation of destructive energy forces that increase the potential impact on the overall economy.

In absence of true answers, yet another strategy is to dismantle and demonize an element of the existing reference model. Retirement, pensions, and health-care-related policies are but a few of these examples. Decade-long mantras are devised to shape and convince public opinion that previously, perfectly congenial and necessary elements become vices and need to be curbed, reduced, or annulled in the general interest of the majority. These strategies usually create many inequalities among living generations that benefited from them and those that are called to contribute to them amidst other hardships without being able to benefit from them.

But have policies that have leveraged repetitious mantras, which have tried to change desired views on the public, produced tangible results and resolved the issues? Are these addressing the dilemmas we are facing on a national or international scale?

In regard to the net of all costs and benefits, has the increase in retirement age, for example, produced any tangible positive outcome to the majority of persons, companies, businesses, investors, pension funds, and real-life issues that real people live every day? Or have they produced an additional layer of complexity to things such as the natural generational turnover, freeing up space for younger generations in the marketplace and creating professional growth and career development possibilities that are the lifeblood of any enterprise and economy? Or is the truth of the matter simply that these issues have become even more multifaceted both in their nature and extent?

To be balanced and perfectly pragmatic, some would argue that if you look at the issues from the prism of the current model, it all makes perfect sense. But are we sure there is no alternative view? Not looking out of the box, the mantra makes sense because the underlying reasons are linked to the weight it has on things such as national debt and the evolving demographic mix. But is this the only perspective from which to look at elements such as this? *Are we sure that this issue, seen from a totally different perspective, could not in reality simply hinder or hide opportunities?*

How realistic is it to think that the large majority of a growing number of hardworking men and women over a certain age who are impacted by these policies will have a chance of finding employment or business opportunities in normal economic conditions before reaching current retirement-age ceilings, let alone in one of the worst economic crises ever? This has nothing to do with persons who wish to remain active. Quite the contrary.

If remedies produce more problems than benefits, can these be called solutions? Are similar thought processes rational, reasonable, or even in the nature of things? What are the end results? What value do they bring to people, businesses, markets, or the economy at large?

Are we sure we are not following models just because these have been valid references in the past and, as such, have become the only reality? Are we sure there are no alternatives that can be more sustainable and viable than the present one?

Do an exponentially growing number of people need to fall below the poverty line and lose their hard-earned investments, businesses, possessions, dignity, hope, and children? Current reality is brutal.

For example, Greek mothers, out of desperation and a need to assure the survival of their children, leave a growing number of children in orphanages. Is this sacrifice justified? Without being idealistic or rhetorical, is this the level of civilization twenty-first-century man wishes to pursue?

Where is the centrality of man in the current paradigm? Historically, every time the centrality of man reached hindrance, the reference model was ultimately superseded by an evolved model.

In today's global crisis, the number of elements that no longer find answers, such as retirement, public debt, markets, jobs, business closures, investments, etc., is growing and will continue to do so ceteris paribus (everything else remaining the same).

Is there any reason we instead do not adopt strategies that improve the economy, our prospects, our lives, and provide hope and concrete answers for our future and that of our future generations?

The current scenario is different from the 1929 crisis. This is a truly global crisis! No one nation, government, or individual can feel exempt from or unaffected by the current crisis—not even those countries that are living an ephemeral moment of glitter and glory.

There are alternatives to the current scenario. The only thing stopping us is our will to make a difference.

EVOLUTION: QUINTESSENTIAL STRATEGY TO LIFE

Evolution is said to be one of the constants in the universe. The universe undergoes constant evolution. The relatively tiny planet on which we live evolves geologically and biologically. Plants, animals, cells, and humans evolve; our lives evolve. Our bodies undergo continuous evolution. Our thoughts evolve on a daily basis. Anything developed by man evolves. Evolution is everywhere and touches everything, not just animals and plants.

Evolution, adaptation, and choosing the appropriate strategies make the difference between success and failure. Anthropologists seem to agree that man as a creature is probably among the weakest in nature in terms of physical strength. Yet this evident impediment that exposed mankind to a very real extinction risk (considering the wilderness of the time) for thousands of years allowed it not only to survive through many cataclysmic events, including an ice age or two, but dominate over the rest of the animal kingdom leveraging his/her intelligence.

Given today's knowledge, it is apparent that mankind seems to have started its voyage, stepping out of a geographical location, be it based on one's beliefs of religious origin or otherwise.

Current archeological knowledge suggests that early man started inching its way from an area around Africa and the Middle East to the four corners of the world. Mankind's initial survival, growth, and success were tied to three fundamental strategies: (1) improve survival and security by keeping in groups, (2) consume what is readily available in nature, and (3) move on to new ground as resources deplete.

As time progressed and knowledge grew, some in these nomadic groups would separate or remain behind and settle. The reasons behind the adoption of this new strategy were probably many; some of them could have been tied to economies of scale, the impossibility of satisfying the needs of ever-growing group members, frustration and exasperation from wandering around, a decreasing need for further migration, or simply a better appreciation for the cyclical events in nature and the invention of agriculture. They may have deemed that those new surroundings would be able to fulfill their future needs as seasons changed, bringing a renewal of life. Independent of the real reason, settlement became the new survival strategy, the new paradigm, the game changer—a precursor in the evolution of mankind.

One thing seems apparent: the migratory strategy that led mankind to the next hunting ground would reach its climax when man literally reached the four corners of the earth and there were few other viable spaces into which to venture. Some scientists suggest some of these intercontinental crossings (e.g., Asia-America, Asia-Australia) were made possible or facilitated by the lowering of ocean levels and glacial bridging (Asia-America) deriving from cyclical ice ages.

At this point venturing back probably entailed entering the vital space occupied by those who had decided to remain behind and settle. And this, perhaps more frequently than not, entailed bloodshed.

It is not important if events evolved in exactly this way. What is important is that mankind, at a certain point in time, faced the challenge of changing their survival strategy. Evolution could no longer be postponed and had to come about in a relatively short time.

The migratory strategy that once seemed to be the only reference model had simply ceased to be a viable strategy for the majority.

These moments of evolutionary change were driven by the imbalance in the cost of continuing an existing strategy. Those who found new ways of survival were those who progressed and found new modalities to thrive, grow, and succeed as individuals, families, villages, city-states, countries, empires, and republics.

Those who staunchly stuck to old paradigms, strategies, models, and ways—though perfectly valid for their success in that time window—slowly fell behind and, in most cases, either simply vanished over time or, at best, meagerly survived in very small groups at the fringes of society.

Simply put, man is the master of his own success or demise. New survival strategies have continuously replaced existing ones that were believed to be the only successful ways. Each strategy is founded on a set of assumptions, rules, thoughts, convictions, etc. They set the limits of that specific strategy or paradigm.

Think of these limits as the confines of a specific play area that, together with the rules of the game, set its foundations. So long as the game is played with the same rules and within that specific arena, everything is fine. However, the minute the game starts requiring different rules, especially if they are exerted by external elements, that particular game can no longer be played in the same way. It becomes a new game or the evolution of an existing game.

Human progress and survival strategy work along the same lines. Those groups of people who are able to anticipate the changes occurring around them become the precursors of evolution, adapting faster and more effectively in the development of a new strategy. This concept is also valid for businesses, investors, managers, employees, and political entities.

Those that evolved become the game changers—the new winners, so to speak—in the game of survival but more importantly in the art of mastering evolution. The rest will become, at best, followers. A residual few will dwindle away in an outwardly spiral.

WHAT HAPPENED TO THE EGYPTIAN, PERSIAN, ROMAN, AND BRITISH EMPIRES?

When visiting places once occupied by great civilizations, a few questions immediately come to mind to many travelers. What happened to these civilizations? Why have they not continued building other pyramids, ziggurats, or temples? Why is there no evidence of continuation? Why and how could the people who built these magnificent monuments simply vanish? Where did they go? What happened to the Egyptians, Persians, Greeks, and Romans? What happened to the British Empire?

As societies evolved, those that chose to explore and adopt new survival strategies became the new game changers of their times. Disputes or wars sometimes ensued, as the new entrants instilled a natural fear in societies surrounding them that held onto old strategies. Ultimately, most of those societies that feared the loss of their previously dominant positions lost these disputes or wars.

The new societies that emerged as the winners immediately filled the void created by those who preceded them in the evolutionary chain. Those that remained unfalteringly tied to models, strategies, and systems that had reached their failure and implosion points succumbed.

The new entrants and the places they inhabited became the center of attraction for all those who mastered a trade and, among these, the best and brightest. Most came from the defeated city or empire. Thousands, if not millions, migrated to the next new land of opportunity, leaving Egypt, Persia, Greece, Rome, etc., devoid of much of their know-how and the possibility of any substantial further progress. Then dust settled on these once-great civilizations over time.

That's where they went. That is why those lands did not continue creating Ur, Sumer, Babylon, Karnack, pyramids, Persepolis, the Parthenon, the Coliseum, and the Westminster Cathedral that once stood as emblems of where the centers of civilization of their own time resided. That is why when you visit museums, such as the Louvre in Paris, and follow the suggested chronological path, it literally takes you across a history of evolution, from the first human settlements and civilizations onward, allowing one to notice how everything seems to fit the pattern of human progress.

One witnesses how everything—from useful objects in day-to-day life, such as pottery, to complex strategies of warfare, to engineering and construction methods, to the arts in the general administration of a state, to writing and record keeping, to channeling water across hundreds of kilometers—evolved over the centuries, as each new civilization added something more to the preceding model. It allowed new ideas to come into being and exploited these.

For example, one notices how the art of building columns progressed from Babylonia and Assyria, to Egypt, to Persia, to Doria, to Corinth, to Athens, and to Rome. Underground irrigation methods, such as the "Qanat," used to transport water over hundreds of kilometers of deserts across the Middle East, gave way to the fundamental science behind the building of spectacular aqueducts in Rome and throughout its empire. Trade across sea and terrestrial routes, such as the Silk Road, brought evolution in textiles, food, tapestry, art, and musical instruments. Each new perspective provided the ground for new ideas and new uses—from noodles to spaghetti, and from gunpowder only used for fireworks to its multiple uses in battle and mining.

Throughout history, the new land of opportunity (the America of its time) would quickly attract the best craftsmen, architects, teachers, scientists, doctors, engineers, workers, and managers—the best of the best in each area of human activity. Growing masses of people were fueled by the passion and desire to improve their lives for themselves and their children, leaving the old state of affairs to the dust of time.

All these men and women had one fundamental trait in common. They were eager to bring about an evolutionary change in their life. They believed that this move would bring them prosperity, especially for their future generations. As time went by, this growth and the search for a new paradigm went hand in hand with a growing need for individual freedom, rights, and more civilized societies.

Every time humanity approached a new dead end, it faced a new evolutionary need for change. All signs indicate that we have reached a step-level evolutionary episode. And if we are not there yet, we are very close.

But then again, does it really matter if we ever see this virtual line or if, in reality, these lines simply don't exist? Does it make a difference knowing where the exact demarcation point is located?

IS IT TIME TO EVOLVE?

We only notice evolution in the brief moments we look back at what no longer exists. Evolution is made up of many small steps. They seem insignificant when looked at singularly on a daily basis, yet they are impressive when we notice the sheer distance covered. Yet if one does not begin the journey, nothing will ever happen, no one will ever go anywhere, and time will consume everything.

The time to change might be of secondary importance for those who begin to sense a need for change is imminent. Some just get stuck in a loop, wondering about evolution. There will be many more though that choose the road to continuance, survival, and progression for themselves and their loved ones.

There have been many evolutionary changes man has had to face, and so far each has been successful. The invention and use of fire, agriculture, steel and other metals, and barter were all unquestionably game changes. Ultimately money allowed trade in ways that bartering could never have achieved. Even religions in many ways faced change in enriching man with an evolved appreciation for the world, spirituality, and its rapport with life and other fellow humans.

In the last decades, the inventions of flight, space exploration, computers, the Internet, mobile communications, nanotechnology, etc., have impacted our lives in numerous and incredible ways. Each invention is undeniably a game changer in its own right. These changes have substantially influenced all of us and will continue to do so in unfathomable and unpredictable ways.

Couple these gigantic technological advancements with the incredible challenges humanity faces with sustainability, natural calamities, and the current global economic crisis, and you have all the elements for a new, evolutionary need for change. Never has man been able to produce so much (e.g., products, services, ideas, processes) through the economy as it has done in the past three or four generations.

According to *The Economist*, the combined economic output from the first century onward does not match that of the twentieth century, let alone that which might be produced in our century (Maddison, UN, & Economist).

Given the global economic crisis, this data alone could be valid enough to suggest we should at least pose legitimate questions as to what we wish to do from now on since the potential for growth is still real. We have to find evolved models of tapping into it.

Today's generations have become so accustomed to seeing innovative solutions (that were science fiction literally only a few years back) pop up nearly on a daily basis that we might not necessarily appreciate the impact they have on our lives, at least in the short term.

To understand the extent of the impact of recent inventions on our lives, think of how many simple day-to-day activities are no longer necessary—for example, entering a telephone booth, dialing a phone number on a circular dial, cranking up a window in a car, inserting or rewinding a music cassette or VHS tape, manually loading garbage trucks, carrying heavy objects in our arms, forcing a typewriter carriage to the next line, licking a stamp, and manually washing dishes or clothes.

Think of how many objects were useful and necessary only a few years back that have dramatically changed shape and are no longer in use.

Theoretically, you may no longer need to buy the following items separately: photographic camera, movie camera, stereo, agenda, telephone, writing pad, magnetic compass, pen, eraser, calculator, map, clock, game cards, board games, navigational system, TV, remote control, CDs, DVDs, books, newspaper, encyclopedias, stopwatch, speakers, and more. These can all be found in your smartphone or tablet.

Think of how many things have influenced our daily behavior and rapport with others only in the last generation: the disproportionate amount of time spent using a smartphone or the Internet, fixating one's thoughts and time on an a screen for an abnormal amount of hours each day, 365 days a year—cell-phone anxiety, the different approach to human interaction moving from the physical to the virtual, the change in our languages and the way we communicate, and the endless search for information on search engines. Yet, the impact of each of these on business, the economy, and the individual is astounding.

Only three decades ago entire stories of buildings pertaining to the same business were filled with persons performing then-useful jobs. These have simply vanished. Yet it is absurd to think of going back.

Our world is changing by the millisecond in every sphere of our life, and yet we try to address our problems with the same reference models of the past. As the theory of relativity applies to the universe, it also seems to touch our very survival strategy.

PATCHES

A tremendous amount of effort seems to go toward patching up the growing amount of cracks and holes that are appearing in a structurally weakened ecosystem-destructive dam (the current economic model) instead of addressing the real issue, the dam itself and the risk it poses.

Do we wish to focus our thoughts, energies, and resources on making adjustments to the dam (i.e., bolting down the turbines or carrying out maintenance on each element of the dam, its tunnels, its wiring system, its internal workings, or its concrete)? Or is it time to ask ourselves if we cannot satisfy the primary needs for which the dam was created using alternative methods that could at the same time take away the hazards?

The incredible events taking place in Greece form a perfect example. A nation of 11 million souls has been declared on the verge of default due to its debts. One of the solutions that are being forced on Greece (as of August 2012) is another massive loan accompanied by the implementation of very harsh austerity measures, driving its economy further toward a standstill, forcing millions into poverty.

Wasn't the original problem a huge debt?

Many dedicate much effort, all driven in perfect goodwill, to study the best forms of austerity measures—repayment timetables, appropriate financial instruments, the best government policies, the effects of a possible spillover, the spread, increased taxes, mass layoffs, etc. But are we losing sight of the bigger picture here?

What is the sense of exacting a heavier burden on Greek citizens or that of many other countries facing similar situations? How can economies exit this self-consuming loop? How many more losses can investors, banks, and businesses be exposed to?

Greece is not the only country with this dilemma. A growing number of other countries are in similar conditions and face problems in honoring their colossal debts within given time frames. The current list of these countries is incredibly long and unfortunately growing.

Has the time then not come to look at the big picture? Is continuing down the path logical or rational? Will it produce any benefit for anyone down the road?

Everything is now interconnected; everything is reliant on everything else producing an additional dichotomy (irreconcilable difference). Prolonged and profound economic recession, mass unemployment, financial market instability, the credit crunch, public debt, business slowdown, etc.—all need to be addressed outside of the straitjackets of the existing models.

The numbers of opposing forces that impede current models to work properly are increasing, shaping, and fomenting the current crisis and will continue doing so with greater virulence.

THE MEGA TSUNAMI

Some are convinced that niche areas, such as the derivatives markets or the emerging markets, are the panacea to all dilemmas, the answer to all economic downturns. To grab a piece of the action, thousands of businesses are relocating and or investing unprecedented amounts of money.

These seemingly new lands of opportunity might be just that after all. If one looks closer, one will notice structural cracks in the many dams erected in haste. The difference is that the cracks are growing at faster rates and with greater dimensions than those that brought about the successive bubble burst leading up to the 2008 financial crisis.

A growing number of economists reasonably question the solidity of the foundations of the economies in emerging nations, arguing that they are set on inappropriate ground, that the cement used in the construction of these might be of lesser quality, and that corners might have been cut in the design to save time and money for speedy exploitation. The suggestion is that, as enormous pressures build up behind these dams, exerting growing pressure on their structures, these forces will ultimately find their way to the weakest points. Once they reach the structural point of failure, some of these dams might burst.

Should this happen, the extent of immediate damage, its propagation, and effects on other financial systems and businesses around the world will be very hard to fathom. It would not be hard to guesstimate though that they will be much bigger than what the world witnessed with the 2008 near-systemic meltdown. Some already have coined different names, such as mega tsunami, reminiscent of recent environmental disasters.

Whether or not this might be the case is not the primary focus of this book. What is important is being cognizant that, in the eventuality of implosive or explosive phenomena in emerging markets or defaulting developed countries, these could have severe systemic effects, only adding complexity to the many challenges already being faced.

In the following chapters we will look at a set number of elements, those that probably have the largest effect on what we see unfolding in front of our eyes each day.

DISAGREEMENT

For centuries economists, philosophers, sociologists, and thinkers gave birth to contrasting models, such as capitalism, socialism, communism, and Marxism. They have written tomes about these and the intricate ways they should operate, with lists of benefits vis-à-vis those of their historical counterparts.

Disagreement on models lie even among those that declare their allegiance to the same general model, generating many differing schools of thought.

As a society we still have not configured a model that could finally put an end to a debacle that seems to repeat itself ad infinitum. Independent of the historical period, the way human societies were configured in these periods, and the economic model used, the end result is a net contraposition between many opposing viewpoints across history.

The current existing economic model is at best the result of compromise among differing points of views. The scope here is not to judge any of the existing models but to see if there is a solution. Is there a different approach, or are we condemned?

Additionally it is to confirm that any new model must need to benefit from the contribution of different legitimate viewpoints.

PART 1:

Structural and Systemic Blocks, Dichotomies, New Variables, and Paradigms

INNOVATION, NEW TECHNOLOGICAL BREAKTHROUGHS, INTERNET, MOBILE TECHNOLOGY, AND NANOTECHNOLOGY

This chapter is not about a judgment on innovation and technology, as they have brought us to where we are today. Rather, it is an attempt to shed light on the different perspectives, opportunities, and critical issues that we will be facing and to address a future that surprisingly is not very distant; in many cases it is already here. Understanding trends will allow us to address the challenges and possibly turn critical issues into opportunities.

To achieve this, the book will first provide a photograph of where we stand, tackle the concerns around this issue, and then investigate the possible opportunities and how we could leverage these to revive the economy and improve long-term prosperity—leveraging technology instead of being negatively impacted by it.

It is self-evident that the invention of things such as the Internet, mobile technology, and nanotechnology has changed our lives from only a few years back. Hence, this chapter will not concentrate on just a single element (e.g. the benefits derived from these), but focus on the areas worth consideration and highlighting, as these need to be addressed if we wish to find a possible solution.

Not too long ago, a dear friend noted, "I found myself laughing about a statement my brother made regarding his use of the Internet. The Internet sort of feels like having Aladdin's lamp. You put a question to it in simple language, and, wham, it comes back with a thousand answers. Most of the time you find what you are looking for among the first two pages." It gathered a laugh or two from most of those who were listening. My friend mentioned he felt his brother was exaggerating.

Only a couple of months later, none present that day were laughing any longer.

A few years back, many businessmen and super-consultants were struggling to understand how they could make money from the Internet. Many entrepreneurs threw massive sums of money at it to the point that a gigantic speculative bubble burst under its own weight, creating one of the biggest financial black holes in the stock market globally.

As in many new feats that focus on the search for the golden vein, many entrepreneurs, consultants, and scholars suffered from multiple defeats. Some became frustrated to the point of going to the other extreme, even predicting the dismay of the new economy, the virtual promised land, and the unavoidable return to the old brick-and-mortar economy.

The truth most always lies in between. When things are new, our eyes are not trained to look beyond the apparent. We fail to see things beyond the adopted models, limiting their potential view. Consequentially, some only focused on being the first, while others in very obvious niche areas took a watch-and-see approach, especially after the first big bust.

It is only a few years later, and today there is hardly anything you cannot buy or do on the Internet. You can purchase anything from shirts to pants, pots, pans, pins, paints, paper, sushi, and your favorite vacation, even choosing your own room and taking a virtual tour beforehand in order to know exactly where you are going. Nothing is out of reach. Those who were born after 1990 might say, "So what?" Yet most of this was actually science fiction to the majority of those born before that date. And it all happened in just a few years.

What is the Internet today? Is it truly very far away from the concept of Aladdin's lamp? Where is it headed? Where is it taking us? Where do we want to go with it? What do we want it to become?

In order to increase its potential benefits, we must also be able to manage advancements and technological breakthroughs productively. Nothing can be left out of control. Indeed, nature works within the framework of very complicated systems that keep it always in balance. The physical world around us responds to the universal laws of physics. The universe also adheres to many yet-to-be-understood laws. Any attempt to leave anything man-made alone to manage itself has demonstrated to be, in most cases, unproductive while in others destructive to man itself.

Among the many advancements, the Internet, for example, is no exception. While it should remain an accessible and free domain—a knowledge, economic, and social (KES) platform open to all—without rules it will be prey to those who hack it, phish it, etc., and use it for scopes that instead of producing benefits might (sometimes even unconsciously) produce damage and harm of unpredictable scale to millions.

Some sources estimate that there are more than 2 billion Internet users across the planet to date. True or not, that's nearly one-third of our planet's total population. Many more are said to own a mobile phone. This interconnection among people has never been reached in human history—and this all happened in only a hand-full of few years.

KES^A AND WEB INCLUSIVITY

Thousands of sites pop up one day to the next, while others disappear just as rapidly as they emerge. The Web emerges around essentially four paradigms. The first three are of human origination and sources, while the fourth potentially might not be:

1. Knowledge: sites that provide/share/disseminate information/data/news;
2. Economic: sites that have an economic end (i.e., selling, buying, promoting);
3. Social: sites that have a social/interactive/networking objective
4. Awareness (discussed later).

Whatever paradigm on which new sites have been founded, most websites are in faster time frames inadvertently superseded by what can be called a more inclusive paradigm and website. In other words, websites lose the uniqueness and innovation to more inclusive websites and paradigms that replace them in ever-faster time frames by a phenomenon that could be named "Web inclusivity." The more a website provides generic "me too" data, the higher its chances of demise and becoming a victim of Web inclusivity. To clarify, the following example can be emblematic.

Not long ago (even as near as the latter half of the 1990s), it used to be that physical distance separated one from his dream destination due to the lack of or access to information, and hence leading to the necessity to avail oneself of the services of expert intermediaries. In many cases people who dedicated their lives to becoming experts in the travel industry traveled to offer their hands-on expertise.

A traveler's choices in many cases were limited to selecting a carrier (land, sea, or air) to get you to your desired destination and, in some cases, not even that. You needed to rely on the expertise of a trustworthy travel agent who could provide you with added-value experience that went beyond the few fancy photographs in glossy brochures. In other words, you needed someone with real hands-on experience with that destination. One's only source of real feedback on a hotel's true adequacy, for example, was only by word of mouth from friends or one's trusted travel professional. After much thought and comparison, you literally took an act of faith, hoping for the best.

Unless you were a seasoned traveler, before the 1980s, questions that would seem banal today were potential showstoppers. How do you estimate your expenses? What amount of traveler's checks do you need? Where do you get cash if you run out of money (this is before the dissemination of ATMs)? What are you going to eat (before fast-food globalization)? How do you get about town? Will there be car-rental companies (only major cities were equipped with such facilities)? If so, will you be able to drive with your state's driver's license? Do you need to obtain an international driver's license? In case of emergency, where is your country's nearest consulate? In terms of language and cultural issues, what happens if you need medical assistance? It might sound strange, but these questions still existed up until the mid-nineties.

In such a small amount of time, technology has evolved. The travel industry, in ways unthinkable till a few years back, has also addressed many dilemmas that impeded travel. Arranging a trip is within everyone's reach nowadays, to such extent that tourism's numbers across the globe have grown n-fold since the 1980s.

Since the invention of the Internet, the concept has evolved dramatically. In the beginning you had to create a vacation, putting all the elements together. You searched for your preferred destination on a limited number of specialized travel websites. Data was not organized in more standard formats, as we find today, and much time was lost finding comparable information. For example, you first investigated those websites that talked about your destination. Then you browsed the websites of the airlines that flew there, checking them one by one. Hence, you looked at each hotel website singularly (if you knew which ones were available locally), then you looked at the car rentals, and so on. It was an exhaustive experience that sometimes could take entire days. At the end you had to go back to your travel agent with the pieces of information that you gathered to make the booking, because in the majority of cases there were no online booking or payment facilities. If there were, the majority of persons did not feel secure making payments on them. And even after checking availabilities, more times than not you ended back at the drawing board or gave up and asked your agent to create the package for you.

In the early days of the Internet's real diffusion (late nineties), these different/unique websites represented different players that were competing against one another, providing alternatives on the Internet.

As months progressed, some entrepreneurs started "bundling" websites containing the same type of complementary services, acting as a virtual search engine (e.g., creating the first level of Web inclusivity, putting together a limited number of airlines, hotels, or car-rental companies). It is very difficult to come by data that could evaluate whether these businesses even had time to benefit from an adequate return on these investments, because in literally no time a higher level of "Web inclusivity" was reached by others. These have gone to the point of enclosing all-inclusive sites under one umbrella, allowing you to also choose your seating on an aircraft, an operation only possible on the airline's site until only a few months ago.

At this rate, is there anything stopping someone from reaching the ultimate level of Web inclusivity, one that will allow you, for example, to create a wish list and let the Web do the rest? Order your choice of dessert on the third evening of your hotel stay in a restaurant outside of your hotel? Make arrangements to have your house cleaned and decide the best house insurance for your family and best deal for the tires on your car that need replacement, all before you leave on vacation?

Is Web inclusivity only affecting the travel sector though? Web inclusivity is not sector-specific. In the real world, things are aggregated into the Web inclusivity paradigm faster than most can think of. And it is happening across all sectors. Web inclusivity is not confined to imaginary lines that separate distinct economic sectors (i.e., travel, retail, banking, real estate, construction).

In theory it's great, is it not? Why go back and forth with many sites when one site can do all?

Is there one reason that will impede the need for increasing Web inclusivity paradigm? Will Web inclusivity become the sole winning strategy or paradigm on the Web?

Is there a single motive that will prevent your preferred search engine or its successor from becoming the single source for everything, from finding the definition of a word to the address of your nearest hairdresser to buying a book, a car, or a house? The Web could even become the medium for your international video calls, your chats, your networks, your business meetings, your post office—whatever you want it to be. It already is, is it not?

Web inclusivity encompasses also such disparate things as the many app's that are being developed and which can be still considered as separate distinct modules.

However provided the massive numbers of these app's that will inundate the market—we may not be too far away form a scenario whereby the end user might just want a fully inclusive bundle of whatever he or she need to do through their preferred medium (tablet, smartphone . . .)—from calling to opening a hotel room door, to using it as a full-remote controller (to manage just about everything from toys to air-conditioning), etc.? Some of these technologies are already here.

Not long ago, visiting different sites meant also obtaining different price possibilities and choices. Higher levels of inclusivity can instantly assess market demand and supply. Would this impact the availability of prices and real choices? To what degree? In what time frames? What then?

But more importantly, how will this affect business, investments, and jobs?

Would this also put challenges on the business models of suppliers and services not known till today, exerting the self-consuming "cost centric"-only logic paradigm (discussed later) even further? How far are we truly from that all-inclusive Web inclusivity paradox?

IS THERE ANYONE WHO WILL NOT BE AFFECTED BY WEB INCLUSIVITY?

So far the Internet has created some jobs while transforming or replacing others. To date, the net effect of the Internet on job creation/loss is a subject of much debate. The crude reality poses a series of genuine interrogations though. How many net jobs losses or increases is the new model really generating? Will Web inclusivity produce a natural extinction for growing numbers of previously crucial human expertise and added value?

Will Web inclusivity only eat up lower levels of Web KES[A]? Will Web inclusivity also consume its own flesh and blood, additional Internet businesses, and jobs? What about brick-and-mortar businesses and jobs? A city, a region, a country's economy?

What happens to all those sites and related jobs that fall out of the new economic loop, where higher levels of Web inclusivity become the winning paradigm?

What happened to the millions of persons who work in the travel agency business or other brick-and-mortar enterprises/sectors? And what will happen to all those working behind the scenes of the websites that might vanish simply because they lose out to more Web-inclusive sites?

Do not these queries hold true for people in all walks of life? Is anyone or anything—investor, business, enterprise, profession, executive, manager, employee, worker, tradesman, representative, politician, billionaire—exempt?

Is there a single reason that enormous databases—say, in the medical field—which are engineered to requirements by professional doctors through software engineers, are able to perform diagnostic tests faster, more efficiently, and effectively (in the comfort of your home)? Might these innovations completely affect the medical world, for example?

What effect would this have on thousands of jobs in the medical field? Would it leave a decreasing number of physicians to simply manage processes, data, and robotics (probotics)? Technology is provided with more and more knowledge and becomes more intelligent—able to performing surgery with minimal supervision, especially those types requiring very long hours and precision. How far away are we from this?

Is there a single reason similar databases and processes with diverse forms of expertise—till this day in the sole dominion of man—are not replicable in all other fields (e.g., civil, mechanical, electrical, aeronautical, astrophysical, molecular, biological, mineral, or geophysical engineering)?

How about the forensic profession (i.e., law, lawyers, solicitors, judges, prosecutors)? How far away are we from automated Web-based processes that run on databases of laws and verdicts? Could simple lawsuits, such as neighborhood and consumer litigation, that currently take up a hefty chunk of the judicial backlog and exert incredible weight both on the judiciary system and the fiscal cost to citizens be able to produce automated judgments/settlements?

This could include the oversight of an automatically assigned judge and lawyers who might not need to be physically located in a courthouse. How far away are we from a stage where the average citizen can file a legal dispute using legally intelligent forms online? The legal application performs instantaneous checks against the updated laws or judgments, providing a first verdict that can be contested later by, say, a professional that adds his contribution.

What about notaries public that, as strange as it might sound, in many countries are still delegated by law to a limited number of exclusive families that for generations have held these posts, passing down their profession to their sons and daughters performing their duties at reasonably high rates that in many cases are determined by law? What effect could the Internet and automation of processes have on these professions? For how much longer could these models survive in the forms we know them today? Will they ultimately be pushed to conform to new modalities?

Is it truly about how much time these processes might take to become reality? Or is it about being able to acknowledge that we are facing change to a degree unprecedented till today in human history?

Is there anything stopping banks and supermarkets or other businesses from becoming even more automated? Literally yesterdays' next-generation e-supermarkets and e-banking are already part of reality today, are they not?

While there may be a return to models that require real persons in some industries, such as call centers (because talking to a machine had become an unacceptable customer experience), these jobs are not able to cover the increasing number of job losses. In many cases, these jobs are the first to be delocalized in faraway cheap-labor heavens. Is there any job you might think of that will not be affected by technological advancement?

What about a pilot? As much as I love the art of flying, in the commercial aviation sector there are advanced plans that will substantially change a pilot's contribution in a cockpit. As for pilots in the military, the new reality has already affected the lives of many professionals that have dedicated a lifetime to this profession. There are currently huge investments unmanned airborne vehicles (UAVs). Pilots sitting at game-like consoles are flying a growing number of sorties over dangerous hostile territory today. They are doing this in rooms sometimes thousands of kilometers away from the physical location they patrol. They supervise and at times steer these UAVs once they reach the vicinity of the target areas—with simple joystick movements. These vehicles theoretically could perform the entire mission (for now some types) without actually needing human intervention. These vehicles are not limited to use in the air; many prototypes and deployed unmanned assets are being used for naval, terrestrial, and undersea operations. Consider that similar vehicles have been deployed on distant planets, such as Mars, in the past two decades.

What effect will this technology have on the thousands of jobs in the armed forces, aviation sector, and the advanced sciences? And what about the companies in their supply chain, adjacent sectors or in seemingly unconnected far-away sectors in left field, such as cameramen who make a living covering breaking-news events from helicopters? What about maintenance crews, airport flight and ground operations crews, and air traffic controllers? What about all the other sectors that in turn form their supply chains?

How about a mechanic's job? Already a mechanic is no longer a profession assimilated with someone who has grease all over him/her. Rather, the person is someone in a clean environment, interacting most times with a computer. Could the future of automation transform this job even further? In the not-so-distant future your car might communicate the chance of failure directly to a manufacturing site in a distant location, prompting you to accept the replacement offer. Should this be resolvable by simple upload of a software update, it will automatically upload the fix; otherwise, it will prompt a maintenance engineer to your address at a time of your choosing that will perform the intervention.

What about a garbage collection crew? We have already witnessed the evolution of this profession in many cities. Until not long ago it was a job previously requiring at least three individuals. At a growing rate, in many instances crews have been reduced to just one person, managing a truck that performs these duties automatically. How will technological evolution transform this job even further? How far are we from a totally automated garbage collection scenario, with minimal remote human supervision?

What about a specialized subsea oil and gas maintenance crew? Was the last mega oil spill in the Gulf of Mexico an example of how this job has been transformed?

How far are we from voice-activated smartphone apps that can provide a walk-through animation of a supermarket ambiance designed to your fantasy that is also cognizant of your home supply levels—your health conditions, your allergies, your weight objectives, or simply your wife's shopping list? Once purchased, the order is processed by remote intelligent warehouses and delivered to your doorstep automatically or by a smiling clerk.

Would this model not be replicable in many other retail stores? What happens to investors or businesses that have large retail facilities? What about those who used to work in supermarkets and their supply chains?

What about a profession as seemingly "technologically unaffected" as that of a policy maker (e.g., a politician)? The question here is not if we will end up with automated leadership but how technological progress impacts a policy maker's mode of operations, choices, challenges, accountability, relationship with constituents, law-making capacity, independence or dependence on new factors, lobbying effectiveness, relations with other government agencies, mandates, responsibilities, remuneration criteria, etc.

Already the number of increasing variables heavily affects the day-to-day life of a head of state both during his elective phase and after taking office (e.g., Twitter, YouTube, online news, blogs). Technological advancements also pose new challenges in the way policy is formed and affected or terminated, as in the case of growing numbers of "tweeted" public sentiment evaluations, campaigns, rallies, and uprisings. Will technology also not affect policy makers' jobs substantially? And what to say about the management and execution of policy and policy making? The greater the government structure, the greater the potential exposure.

Many are fixated on the fate of billionaires and the tycoons who might be seen as having barely a chance of being affected by any of this. Incredibly and paradoxically the level of exposure to growingly numerous risks that extremely wealthy individuals, estates, trusts or concerns face through Web inclusivity and in general innovation and new variables—is more than might be apparent at first glance and potentially more devastating than can be imagined and more time sensitive than can be appreciated. Though it is hard to establish a priori to what degree, as this depends on each case, it would not be so unreasonable to guesstimate that the level of exposure theoretically might be somewhat proportional to their wealth.

Whose job will not be affected directly or indirectly? Whose business model will not be transformed? Whose investments might not be touched? Does not "when this will happen" become secondary priority? But even more importantly, do our current economic models have the answer? Will existing legacy or hybrid models (discussed later) be able to address these issues?

Have government policies and reforms been able to address the issue of potential impact of Web inclusivity on the continuous spiral of joblessness, business closures, investment evaporation, and economic meltdown?

Web inclusivity is not only about the Web but also about automation, processes, human interaction, societies, individuals, and everything that concerns our very human way of life.

What is foreseen by today's policies/models/reforms to address the negative DNA changing effects/impact of all these on businesses, jobs, investments, markets, and entire economies?

Are we all doomed to sit at home? How is the economy to provide sustenance and business? How are policy makers going to provide a basis for jobs for the growing numbers of unemployed? How are they going to address business leaders, entrepreneurs, investors, owners, executives, and employees that lose their source of income? How will they stop business closures? Should we turn back technology? Stop advancement? Go back to twenty years ago?

Fortunately, we might not have to, should we wish to open our horizons beyond the current model(s) that naturally lock us in that world—a context that is no longer consistent with today's and tomorrow's reality, challenges, and opportunities.

THE "K" IN KES[A]

So far among the plethora of the uncountable new variables, advances, and innovations, we have only touched on Web inclusivity. Let's now talk about a few more variables; among these is the K in KES[A]: knowledge.

Another aspect that is taking form and is bound to shape and transform the way we live are all those aspects that will impact human knowledge. This has many dimensions to it, and it is not limited to Internet or Web inclusivity. Let us analyze the major ones here.

One aspect of knowledge is the raw information/data in itself and anything digitally stored (e.g., your name and birth date, the formula for calculating the orbit of Mars, the definition of legal terminology, the photograph of an object, the blueprint of a skyscraper, highly sensitive government data, the molecular composition of elements, the wealth of information in streaming format).

The second aspect of knowledge has to do with not only how information, data, and knowledge are processed but also the results of this elaboration. Raw data gives way to databases and their management. Elaborations use the raw data to process information and the result of this elaboration, together with a third aspect—that of the results of the elaboration of a human brain—all to be stored in databases or clouds.

Software and applications are moving away from the need to be physically associated with one's personal medium of connectivity that processed the data you fed it. It used to be that your computer needed software you physically purchased and installed to process the data you provided it with and which henceforth resided on your computer.

This concept has evolved, and today your preferred medium (e.g., tablets, smartphones) can download the applications you need or run them remotely in a cloud. This concept, however, is already old news independent of its recent commercial availability.

Clouds, as we know them today, are a virtual place on a distant server that runs applications and provides storage space.

In the not-too-distant future there will probably be no real need for the smart mediums we use today, since all you might ever need will be in the cloud—literally everything from your work applications, your personal applications, your work data, your personal data, your photographs, your films, your music, everything (even data you have deleted). It is only logical to think that, as time goes by, each element in the cloud might end up having a price tag associated with it—even your own data.

Already some tablets of the latest generation come less equipped with easy and fast transfer possibilities of your private data to a physically separate personal storage facility. In most cases you still can save personal data on your hard drive, but you have to go through an increasingly unnerving series of transfers.

Clouds in cyberspace make sense commercially, because they are children of the same paradigm: Web inclusivity. In the not-so-distant future your medium will probably move toward becoming a mere instrument for sending and/or receiving all matters concerning your life. This medium might not even need to be visible in its standby state, as we will see later.

This knowledge dimension also includes something extremely important. It forms the repository of all thinking and its evolution. In other words, it's a place where all our (humanity's) knowledge, know-how, ideas, inventions, thoughts, strategies, perceptions, feelings, moods, fears, hopes, rage, doubts, questions, and movements reside.

How will this enormous repository influence our lives? What implications might these events have on our existing models, lives, interactions, businesses, jobs, investments, markets, and economies?

In proving their concerns, recently two biologists made headlines by disclosing how easy it had been for them to download all the information necessary from the Web to reactivate the polio virus using every day, easily acquirable lab machinery.

The other aspect of knowledge deals with the third dimension of data, information, results of elaboration and in general inclusive-info henceforth (II) or better yet its:

- Denial—e.g.: II can be rendered fully or partially unavailable without prior notice with incalculable domino effects on systems, applications, reports . . . that depended on this II;
- Manipulation—e.g.: II is exposed to manipulation in ways that physically printed data could not be whereas a single modification from a single input source can;
- Visibility—e.g.: visibility over II can be controlled giving providing different perspectives over II;
- Completeness—e.g.: the level of comprehensiveness of II can be controlled;
- Original source validation—e.g.: as everyone relies on potentially same subset of II—this becomes an assumed truth;
- Accuracy—e.g.: the previous point gives way to exposure to inaccuracy;

- Veridicity (truthfulness) e.g.: II under KES^A increases exposure to possibility of falseness and false positives phenomena;
- II overkill e.g.: exposure to abundance of II—hard to find what is relevant;
- Time theft and focus inhibition—e.g.: the above points could lead to exposure to wanted or unwanted unproductive time spent in searching, being detoured to unnecessary II, dispersion of energies and inhibiting focus and concentration;
- Etc.

Extrapolating this concept to higher levels, if the axiom that has held true throughout human history—that information is power—would whoever has access to segments of the overall KES^A, its transportation and distribution means, and its elaboration or storage unequivocally hold potential power?

THE "E" IN KES[A]

Here we talk about the economic aspects of KES[A]. Earlier we noticed how business, jobs, and processes have been affected by Web inclusivity. But is that the only economic impact we can expect?

Think of the interactions that lead to business opportunities and their development, the joining of forces that create investments, a return on investment, how they translate into compensation, etc. All of these will be impacted. Moreover, think about the dynamics and processes that currently translate into offers, orders, production, and payments. To what extent might these evolve? What about our hard-earned savings?

Who will produce what? Where? How? With what? With whom? For whom?

There is much more to be said here also but given the books central theme it is best to elaborate this in the manner it deserves in specific book and or paper.

THE "S" IN KES[A]

Let us now touch on the S in KES[A]: the social dimension. We are talking about the world of social networks, where at a growing scale many interact with others. This dimension does not touch one post on these websites (e.g., photos, opinions, conversations), because these belong to the knowledge domain.

What we are talking about here is subtler. It is about whom one connects with, the quality of the interaction, the purposes of the interaction, and the type of the interaction among other things. Actions and reactions spark not only with reference to the impact between the two connecting persons but the cascading effects that they have on the general behavior of the masses or sub-segments of it.

There are already applications that sense the general mood or communication trends of society and sub-segments of it (e.g., applications that hone in on communications among the hacker communities to anticipate attacks on certain websites). Independently of what is being sensed or whether or not these activities are limited only to sensing on behalf of some scientific institute for academic purposes or if they go beyond this for verifying reactions of groups to certain inputs, it is not impossible, but it is not the focus of this book.

The question rather is what effect this has on everything else. And are our current socioeconomic models geared to face this additional challenge? With what instruments? And how? To reach what objectives?

Social networks are currently the property of companies that have for now a purely lucrative scope. What about the unlawful or uncontrolled use or divulgation of this information or the sale of these companies that manage and "own" this data (your data)?

These are just a fraction of the legitimate questions that need to be addressed sooner or later.

THE "A" IN KES^A

The last element composing KES^A is awareness. I have elected to discuss this only very briefly in this book not only because it will fill a book of its own but primarily because the risk associated with it is not yet felt or perceived as imminent. Right or wrong, it is not the central theme, because for now it is a thought, one worth initial investigation or possible intellectual consideration.

I have not seen much evidence of it in recent literature, except some notions of it maybe in science fiction—or I might not have looked in the right places. Yet there are elements all around us that might suggest the possibility of such an eventuality not being too far-fetched after all, or at least be worth a reflection.

While navigating the Web in the early days (only a couple of decades ago), each search was a unique transaction, building only a bidirectional connection and creating rudimentary synapses between two elements, which probably quit existing the moment the transaction ended.

This happened in closed-network environments, involving very limited resources and connecting to a single server or a limited number of rudimentary servers/PCs.

Today, at an increasing rate, each search is more of a stream of information and connections rather than a unique query/response episode. It feels and looks like a flow, an interaction with one or more applications, creating an incalculable number of synapses.

One's transaction is even anticipated in the search, producing responses even before there is time to finish typing the first letters of a query. The Web today is linked to our mobile applications, creating numerous additional connections to yet other servers and more intelligent applications that are growing and sharing data each day.

Today data continues to be elaborated. Additional intelligence is being developed even when we are not actively using the system, think we have deleted or trashed it or are completely disconnected. This information flows and its eventual successive elaboration occurs without human intervention or control from one application to another, creating new nodes of interconnecting inclusive-info and its further elaboration.

And this is not limited to our own personal data, which might reside on social networks or our laptop/tablet/smartphone. It includes data, applications, the results of elaborations, our reaction and feedback to it, etc. (inclusive-info) that are kept on servers across the world. It goes from the inclusive-info generated /provided by grocery store down the street, to the company that produces buttons, to those that produce light-bulbs, to one's bank, to the company that produces electricity, to the one that controls the local power grid, to the accountant, to the law enforcement agencies, to the ministries of finance, to the aircraft manufacturer, to the shipbuilder, to the defense contractor, to the intelligence community, to the country's most sensitive data, to the office of the highest-ranking public officials, and to the office of the president.

In this process, the amount of connections and synapses are probably no longer calculable, as they grow exponentially with each second.

It is not uncommon to find a growing number of industrial and nonindustrial processes linked up to Web-based applications that serve to control them (e.g., presses, robotics) and to produce data from these processes.

These applications are, in most cases, linked to others that govern other areas within a company, such as finance and senior management decision-making cockpits.

The applications are also connected to a growing number of outside concerns, such as suppliers, customer systems, and other industrial processes, which are connected to other applications and servers both within and outside their companies—in a virtual link that could go around the world, creating more connections and more synapses.

This connectivity enables us to purchase something online that is produced from scratch and invoiced immediately. This interconnectivity also allows the use of data by many concerns.

The "A" in KES^A refers to awareness. It is an awareness acquired by humans who use the systems. Yet is this the only type of awareness possible?

This notion goes beyond a new concept called "super intelligence (artificial intelligence)" of mocynet and anything electronic. We need to be cognizant that in 1997 a computer called Deep Blue beat Gary Kasparov, the world's best chess player, at his own game. What today is called the dimension of digital minds could theoretically be superseded by awareness.

MOBINT: MOBILE AND INTERNET TECHNOLOGY

Mobility is probably the true step-level revolution within the Internet revolution. It gave the Internet its legs to walk with you and be present wherever you are.

At this rate of convergence, when will we, for example, end up needing only one medium that does it all, one that can change its physical shape to fit different needs?

"Mobint," we could call it, is the convergence between mobile technology and the Internet. It provides directions to your newly found restaurant and access to your favorite online book or movie. You can receive all your e-mails without necessarily having to transport your PC along with you. You can even check in on a plane with it. In today's world you can even know if your refrigerator is running out of milk and open your garage door with a simple app.

A group of professors and researchers at the Massachusetts Institute of Technology are working on a new concept called "reality mining." The applications they have developed are based on the historic movements of your cell phone. They can tell not only where you went but also how long you stayed in a particular room of a house, at what exact time you walked out of a room to walk into another room, with whom you might have been (if they were tracking other phones as well), and when you stepped out of your own house. Among other things they can tell if you were running, jogging, or walking.

What is fascinating is that, should you wish to sign up for the program on a voluntary basis, they can predict your future movements with a declared accuracy of around 95 percent.

In conducting their study on a group of volunteers, they noticed common behavioral patterns of persons who did not know each other. In the long run, for example, these patterns could make them, for example, prone to health problems such as diabetes. In other words, they sustain that by sharing your movement information. They could advise you on potentially hazardous behaviors that increase your potential risk and exposure to certain health problems.

The main concern is around privacy and the ability to exercise one's rights. That should include using one's proprietary data as one pleases. The paradox here is that our private information is already available to those who want to access it. Billions are made by companies that provide this information or use it. Can we change the model?

People have a growing number of questions. For instance, if others are free to sell our information, why aren't we benefiting from this or managing its distribution?

There are many schools of thought here. Some argue it would be a source of income. Others argue that if you have nothing to hide, why should you be worried in the first place? Still others argue that one's perception of oneself might be one thing, whereas the way the information is used or elaborated—and, hence, the way you end up being perceived and exposed to judgment by others—might be a totally different story. How many persons have lost their jobs because of what they deemed a perfectly normal life routine posted on the Internet?

e-Money and e-Wallets

Virtual money is already a reality. If not already available in some parts of the world, in the not-too-distant future a growing number of individuals and businesses will also be able to pay with their smartphone at the supermarket, movie theater, etc. Will this mean the end of credit and debit cards?

Will this entail more synergies, mergers, cuts, and Web inclusivity in the business model? Will it force more businesses to close, generating more job losses? What impact will these advances have on existing and future business models?

Though no one has that sort of a view into the future, it is reasonably likely that these transformations will impact the financial industry. But is that the real extent of the impact on the financial world, as we know it today? Will the financial world be impacted beyond the credit card business, home banking, and ATMs?

Networked Intelligent Business Systems and Apps

In the not-so-distant future, a company that manufactures widgets and needs fifty kilograms of a specific item will simply need to type in a request for it on the Web-inclusive app to immediately find three suppliers that have confirmed their product availability. How will this impact intermediaries, agents, other websites, applications? What further implications might this have on known industrial or business models, processes, investments, and employment?

e-Retail

Web inclusivity is a paradox that has impacted the retail business heavily in the past years. The official numbers of Internet sales on Web-inclusive websites is growing exponentially all over the world. Websites that were originally set up to sell only a specific item (e.g., books) have now become the epicenter for just about anything one might wish to buy or to sell!

Where is all this taking us? Will physical retail disappear? To answer these questions, let's extrapolate on the current model to a possible not-so-distant future on a type of merchandise that might still be a bit harder to separate from the physicality of a retail store: i.e., clothing.

Different from a camera that once you've investigated and identified you can literally buy on the Internet—not only in your own country but in a country that offers it at a substantially lower price (even considering transportation)—in order to buy clothing you are still, even though to an increasingly less extent, in need of a physical store. This is because you might wish to try on the clothing, compare it to other items, experience the joy of shopping, etc. But what if, in the near future, the manufacturer or designer gives you an opportunity to bypass the current retail model that needs your physical presence?

Should a shopper wish to purchase a nice skirt shown in a Web catalog, an advertisement, or simply seen in a shop, is there any real impediment that she could do this, providing her digitalized body scan directly with apps on a smartphone, into the factory in an interactive modality so that the person can immediately see the effect on a digitalized version of herself with the possibility of personalizing the skirt to best fit her specific requirements with an endless selection of buttons, zips, colors, accessories, etc., that will produce (heaven knows where in the world) a perfectly custom tailor-made skirt (giving the perception it is no longer mass produced), bypassing all the existing intermediaries at considerably less costs?

What will happen to the retail industry? What will be their business model? What night be the *consequences to other industries in the supply chain or adjacent sectors such as construction and real-estate, the publishing, advertising industries and their supply chains?* What might the impact be in terms of additional businesses closures and unemployment? What about the investors? The answers that emerge seem crudely to point toward one conclusion: the gravitational pull of the law of inclusivity.

In the same way the gravitational force that pulls particles and atoms together to form stars, planets, and galaxies, Web inclusivity seems to be governed by the same physical laws. It seems it will pull everything together. Independent of how many sites we will populate it with in the future, is Web inclusivity the Internet's natural essence?

Are the systemic shortcoming and dichotomy of the current model more evident now? Is it limited to single industrial sectors, groups of individuals, echelon, the economy, or the nation?

How does this now change the perception BRIC (Brazil, Russia, India, China), or other healthier economies? Will this not touch investors as well? Are we not all in similar boats—just distanced temporally? Are the current economic models geared to address these issues, or have they provided effective remedies? Can we afford to stick to these existing models? Are we trying to resolve issues and challenges that have a different DNA than our current model?

Considerations on the Law of Inclusivity

Unless conspiracy theorists and doomsday catastrophist are right that there is no lasting solution in sight, there is a way out. Before we seek a solution, we need to make an important set of considerations:

- Internet and mobility bring many opportunities but have their shortcomings;

- Web inclusivity is a reality, and it must be considered and addressed;
- Mobint and Web inclusivity continue to impact our lives dramatically in all spheres, from investments to business to employment to KES^A;
- Mobint and KES^A are variables formed from a different/ evolved DNA;
- These variables constitute game- and paradigm-changing dichotomies and systemic blocks to our existing models;
- Our existing models have difficulty in appropriately addressing new variables and, in a growing number of cases, are not equipped to tackle the many new challenges posed by technological advancements;
- But in the same way each coin has two faces, these variables and innovations also open the door to many opportunities;
- The successful strategy lies in understanding how they operate and how they affect our lives. Once this is achieved, understand how to leverage their strengths, manage them, and exploit their true potential in unleashing benefits, opportunities, jobs, remuneration, investment possibilities, and long-term development and prosperity.

NANOTECHNOLOGY

Nanotechnology introduces another paradigm-changing element. The term "nano" refers to the size of miniaturized technology. A nanometer is equivalent to one-billionth of a meter. So small that in some cases solutions are developed at atomic levels. Miniaturized technology is best known for things such as the electronic circuit boards that reside in a computer's CPU or other current-day electronic equipment.

Recent innovations and inventions are opening the way to an incalculable myriad of applications, useful from both a scientific and daily point of view.

Nanotechnology will bring the further miniaturization of products and processes down to scales in the nanometer range. Current technological theorists state that this will dramatically impact the need for resources to build and supply the factories, hospitals, offices, infrastructures of tomorrow, and most of the machinery needed to run them.

In other words, the reduction in size means saving trillions of tons of raw material used for the production of the same products. It also impacts manufacturing processes that, in turn, affect how everything is organized, the amount of physical space needed, energy consumption requirements, the business models, the final size of these products and employment.

At the same time, one could venture to say that the move toward miniaturization is probably one of the first concrete moves of humanity toward real sustainability. Imagine how many things would not be possible today had we not reached this level of technological breakthrough and how many things might be possible tomorrow.

Nanotechnology has as many benefits as it does shortcomings. Much work still needs to be done to make it safer, non-hazardous to human health, and controllable.

In the field of medicine, for example, things impossible only last year could become possible by working at molecular levels in healing and combating viruses or tumors—at dimensions either equivalent to or infinitely smaller than the viruses—becoming a virus's own virus or act as a transportation vehicle for delivering medicine to specific cells while saving the rest of our healthy cells by putting them out of harm's way from the drastic side effects of many medicines or that of alternative invasive surgery.

Imagine nano-robots that destroy a tumor, down to the last cell, and then apply only a finite level of chemo- or biotherapy to those cells that need it. Scientists will finally be able to study the inner workings of maladies that have plagued mankind in ways unfathomable till today and finally provide real answers to what today are incurable illnesses.

It is not hard to imagine entire production processes will be miniaturized, drastically reducing the need for production space, costs, and raw material. New performance material will emerge for new applications, affecting every sphere of our lives. Production processes might end up being cleaner (if for example they are done under vacuum or sealed) and less damaging to the environment, providing new answers and solutions to previously irresolvable or economically nonviable investments and business enterprises, employment, etc.

On the other hand, new challenges will emerge: how to control nanostructures from being dispersed outside their needed space of operations and, only for the time necessary, preventing them from becoming airborne or waterborne hazards involuntarily entering ecosystems or sensitive membranes of the body, such as the lungs or the brain.

Let's start by seeing what some of the concerns and challenges surrounding nanotechnology today are.

Areas of Current Concerns, Risks, and Needed Improvement

According to a report produced by the US Government Accountability Office (US GAO), the following is a non-exhaustive list of findings by different research conducted to evaluate different aspects of nanotechnology (below are excerpts from this study):

1. Properties, surface, reactions, and interactions of nanomaterial. The amount of information and data available is still insufficient with regard to unfamiliar properties/types/interactions/reactions that can materialize at nano scales, (e.g., chemical, photoactive, electrical, magnetic, thermal, mechanical, optical).

It would seem that at those atomic levels, properties and interactions "could differ in important ways from the properties of conventionally scaled materials." Studies carried out would indicate that some nano-scale particles, for example, may be potentially explosive and/or photoactive—meaning that sunlight might trigger chemical reactions in them."

Additionally, given their very small dimensions, nanomaterials can enter the human body through three primary routes: inhalation, ingestion, and dermal (skin) penetration. In addition to humans, the environment may also be exposed to nanomaterials through releases into the water, air, and soil during the manufacture, use, or disposal of these materials.

Studies are being conducted to evaluate how the size of nanomaterial might affect health. As stated by GOA's report, "In some cases size may pose a risk to human health because these materials may be able to penetrate cell walls, causing cell inflammation and potentially leading to certain diseases. However, according to EPA, the small particle size may also cause the nanomaterials to agglomerate, which may make it more difficult for them to penetrate deep lung tissue;"

2. Shape. "The shape of nano-materials may be connected to the type of health risks they may pose. For example, some carbon nanotubes resemble asbestos fibers. When inhaled by people, asbestos fibers are known to cause mesothelioma . . . This similarity has caused researchers to question if exposure to such nanomaterials may lead to a similar disease;"

3. Militarized use. There are many applications where size and the other qualities offered by nanotechnology can be a strategic advantage of unfathomable destructive capability. On the other hand, the problem is the uncontrollability associated with size—hence, its unwanted or dispersion.

Opportunities

According to the same report, "the world market for nanotechnology-related products is growing and is expected to total between $1 trillion and $2.6 trillion by 2015."

Nanotechnology is not science fiction. It already affects our daily lives in ways that might surprise. Additionally, nanomaterials are not only the result of man-made material. As the GAO report states, "nanomaterials can occur naturally, be created incidentally, or be manufactured intentionally . . . naturally occurring nanomaterials can be found in volcanic ash, forest fire smoke, and ocean spray.

Incidental nanomaterials are by products of industrial processes, such as mining and metal working, and combustion engines, such as those used in cars, trucks, and some trains."

Man-made nanomaterials instead are developed for a particular application, "such as improved strength, decreased weight, or increased electrical conductivity."

The report goes on to provide concrete examples of nanotechnology uses in different sectors:

Automotive

Current Uses	Future Uses
Coatings for body and engine	Self-cleaning, self-healing paints
Bumpers	Electrodes and electrical conductors that contain movable electric charges
Auto parts that incorporate composites	New additives to improve fuel efficiency, cleaner burners, less noxious gases
Batteries with increasing efficiency	New lubricants (alternative to oil-based) to reduce engine and parts wear
	New material with ability to withstand a stretching force without breaking, about one hundred times greater than that of steel at one-sixth the weight

Advantages include reduced weight, increased strength, fire resistance, ability to block ultraviolet (UV) light, and promotion of self-cleaning without altering the transparency.

"For example, coatings containing nanoparticles make surfaces stronger, smoother, more scratch and stain resistant, waterproof, or some combination of these and other properties."

Aerospace and Defense and Civil Applications

Below are some examples of areas of possible application of nanomaterials in aerospace and defense:

- sensors for different types of applications (i.e., monitor a person's condition, or automatically dispense drugs);
- stronger and lighter aircraft bodies that are better protected against lightning and fire;
- microbe-free interiors of aircraft and clean rooms;
- surveillance from micro-platforms;
- clothing material that could potentially change color or match mood or environment, or become rigid casts to protect injuries, or help block bullets and chemical and/or biological agents;
- Nano weapons or delivery systems.

Electronics

In the electronics sector, lead-free, conductive adhesives could eliminate tons of toxic and leaded solder used every year by some industries, leading to more efficient and longer-lasting data storage with estimated storage capacity of one terabyte per square inch, and micro-batteries may open the door to many new applications.

Energy and Environment

Applications here can range from cleaning up waste to substituting nonrenewable resources with renewable ones, to reducing pollution, to increasing the efficiency of solar power generation.

"Increased surface area of various types of ceramic or metal nanomaterials for example can result in the rapid reduction of contaminant concentrations in soil, water, and air, as pollutants or toxins in these media react with the nanomaterials."

In the future, nanomaterials could help deliver alternative forms of energy, cleaner water, and more efficient energy transmission. Using nano-scale catalysts, hydrogen could be produced from water more efficiently.

For example, a company has developed a photo electrode that uses nano-scale material and converts sunlight into hydrogen six times more efficiently than its conventionally scaled competitor.

In addition, nanotechnology-enabled water desalination and filtration systems may offer affordable, scalable, and portable water filtration in the future. Filters have the potential to allow water molecules to pass through, but screen out salt ions, bacteria, viruses, heavy metals, and organic material.

Nanomaterial could improve the efficiency of energy transmission by increasing the capacity and durability of insulation for underground electrical cables. This would allow cables of smaller diameter to carry the same power or more power (as much as one hundred times more) as larger cables and to last longer whilst reducing transmission losses, saving billions of dollars in fuel consumption (i.e., equivalent to 24 million barrels of oil just in the United States, according to the study).

Food Production and Agriculture

Examples of applications in this sector ranging from strong oxygen and carbon dioxide barriers have been used in plastic bottles and films for packaging food and beverages and "encapsulation" (a means of delivering another material inside the human body to target nutrients, release drugs on a controlled schedule, and mask tastes—for example, some vitamins can be difficult to deliver in beverages because they degrade and may not be easily absorbed by the body).

In the future, manufactured nanomaterials could be used to enhance agriculture; monitor food quality and freshness; improve the ability to track food products from point of origin to retail sale; and modify the taste, texture, and fat content of food.

Nanomaterials are being developed to more efficiently and safely administer pesticides, herbicides, and fertilizers by controlling more precisely when and where they are released and in which quantities.

Sensors have been developed that can detect bacteria such as salmonella in water and liquid food and contamination of crops such as spinach, lettuce, and tomatoes, potentially reducing the spread of food-borne illnesses.

Nano radio-frequency identification tags could be integrated into packaging for food products, potentially result in improved food security and better inventory tracking and management.

Housing and Construction

"Materials and coatings are currently making buildings and homes cleaner and stronger." In the future they could improve: energy efficiency and insulation, protective coatings, antifogging, self-cleaning windows, lighter, tougher and more durable material, air purification products and energy-efficient air-conditioning systems, solar energy capture and intelligent energy release, and self-healing, incorporating "nano-containers with a repair substance . . . designed to open and release its repair material to fill the gap and seal the crack."

Medical

Nano-scale sensors could be used to identify biomarkers, such as altered genes and early indicators of cancer, and show presence, location, and contours of cardiovascular and neurological diseases and small tumors. They could track particles to the site of a tumor, resulting in earlier detection of tumors.

Nano-instruments could allow continuous and detailed health monitoring, while other applications could include the following:

- producing enhanced images from deep inside human tissue used to guide surgical procedures and monitor the effectiveness of nonsurgical therapies in reversing the disease or slowing its progression;
- drug delivery and accuracy, additionally turning a drug into a multifunctional tool or platform for diagnosis and treatment;
- antimicrobial wound dressings, requiring fewer dressing changes for patients, which can result in pain;
- delivery platforms that can produce targeted interventions such as the one suggested by the National Institutes of Health: "gold nano-shells to simultaneously image and destroy cancer cells using infrared selectively . . . killing tumor cells without disturbing neighboring healthy cells . . . potentially reducing the amount of chemotherapy" to deliver molecules and growth factors to promote better healing for burns and wounds that heal without scars;
- healing mesh scaffolds to treat bone, nerve, cartilage, and muscle injuries, improving healing or stopping the flow of blood and other liquids.

Other Nano Applications

- personal care and cosmetics products for aesthetic purposes;
- performance improvement and reinforcement of a variety of sporting goods, such as bicycle frames, tennis rackets, baseball bats, hockey sticks, skis, and tennis balls;
- new water- and stain-resistant, power-generating clothing.

Robotics

Mere science fiction until a few years ago, it is an ever-growing presence in many industries, with an increasing level of use in new and different processes. Advanced robotics are replacing processes not only in manufacturing and mining but also in hospitals and other places where there are particularly dangerous working conditions.

Robotics are used to perform ever-increasing numbers of tasks previously performed by man, with undesired consequences on his health. Robotics are also used increasingly in advanced studies, from outer space explorations, to deep ocean surveys, maintenance, and salvage operations.

A form of robotics is used in unmanned vehicles that have different applications in military and civilian fields. For now each of these is mission specific. For example, they can only fly on intelligence-gathering missions over enemy territory. Alternatively, they can act as mini helicopters with the added benefit derived from hovering. They can alternatively be used as terrestrial vehicles to search and destroy explosive devices. They can be waterborne, acting as fast-moving patrol boats, or alternatively be used to do underwater maintenance work for oil companies.

Other Technological Advancements/Innovations

Our lives are being affected in many other areas, as well. Advancement is touching just about every aspect of our lives, most times with paradigm- and game-changing impacts. Below are just a few other examples.

Additive Manufacturing

Additive manufacturing, though something still in its infancy, is already being put to use in real-world applications. This current manufacturing process usually starts out with a slab of material (such as a sheet of aluminum), which is then machined down to shed off and create great levels of waste and raw material. Additive manufacturing uses a revolutionary technique that flips the entire model around.

It works at molecular levels, building objects that have been designed on a PC using advanced 3-D technology to literally create the object from a printer that, instead of spraying ink, sprays tiny particles of matter. As the particles settle row after row, the "printer head" moves back and forth, stacking the rows of fused material one on top of the other until the object materializes in front of your eyes from the bottom up!

Exoskeleton Applications

This technology is already in use and will have many possible applications in diverse fields. In the medical field it could help paraplegics or other differently abled persons to improve their freedom of movement and quality of life.

In construction, mining, and labor-intensive industries it could reduce exposure of workers to injury, improving delivery timetables and increasing the type of task that could be achieved.

In the fields of applied sciences, research, mining, marine applications, or anything requiring significant amounts of muscle energy (but not enough to require specific larger machinery), this application could provide new answers.

Mind-Activated Applications and Processes and Mind Capability Augmentation

This technology is no longer science fiction. Several researchers, universities, and institutions around the world are making the final tweaks to these applications, opening the way to currently unpredictable uses, such as allowing differently abled persons to perform tasks, see, and hear—not possible only a few years ago. Its industrial and personal uses are theoretically endless, and anyone's guess is good.

There are also many advanced studies that have yielded concrete results in the area mind capability augmentation. Test thus far concluded that expert capability can be acquired artificially via electromagnetic stimulation to the brain through new applications. This stimulus seems augment synapse generation or activity in specific areas of the brain allowing a person to acquire capability that would otherwise require years of training to develop. The example here was with reference to creating expert capability in intelligence analysts in evaluating aerial photographs and finding enemy targets in a very limited timeframe (weeks?)—that would have otherwise required years of training and experience to develop.

The degree to which this might be achievable (without causing undesired side effects) might imply a paradigm shift in human learning un-paralleled in history—completely altering many of our millennia old dogmas, models, and convictions not only in the area of education.

Next-Generation Alternative Energy

Many new advances in this arena are making headlines each day. New technology is allowing for instance, a substantial reduction in solar panel sizes and costs while increasing performance levels n-fold. In another example, the US Navy Research Laboratory believes it may be possible to make jet fuel (JP-5) onboard ships derived from seawater (IHS Janes International News Briefs).

Undeniably, new technology development and commerciability require a phased rollout. Their use or the time frames involved are no longer in question. The questions rather are how these will impact our existing models. Which existing models are geared to address and leverage these new paradigm-changing variables? How will we be able to exploit the opportunities these offer to create sustainable long-term development, prosperity, and well-being concretely if our current models cannot provide answers?

ADDITIONAL CONSIDERATIONS ON INNOVATION

What could be defined as the law of "Technological Innovation Advancement and Inclusivity," or TIAI (which encapsulates Web + Mobint + Nano + Robotics technology and other advancements), contemplates the merging of new technology into something that might go beyond the tablets and smartphones we have become accustomed to, since only a few years ago.

Innovation in nanotechnology might bring about mediums that might be invisible to the naked eye in their stand-by state but which can be enlarged simply by our hand motions, becoming virtual screens to the size necessary for different uses—from watching TV in 3D on a larger than the current sixty-inch displays, which we can temporarily hang or place where we wish, to converting it into a picture-in-picture screens where you can develop your thoughts into without having to type them while watching the news, receiving an e-mail, etc.

It might allow you to reduce the size of the display back down again to a handheld to access any information you might need at any time—for example, on a plane—or size it down to an object as small as a coin or less that could become your Skype phone on the move without the need to having a physically visible smartphone, TV, tablet, PC, movie and picture camera, wallet, ID, driver's license, personal medical data, document container, music/film/picture database, social networks connector, travel agent, personal assistant, trainer, medical advisor, idea manager, calendar, apps list, stereo system, etc. It could be whatever you would like it to be.

So how and where do we go from here? How many businesses, investments, and jobs will be lost or gained from these new innovations? What impact will these innovations have on the economy at large, independent of geographical location? Will there be an economy, as we know it?

What shape or form will our economies take in the near future? Is this the end of the road? Or the beginning of a new era?

Without being ingenuous about things, is it now clear why it does not really make a difference what China or India or Russia or Brazil are up to today, if they are using the same reference model? Our destinies are interconnected on a planetary scale more than we might wish to think. Once the current economic model peaks (in my modest opinion it we are possibly very close), it will produce the same effects on the neo-economic giants as it did with developed ones—with an impact relative to their sizes or, even worse, if unknown cumulative effects come into play.

As I write each sentence, entire echelons of society are disappearing on a global scale—the middle class being the first and most affected in the immediate term. Should things remain unchanged, are we sure that there could be persons who might not remain unaffected by it? To what degree?

REACTIONS, IMPLICATIONS, AND EFFECTS

There are several natural reactions to advancement, technology, and innovation. They include curiosity, reactionary, conspiracy, opportunistic, contemplative, ironic, cynical, extremist, religious, etc.

Productive in healthy debates, each of the above stances might or might not add anything to the equation of how to address a step-level evolutionary transformation that is already taking place.

It is imperative to understand how these innovations will continue to transform our lives, beyond what has been discussed thus far, i.e.: investments, business models, employment, processes, etc., and their implications. This exercise alone is not sufficient. We must understand how each of these innovations affect other elements making up the existing economic model. These include: public debt, taxes and fiscal policy, monetary policy, economic policy, pensions and retirement, markets, banking, financial services, manufacturing, retail and all other sectors, international trade, and so on.

In performing this evolutionary protocol for each of the above elements, each time there is a paradigm-changing innovation, we will need to find how each innovation impacts the existing economic model and begin to create a new framework to understand what choices we have in order to take action and transform challenges in opportunities, opening a new chapter in progress, prosperity, and human evolution.

MONEY

We all have been accustomed to the images of large presses located in the inner meanders of Fort Knox-like buildings. Behind enormous, protected vaults, several feet thick, security-cleared employees and highly skilled technicians use special paper, ink and embossing made with secretive formulas and processes to print money.

Employees are searched routinely at different checkpoints in the building. Cameras follow their every action. Armed guards are everywhere. The picture might be more or less as described, based upon the country, but in many cases one might be surprised to find out that in reality the task of printing money is simply assigned to a country's mint that in some cases operates in incredibly ordinary buildings with an adequate level of security.

The cost of the presses and the processes involved is so high that some countries don't even bother printing money themselves and outsource the physical production of their currency to other mints, such as those of the United States.

We just covered the creation of physical paper money and coins. The amount of physical money in circulation at any given moment is very limited. In replace cases new money is printed only to supplant used and damaged currency.

Physical currency only makes up a very small percentage of total money circulating in an economy. The vast majority of money is nonphysical. This nonphysical money has no material connotation to it. It is simply represented by a number in a computer. With limited exceptions, and unless it is an illicit business, an employer, for example, does not use physical money to pay his employees unless they specifically ask for it. Banks don't use physical money to give out large loans. Financial institutions and businesses of all kinds around the globe do not use physical money to perform their transactions.

Think of it when you receive your paycheck. Your hard-earned money is literally represented by the ink that forms the numbers you see at the bottom of your pay slip.

If you query your bank account at an ATM or on your PC, your money takes the form of the pixels that are illuminated on the screen. These are just bits and bytes stored in a server somewhere (that could even be located on some distant island nation).

It would be too hard and expensive to print and store all the money that is needed in an economy. Like with gold and silver, the mere idea of printing money to cover all transactions in an economy had to be given up a long time ago because it was physically impossible. The vast majority of the trillions that make the world go round in economic terms and are exchanged on a daily basis around the world are all virtual, digital numbers on screens, binary digits in servers—representing an adaptation to evolved needs.

For all practical purposes, money is virtual, and this modality of paying and receiving money keeps the system working. Your credit and debit cards generate transactions that are not in paper bills (except for when you request cash advances). Your bills are now paid mostly via a noncash modality. The majority of transactions nowadays across the globe use virtual money.

The nonphysical nature of money is not a new concept. Merchants as far back as biblical time used rudimentary promissory notes (IOUs). As early as the seventeenth century, rudimentary ancestors of checks were used with growing frequency to settle payments even across borders. Our credit and debit cards are just natural evolutions of such transaction modalities.

In the not-so-distant past, before the invention of computers, virtual money was represented by mere physical entries made by a vast number of clerks on general ledger accounts in one's bank that reconciled accounts between them and their central banks. With the introduction of information and communication technology and the Web, reconciliations take place in a matter of hours, and that is only due to the server's processing capability. Paper money is fast becoming a thing of the past. Banks are not obligated to maintain large sums of cash. The only cash they need to maintain is what the central banks designate them to have. So should there be a reason for a bank rush tomorrow morning, you might be better off not risking getting hurt in the midst of an angry mob, because there will not be enough cash to be distributed—even though you are legally entitled to it.

In today's world nothing backs up money. And since 1971, after President Nixon's decree, money derives its value only from the significance that individuals and societies bestow upon it around the world. It is as physical as thin air or smoke.

It is not backed by gold or any other thing of material value. Even in its physical form, the paper on which the currency is printed is of relatively insignificant value. Its effective cost is linked to the expense incurred in making it harder to counterfeit.

Money is no longer tied to physical collateral such as gold because of the limited amount of gold in an economy at any given point in time. A currency's link to any form of collateral would limit an economy's capacity to grow. Just as it happened in the past with other mediums of exchange that limited trade (e.g., barter), the rule was simply changed.

Hence, money remains a mere instrument, enabling the exchange of goods and services between individuals. Therefore, there is no reason that it could not take any shape or form (physical or nonphysical) so long as it performs its primary task.

But how is nonphysical money generated? What provides its importance?

HOW IS MONEY GENERATED?

In essence there is no magic, no alchemy, no complicated mathematical formula involved in money's creation or providing its importance. People give money its relevance and weight. It has always been so. In fact, even in times when its value was tied to gold, there have been several moments when simple loss of faith in its value led to a currency's devaluation. Though economists differ in their theories of how money is created, the following seems to be the most prevalent in current economics literature. There is no bias here as to who is more or less right, since this might be of little relevance to the main issues—namely, the economic crisis and how to resolve it.

As asserted by many economists, in today's economy and in most parts of the world, banks create money every time they generate a loan. As John Kenneth Galbraith put it, "the process is so simple that the mind is repelled." In fact, contrary to common belief, it is much simpler than one might think.

Before we start though, it is best to understand the main elements making up the puzzle.

"Demand deposit" is the technical name given to bank accounts. The money that you place in the bank account must be given back to you at your demand. It represents a legal claim that a customer has against his bank, since the deposit represents a liability of the bank toward the customer. It is the customer's money.

Central banks, Federal Reserve Banks or in general Monetary Authorities represent the central nervous system of the banking system and are, in most cases, responsible for the monetary policy of a country (we will elaborate on this later). In the United States, the Federal Reserve System is the central bank. It was created in 1913 and is made up of twelve Federal Reserve District Banks. It is the bank for other banks, offering more or less the same type of services that commercial banks offer to their customers (i.e., loans, deposit accounts, and check-clearing services). In fact, each commercial bank must hold a "reserve account" in its Federal Reserve District Bank.

Commercial banks are privately held banks. Not all commercial banks are members of the Federal Reserve System or their central banks. Only member banks can obtain loans directly from the Federal Reserve or central banks at a discounted rate. Commercial banks can lend to their customers and also to one another, and they do so at a rate that allows them to make some money.

Now that the terminology is clearer, let's see how the system operates in normal conditions. Each time you write a check or pay a bill via the Internet, two things happen:

- At the commercial bank level, the balance of your bank account drops by the amount paid, while that of the service provider increases;
- At the central bank or Federal Reserve Bank level, the reserve accounts of the two banks (your bank and that of, say, the service provider) are affected by the same amounts in diametrically opposed ways. This is done electronically and does not involve any physical movement of paper bills or coins.

In this example, the total amount of money circulating in the economy (what is technically known as the total money stock) is not affected. No money has been generated because no value was added to the amounts exchanged.

So when and how is money generated in the current system? One of the primary ways money is generated through the banking system is when money is created at a commercial bank level, when a bank grants a loan (McKenzie, Tullok, & et al).

Every time you ask for a loan and the bank approves it, the bank provides those funds to you via your preferred instrument—a cashier's check, credit on your account balance, or an electronic fund transfer directly to an account—a bank creates new money. It creates new money by simply writing a check or inserting the number of dollars to be credited or electronically transferred in the appropriate fields in a computer!

The instance it does so, the bank generates money, literally from thin air. Contrary to common belief, banks do not necessarily lend out other people's money when they loan money. This action instantly increases the amount of money circulating in the economy by the same amount. It is for this reason that economists say that banks generate money when they give out loans.

The only thing stopping banks from going overboard with this (i.e., generating all the money it wants) is that banks are restricted as to how much money they can create by two factors: the total amount of deposits they hold for customers and reserve requirements.

The reserve requirement is usually expressed as a percentage of a bank's total demand deposits that cannot be loaned out and must be held on deposit with the Federal Reserve or in cash in the bank's vault. Reserve requirements can be changed by the central banks at any given time.

Reserve requirements have nothing to do with the financial standing of banks or ensuring that banks can meet demand deposit requests. They simply exist to restrict the amount of money banks can create. But if this is true, then is the system continuously generating money? No.

Acting as counterweight to the money generation process—on the exact opposite end of the scale—as money is generated in the system, money is also eliminated by the system each time a loan is paid back, be it as an installment or in a lump sum.

As absurd as it might sound if a bank is in a situation whereby in limited periods of time it receives more loan repayments than it has requests for loans, it will not be able to create as much money as it potentially could. In fact, some bankers and economists dispute the necessity for reserve requirements and affirm that banks' restraints in generating money should be limited only to their profitability and credit standing.

Each loan generates a demand in the system that goes up the chain to the ultimate level of the central bank or the Federal Reserve. The demand for the loan (together with the aggregated demand for all other loans in the country) generates digital accounting entries upstream in the accounts of banks that are members of their relative central banks/Federal Reserve. This process allows the central banks/Federal Reserve Banks that accumulate this data to control the flow of money into the economy (theoretically in line with a country's monetary policy) through a number of ways, increasing or easing the legal reserve requirements, as previously stated.

The money creation process is prone to problems. The control of the money supply in an economy is not as easy as it might sound. Central banks/Federal Reserve have three main tools at their disposal to control money generation and availability in an economy:

1. The first is something we have already discussed—modifying the reserve requirements of commercial banks;

2. The second is a control over loans that central banks can make to commercial banks at discounted rates. These loans take the form of digital accounting entries a central bank makes on the reserve account of a commercial bank. This digital entry increases the commercial bank's capability in creating money. The commercial bank, in this case, simply commits to repaying this virtual debt. Where does the central bank/ Federal Reserve get the money to loan? Among other things, it essentially simply creates a digital entry in a computer, crediting the commercial bank's reserve account that it holds with the central bank and simply accepting the IOU from the commercial bank as collateral. A very generic analogy could be an imaginary scenario whereby you could ask your father for a loan, and he prints the money from his printer or sends a digital entry to your bank account and provides you with the money, accepting your IOU;

3. And the third is achieved through the purchase or sale of government bonds or notes by a central bank/Federal Reserve. Government bonds or notes are also created by a central bank within the context of a monetary policy. When a central bank buys the bonds it has printed and issued, it increases the amount of money in circulation and reduces or eliminates money in circulation when it sells/issues bonds.

De facto the two key assumptions behind the balanced functioning of the system are: loans are continually issued in a normally functioning economy, and these loans are ultimately paid back.

Here are some examples of legitimate questions posed by growing numbers of experts, business leaders and individuals:

- Do these key assumptions still hold validity today? If central or Federal Reserve Banks have provided the banking system with injections of money, why then are these not being distributed into the real economy? Would these have not helped reduce the number of defaulting payments as the economy sheds businesses and jobs in a catch-22 vortex?;

- If the banking system generates money virtually, why should a bank be able to strap the customer into incredibly unbalanced and arbitrary contracts, take out a mortgage and/or collateral sometimes (depending on the country you live in) in excess of n times the value of the purchased asset, exercise the right to unilaterally change the clauses at any moment, legally alienate customers' loans, sell them off to third parties, transform them into other types of negotiable paper, reverse-insure them (e.g., benefiting in case your house goes on fire), and bundle them into toxic assets that it sells back to the same customer under a form of a retirement fund, investment or insurance? This is all done without the customer's realistic right to disagree, mitigate, share some of the potential benefits, or counterbalance the risk;

- In the unfortunate case of a defaulting customer, the bank is legally entitled to exercise its right to unilaterally force a business into liquidation or simply sell off a customer's lifelong investments and enterprises or repossess and foreclose at will, with realistically little legal appeal.

This is yet another systemic dichotomy, the effects of which we witness on the news and all around the world. *The underlying message is not to jettison everything*; instead, it is to ask ourselves what can be done better: *to find a solution, a better model, one that could be more beneficial and remunerative to all stakeholders, whilst putting much needed systemic stability and credibility back into the system?*

The virtuality of money and its current generation modality are not a problem but a key to the solution. Fortunately it is occurring in the right temporal evolutionary moment, facilitating the path toward a solution and apt to address the new paradigms and variables. The emergence of new phenomena such as Bitcoin are just the tip of the iceberg.

INVESTMENT BANKING AND FINANCIAL MARKETS

From the perspective of investment banks and investors, the early 1980s were a fascinating period. The economy and the stock markets were booming. People everywhere and from every walk of life seemed to be benefiting from the bonanza. Yet in analyzing the numbers on a daily basis, trends emerged and questions started to form. For example, though markets were booming in those years, it was not hard to spot huge losses now and then in single transactions within a given portfolio. Everything, though, seemed to be within the norm, it appeared. Day-to-day investment decisions and strategies would impact the overall performance of a portfolio only to a certain degree, and so long as the portfolio on the whole was making money, it didn't really matter if a few of the assets making up the portfolio were not performing well. Others would be identified to replace the former.

As the markets became more volatile toward the middle to late 1980s, and losses grew both in size and frequency, the primary dilemma became how to limit these losses. One of the mitigating strategies bankers used to address this concern was the hiring of bright math graduates to write algorithms for programmers to code into the computers that could attempt to stop the loss as prices fell beyond certain acceptable limits. It was not long before most investment banking firms had their version of such presumably fail-safe software.

Yet one of the doubts became, if everyone had similar logic running their computers, what would happen if markets, for one reason or another, showed downturns simultaneously? Would you not end up with a runaway scenario? The situation and the answer did not take long to materialize.

Only a couple of years later, on the morning of Monday, October 19, 1987, the impossible scenario materialized. While passing through a company canteen area, I noticed my colleagues were gathering around a couple of TV monitors that hung from the ceiling. My eyes soon caught the glimpse of a "Breaking News" banner that slid below the reporter. The world had just experienced the worst stock market crash since the great one in 1929.

The crash would later be defined as a major systemic crash (Carlson & Mark 2007) with "programmed trading" as one of its major contributing elements (Katzenbach 1987), along with other elements such as inflated prices, market psychology, foreign exchange, interest rates, etc.

Reportedly, following the market crash in 1987, thirty-three economists from around the world met in Washington, DC, in December of that year. In a joint press release, they made an ominous global economic forecast that "unless more decisive action is taken to correct existing imbalances at their roots . . . the next few years could be the most troubled since the 1930s." In the 1987 market crash, billions of dollars literally evaporated.

What had happened to those funds? To the investors? To the savings of thousands who worked with those companies that had invested in those funds for decades?

The fundamental queries evolved. They were no longer tied to what had just happened or how it happened, as it was already history, but to those concerning the future, the bigger picture, and the seemingly cyclical nature of stock market crashes.

Assuming corrective measures and policies would soon be adopted by policy makers to impede recurrences and protect the interest of the many investors, individuals, and businesses, everything could return to normal. And so long as everyone continued investing their money in the funds, and funds hopefully performed well, the situation would resume normality.

Yet all of this reasoning was based on a set of fundamental assumptions: the market would adopt and implement strategies to mitigate the risks from crashes; the aging population issues would find an equilibrium; the majority of people investing in the funds far outnumbered (both in numbers and weight of investments) the ones retiring and, hence, needing pensions (taking money out of the system).

Notwithstanding the good-willed motivations of many in the immediate aftermath of the crash, it is factual knowledge that, apart from a very shy attempt to mitigate the risk from future crashes, the attractive lure of riches to be made from a new buzzword promising a new era in real estate and a panacea from the "new economy" and the exploitation of the Internet soon took over the interest of the "money that counts."

So attractive was this lure that the last assumption on the list seemed to be irrelevant. Although theoretically well elaborated, in the real world the question still remained. What would happen the minute the first large wave of retirees (especially the baby boomer generation) moved out of the system and rightfully started demanding pension payments, becoming de facto nonproductive elements to private pension funds? How long before the scale tipped, rendering the whole paradigm economically less attractive, or even senseless in some cases, from a purely entrepreneurial point of view? Might this be the reason pensions, retirement, and other related elements have become stigmatized in the last few years?

It is important to note that this is not about demonizing private pension funds, since they are a valuable asset to all of us. Paradoxically they potentially form one of the many elements making up a possible solution, but it is the underlying foundation on which the paradigm resides that needs to be evaluated should we wish these to evolve into truly successful models and businesses in the future.

In the years that followed the 1987 crash, the concept of privately run pension funds made its way to other countries outside the United States. Quite simultaneously in the late 1980s, all across the Western world, much effort, energy, and massive amounts of money would be spent (and continue being spent) on lobbying national and foreign governments to liberalize previously state-run pension systems and funds (to be fair, some of these even doing quite well) worth billions of dollars in each country. This was a massive campaign in a growing manner on a global scale.

It is objectively difficult to think of a period in the last twenty-five years when pensions were not an item on the political agenda in the United States, Europe, and other countries. Some even wonder if (from a very generic and macroscopic point of view) this was all a move to redirect fresh monies into private pension funds to offset the losses incurred in 1987 and successive crashes that followed. In other words, was this a way to fill the gigantic holes created by the crashes of 1987 and those that followed?

Independent of the validity of such concerns, pensions and retirement were and are continuously on the news as a couple of the most important issues to be resolved. The consensus-creation bandwagon promoting it has become a repetitious mantra that has lasted over twenty years. The effect of this mantra has been sublimely genial. The more talk is made around privatizing pensions, increasing retirement age, and reducing pensions, the more it has (in good or in bad) become the truth!

Again, the issue is not about public versus private pension funds, or any of these being a vice with respect to the other. *To the contrary, given they deal with people's pensions, private pension funds can positively contribute to the healthy running of economies. In achieving just this though, a few challenges need to be addressed to make them produce even more benefits with greater business potential to all stakeholders sustainably over the long term.*

Seen from this new perspective then, are we sure that pensions are truly the real demons (i.e., one of the major threats to national economies and debts)? Are remedies such as increasing retirement age beneficial or truly necessary? *Or might we be looking at the problem only through the prism of the currently boxed model and seeing a problem, where in reality there could be a series of opportunities?*

What about the following considerations being posed by a growing number of economists and professionals from all walks of life?

1. Can markets and retirement pension funds leverage new opportunities?
2. Can decreasing workforce fund the growing numbers of the aging population?
3. What about the increasingly limited job market for the older age group?
4. And what about less long-term job potential for the younger generations?
5. How will growingly precarious situations of heads of family units in very delicate age groups (forty to sixty) who are still providing for entire family units with either growing children or unemployed generations to sustain be addressed?
6. How can policy address inequality in treatment and unjust practices (i.e., better deals for those generations who were able to retire earlier than others), leaving younger generations with a scenario that shifts continuously further, beyond realistic reach?

7. Why should younger generations be expected to contribute to the pension systems—or anyone else, for that matter?

8. Beyond a certain limit, could an ineffective retirement system remain unquestioned? Could paying into social security, state retirement insurance, or private insurance funds become nonsensical if there is no real prospect for payback in the future? Should we insist on continuing down this path, would a "systemic backfire" not become a possibility?

Furthermore, what if retirement issues fail to deliver some of the tangible and intangible benefits these valuable systems were intended to produce in the first place? Examples include relative peace of mind to young and old alike, a positive outlook for the future, added incentive to keep families together to create a positive social fallout, and a natural turnover mechanism to free up jobs for younger generations that could benefit from longer-term horizons and invigorate economic development. Job creation for younger generations is the lifeblood to continued evolution and success.

And as absurd as it might sound now, seen from a different perspective and an evolved model, it would create even more revenue, producing more opportunities for those who enter into retirement. Privatizing retirement funds per se is not the malady but an opportunity if done appropriately.

If things do not evolve, however, how will private concerns pay off pensions worth billions of dollars, sterling pounds, euros, shekels, rials, renminbis, etc., from funds that cyclically evaporate in the different bubble bursts?

All of this does not consider the exposure to market volatility and or natural devaluation of growing numbers of stocks, bonds, and other financial instruments that are linked to real businesses. The persistence of the financial crisis, loss of business opportunities, reduction in sales and revenues, growing imparity in cost structures and emerging markets, the effects of the credit crunch, etc., will inevitably devalue companies' equity values, producing waves of potentially devastating knock-on effects on markets and their satiability.

Must we go down this path, or can we leverage new perspectives to provide a turnaround?

MARKETS

Till not long ago, markets where physical places where physical goods where bought and sold. In today's economies, the markets go beyond the physical, increasingly transforming themselves and what they offer into virtual transactions concerning just about anything that can be bought or sold, even without money. While investments can be made in just about anything virtually, they still have a physical impact on just about all aspects of our lives, creating a new dichotomy—another aspect our current economic models have difficulty addressing.

Investments can be made in pension funds, other funds, financial markets, stock markets, bond markets, money markets, derivatives, futures, insurance and reinsurance markets, foreign exchange markets, etc. Other markets example, cover investments not only in corn, rye, meat, wheat, fruit, milk, orange juice, and just about anything one eats or consumes, but also in all the raw material that goes into the things one purchases—from bridges to skyscrapers, cars, printers, and forks.

There are markets for everything, including the water we drink. There are even markets for ideas, inventions, patents, trademarks, and anything you can imagine. In the derivatives markets, for example, investments can be made based on bets on any sort of outcome.

Before becoming the intricate model we know today, the market was a man-made concept, a necessity that dates back to the formation of the first human settlements along the major fertile zones, such as the Tigris, Euphrates, Nile, Indus, and Yangtze Rivers. In their true-to-form essence, they are at the base of what makes our human societies function and provide our livelihood. They are based on a fairly simple set of logic, such as demand and supply.

Problems arise when a market that should be free in theory and should function by these very simple axioms is forced into behaving in a distorted fashion. The example of oranges is emblematic. In years when production was higher than foreseen, it induced prices of oranges to fall. In an effort to counter the vertiginous fall in prices, orange producers literally destroyed millions of tons of produce by running bulldozers over piles of oranges in order to force prices to resume acceptable levels.

Fortunately, after much bad press, this practice is vanishing in some parts of the world. In recent years, secondary markets have arisen that buy the excess produce, freeze it, and store it in large warehouses, sometimes for years, and sell it back to supermarkets when supply is lower. Apples that are mature in their core while seemingly fresh on the outside are a good example of these.

Generically, market distortion appears when the price(s) for a particular instrument (e.g. stock, bond, etc.) becomes overvalued or undervalued with respect to what it would normally be valued at in normal trading conditions during a specific timeframe.

These distortions could be implicitly or explicitly forced onto the market or simply be the result of an excessive demand and supply mix.

Every time we—as perfect, morally correct, good willed, and honest citizens, individuals, mothers, fathers, grandparents, young professionals, trustees, renown businesspersons, and perfectly humble priests of any faith—go to our banks, post offices, savings and loans, insurers, trusted brokers, pension fund managers, employers, or cooperatives to ask how we can invest our hard-earned money to yield a return for the well-being of the persons or businesses we represent, we become an integral part of the system and its frontline players. For that matter, any time we go to the supermarket and complain about the cost of something and decide on a cheaper alternative, we unconsciously induce a market reaction to accommodate the customer's need.

With the exception of deliberate criminal speculation, who can we condemn? In the cyclical distortions witnessed in the last decades was the market at fault, or is it our behavior or the combination of both? If we seek to address this issue and mitigate the exposure to such excessive, potentially economy-breaking phenomenon the answer might reside in, for example, in adopting a strategy that allows us to comprehend how to make things work better in the future—understanding, for instance, if there are ways to distinguish or separate purely speculative transactions from true investments in real economy independently of how virtual this might become in the future.

SPECULATION: IS THERE ANOTHER MARKET BUBBLE ABOUT TO BURST?

In the Random House English dictionary, the term *speculation* is defined as "to engage in any business transaction involving considerable risk for a chance of large gains." "Considerable risk" and "large gains" seem to be the discriminating elements in the above definition. But are these terms not relative, subjective, and ambiguous?

This is probably why it is hard to pinpoint who or what can be considered a speculator. We probably are cognizant of who a speculator is, in most cases, only after the fact, because we have at that point a means of comparison, each of us with our own yardstick.

There must be other elements that concur in making a specific act more speculative than others. Yet even if we were able to quantify these variables, we will probably not find full consensus.

So what makes the work of a speculator different? An element that could put a degree of acceptance (or rejection) on the behavior might be the impact the action has on the vast majority of persons in the context of where this takes place.

During the period of prolonged growth and relative peace of mind after World War II, an unprecedented sum of money accumulated in the form of available liquidity, fixed-income investments, and savings that are claimed by some experts to have "reached $70 trillion worldwide . . . and roughly doubled in size from 2000 to 2007."

It is hard to evaluate the degree of accuracy of such statements, yet it is acceptable to think that very large sums of liquidity had been accumulating, seeking lucrative investments in markets, especially those stemming from successful business windfalls in China, India, and, in general, all emerging markets; profits from rising oil revenues; and those being made via the introduction of new creative financial instruments (now known as toxic assets).

This boom-and-bonanza scenario peaked just before the near-systemic meltdown of 2008, and the rest is unfortunately history. The effects have translated into an unparalleled prolonged recession with which we are confronted today.

The January 2011 Financial Crisis Inquiry Commission reports that the immediate effects of the crisis involved a number in excess of two hundred institutions:

1. The five largest US investment banks with total liabilities worth $4 trillion;
2. Lehman Brothers bankruptcy;
3. The absorption of Bear Stearns and Merrill Lynch by other financial institutions;
4. Bailout of Goldman Sachs and Morgan Stanley;
5. Insolvency of approximately 102 US banks;
6. Drop in US housing prices from 2006 to 2010, which rivaled that of the Great Depression;
7. Drastic drops in the stock markets around the world (e.g., S&P, MIB, FTSE100).

This does not consider the long-standing negative effects on economies internationally.

Since then, central banks in developed nations have jumped in several times, injecting literally trillions of dollars into the effected countries' banking systems and a few large corporations through "facilities" of different nature. With the benefit of hindsight, was the strategy of providing the banking system bailouts and large injections at optimal rates wrong?

Some economists ask if the money provided by central banks have created economic stimulus better if it was also provided as direct loans/financing to otherwise healthy corporations and businesses so that they could pull the rest of the economy along? Might this have not achieved the additional result of distributing exposure to risks?

Might the large sums available to banks and financial institutions be mostly used to consolidate their positions while also investing in higher-yield financial instruments/markets? Moreover notwithstanding all the above an impressive amount of private money is still seeking ways to be invested globally. If this is a viable possiblity provided the amounts involved, might we be moving toward another bubble about to burst?

Should we look at the growth of the primary market indexes around the world over a five-year historical horizon, a curious pattern seems to be forming. Each of these primary indexes seems to indicate that they have reached the same levels before the financial crisis in 2008 in a near-perfect V-shaped format.

This could be good news, and the auspice is that it is exactly that. Yet there is reasonable doubt that we could be in front of yet another bubble. One of the differences between 2008 and today is that in 2008 there was still a real economy. Many businesses were still open, and that provided today's unemployed real jobs.

Additionally, more and more financial experts and analysts have lately noticed a curious and allarming similarity between trends of the sotck market in the periods leading to the 1929 stock market crash and the Dow Jone's performance index (eg. www.mcoscillator. com). Is there anything that can be done to prevent another bubble to burst? Governments have taken many steps to introduce mechanisms and instruments to reduce these eventualities. In the United States, for example, some of these have translated into the Dodd-Frank Wall Street Reform and Consumer Protection Acts of 2010 (discussed later).

But in today's economic environment, do we need to arrive at a physical burst of a bubble for the repercussions of the underlying motives to hit the already-frail recessive and emerging economies? How far can we stretch the model? What effect will it have on investors, businesses, jobs, and debt?

WHAT IS HAPPENING TO OUR BANKS?

Though the stock market had crashed in 1987, with some exceptions, real economies seemed to be still working at least adequately. The two worlds (banking/financial markets and industry) seemed to be able to coexist one in need of the other.

In those years there were major differences between the US and European banking systems. While the United States was moving toward a more deregulated scenario, the European system at the time remained mostly regulated and conservative in its approach.

The exception to the rule in Europe was England, which probably wished to pursue a pivotal role in banking and had started focusing the country's niche capabilities away from industry and toward the financial sector, starting with Mrs. Thatcher's government.

Many economists and historians suggest that, while it could have made sense at the time, its repercussions on the country have been unfortunate and reverberate in the UK's economy till this day. Over the last decades, the country witnessed a dismantling of its once-glorious industrial base, focusing its economy primarily on financial services and, hence, possibly putting most of the eggs in one basket. Fortunately, however, there seem to be recent moves to improve this imbalance, but these have come at a cost.

For the most part, in many European countries in the late seventies/early eighties, financing even for day-to-day business needs was not as seamless or as easily accessible as it was in the United States, forcing businesses and individuals to find alternatives.

In many parts of the world, including Europe, consumer credit was still at its prime in the 1980s, with both credit and debit cards given to a limited number of persons and accepted only by certain retail sectors (i.e., major hotels, car-rental companies). Financing, leasing, and other consumer credit instruments were just beginning to make their way into the European market. The majority of persons simply bought what they could afford. One either had the money to buy a car, or one did not. One paid in either cash or a check.

These were also years of reasonably high interest rates in some of these countries, where the primary focus from both the consumers' and the banks' point of view was to invest in high-yield financial instruments rather than asking for a loan.

Given the credit crunch, businesses that needed financing came up with innovative ways of working alongside policy makers and unions to resolve short- to medium-term liquidity needs. In some European countries, such as Italy, businesses were allowed to distribute yearly salaries in thirteen or even sixteen installments. As bizarre as it might sound, the system did provide win-wins.

Even though not a true financing instrument, another mechanism allowed the employer to set aside a portion of the yearly gross salary (one-twelfth) in an interest-earning company account called the *Trattamento Fine Rapporto*, a sort of mini pension that the employee could use only at the end of his contractual rapport with the employer or for extraordinary needs, such as emergency health-related expenses, a marriage, or the acquisition of a first home.

Without being judgmental, businesses had access to liquidity without the need to resort to costly financing at exorbitant rates.

Employees, on the other hand, found "double" paychecks in critical months such as July and December (just before vacations and major deadlines with taxes) and substantial sums in case of retirement, termination, or needy periods.

The above examples have been made not to denote a preference nor suggest eventual elements of a possible future solution but to demonstrate that different models and perspectives can coexist.

In those years, European bankers were seemingly happy with the state of affairs, as their institutions were seen as relatively sound, where people would deposit their savings and be moderately remunerated for it. New to the system though was access of the general public to the new stock market game that was becoming ever-more lucrative to their clientele in the early 1980s as the stock market fashion, trend, and boom made its way across the Atlantic Ocean. It became accessible to the masses with the introduction of new technology.

These were also years in which there was still international trade rather than the global market. In this scenario, banks played their legacy roles in providing letters of credit and foreign exchange facilities to the import-export business.

Economists, bankers, and entrepreneurs alike logically knew that if there was going to be international growth, this could only be achieved through an international banking system and network with the least systemic imbalances and a more open approach to financing for businesses and consumers.

To this pressure we must add the following: increasing numbers of people were lured by the hope of potentially making easy profits in markets. The demand for newer services from banks that addressed this specific need grew exponentially. Initially reluctant governments across Europe pressured by lobbies from both the consumers and business started approving legislation with a stepped approach. These factors all contributed to fueling a growing necessity for requiring liberalization within the banking sectors across Europe and later in other parts of the world.

Together with incentives, this provided the tools for many businesses in the United States and Europe to expand even more internationally. The numbers of "multinationals" grew quite simultaneously. Ramifications of geographically distributed subsidiaries worldwide grew exponentially in those years, hiring both local workforce and expatriates.

The banking system grew n-fold globally. Mergers between historically separate banks ensued internationally. In a few years, banking products and service offerings in international markets rivaled those of the United States and became accessible to an ever-wider business and consumer base with unprecedented competition to attract more customers.

The disparity among banking systems across the globe, at least on several major issues, was substantially reduced, at least in some developing and developed nations. Among the differences remaining was the approach to risk aversion.

While most international banks jumped on the wave of the real estate and Internet bubbles that affected most of the globe, some steps were taken in terms of caution and diffidence toward overexposure. The real estate bubble burst that hit the banks since the 1980s created huge holes in the system. These holes would be partially filled by the successive bubbles and bailouts by taxpayers, such as the one regarding the US Savings and Loan crisis is the late 1980s.

Pressured by large stakeholders and investors for better returns, banks were forced to invent new means of making money. The result was a plethora of new products and services that the banking world introduced in the last ten to fifteen years. The list of creative instruments is long; it goes from subprime lending to toxic assets to very highly speculative derivatives.

Numerous books have been written on the subjects, so it would be superfluous to delve into these, as the relevance of defining these instruments for the nth time when others have done a magnificent job at it will add little to finding a solution.

In the meantime, the invention of the Internet opened a new window to the stock market to the public at large, exponentially increasing both available funds to be invested and the potential exposure simultaneously. What happened next is public knowledge.

The US Treasury Department (US Treasury 2012) reported,

> *By September 2008, for the first time in 80 years, the U.S. financial system was at risk of collapse, and we faced the very real threat of a second Great Depression. Our system of regulation and supervision had failed to constrain the excessive use of debt and the level of risk in the financial system, and the United States entered this crisis without adequate tools to manage it. The Treasury Department, the Federal Reserve, the FDIC, and other federal government agencies undertook an array of emergency actions to prevent a collapse and the dangers posed to consumers, businesses, and the broader economy. However, the severe conditions our nation faced required additional resources and authorities. Therefore, in late September the Bush Administration proposed the Emergency Economic Stabilization Act of 2008 (EESA), and with the support of Democrats and Republicans in Congress, it was enacted into law on October 3, 2008.*

As billions evaporated during the crash, a mega hole was generated. This hole had to be filled, at least partially, by what has come to be known as the Troubled Asset Relief Program (TARP). Signed by President Bush in October 2008, the program was originally designed to address the subprime mortgage crisis and stop the financial system meltdown. According to the US Treasury,

- the beneficiaries were not limited to banks but also to corporations in the insurance and automotive industries, small businesses, and some 850,000 homeowners through the Home Affordable Modification Program (HAMP) across the United States;
- taxpayers have already recuperated 81 percent of the TARP money so far, and programs are in place to achieve the full 100 percent payback;
- the total cost of TARP is forecasted to be $70 billion; and
- TARP has resulted in $10 billion in profits for taxpayers.

In spite of all the above, the program has sparked much debate and controversy, especially among bankers, economists, and lawmakers.

The "Final Report of the Congressional Oversight Panel for TARP March 16, 2011 Executive Summary" (Congressional Oversight Panel, 2011) said,

> "The stock market had endured triple digit swings. Major financial institutions . . . had collapsed, sowing panic throughout the financial markets. The economy was hemorrhaging jobs, and foreclosures were escalating with no end in sight. Federal Reserve Chairman Ben Bernanke has said that the nation was on course for a cataclysm that could have rivaled or surpassed the Great Depression.

The TARP . . . provided critical support to markets in a critical moment . . . by providing capital to banks but, more significantly, by demonstrating that the United States would take any action necessary to prevent the collapse of its financial system.

The Congressional Budget Office (CBO) estimates that the TARP will cost less than expected in part because it will accomplish far less than envisioned for American homeowners.

If the financial system had suffered another shock on the road to recovery, taxpayers would have faced staggering losses.

The Panel emphasized that the TARP's cost cannot be measured merely in dollars. Other costs include its distortion of the financial marketplace through its implicit guarantee of too big to fail banks . . . 18 very large financial institutions received $208.6 billion in TARP funding almost overnight, in many cases without having to apply for funding or to demonstrate an ability to repay taxpayers.

By protecting very large banks from insolvency and collapse, the TARP also created moral hazard: very large financial institutions may now rationally decide to take inflated risks because they expect that, if their gamble fails, taxpayers will bear the loss. Ironically, these inflated risks may create even greater systemic risk and increase the likelihood of future crises and bailouts.

Intervention in the automotive industry . . . extended the too big to fail guarantee and its associated moral hazard to non-financial firms. The implication may seem to be that any company in America can receive a government backstop, so long as its collapse would cost enough jobs or deal enough economic damage.

The TARP is now widely perceived . . . as having bailed out Wall Street banks and domestic automotive manufacturers while doing little for the 13.9 million workers who are unemployed, the 2.4 million homeowners who are at immediate risk of foreclosure, or the countless families otherwise struggling to make ends meet.

. . . although shareholders suffered dilution of their stock. To the public, this may appear to be evidence that Wall Street banks and bankers can retain their profits in boom years but shift their losses to taxpayers during a bust—an arrangement that undermines the market discipline necessary to a free economy.

Beginning with its very first report, the Panel has expressed concerns about the lack of transparency in the TARP. In perhaps the most profound violation of the principle of transparency, in the TARP's earliest days it was decided to push tens of billions of dollars to very large financial institutions without requiring banks to reveal how the money was used. The public will never know to what purpose its money was put.

In some cases, relevant data were never collected in the first place. Without adequate data collection, Treasury lacked the information needed to spot trends, determine which programs are succeeding and which are failing, and make necessary changes, articulate clear goals or to update its goals as programs have evolved. For example, the Home Affordable Modification Program in early 2009, as asserted by the president should have prevented three to four million foreclosures. The program now appears on track to help only 700,000 to 800,000 homeowners.

On the Role of Oversight. Between the efforts of the Congressional Oversight Panel, SIGTARP, the GAO, the U.S. Congress, and many journalists and private citizens, the TARP has become one of the most thoroughly scrutinized government programs in U.S. history. Such close scrutiny inevitably begets criticism, and in the case of the TARP—a program born out of ugly necessity—the criticism was always likely to be harsh. In the midst of a crisis, perfect solutions do not exist; every possible action carries regrettable consequences, and even the best decisions will be subject to critiques and second-guessing.

Yet there can be no question that oversight has improved the TARP and increased taxpayer returns. For example, in July 2009, the Panel reported that Treasury's method for selling stock options gained through the CPP appeared to be recovering only 66 percent of the warrants' estimated worth. Due in part to pressure generated by the Panel's work, Treasury changed its approach, and subsequent sales recovered 103 cents on the dollar, contributing to $8.6 billion in returns to taxpayers.

Careful, skeptical review of the government's actions and their consequences—even when this review is uncomfortable—is an indispensable step toward preserving the public trust and ensuring the effective use of taxpayer money".

On January 9, 2009, the same panel concluded,

"In particular, the Panel sees no evidence that the U.S. Treasury has used TARP funds to support the housing market by avoiding preventable foreclosures . . . Although half the money has not yet been received by the banks, hundreds of billions of dollars have been injected into the marketplace with no demonstrable effects on lending."

Bailouts were not limited to the United States. In order to stop the virus and the ensuing hemorrhage, these were also deemed necessary for some banks in Europe, where, for example, the Irish government had to step in to avoid a systemic infection.

On the other hand, Iceland's government, for example, pressured by its citizens to call a referendum, had to exclude any bailout of the banks.

Exhaustive stress tests were conducted on the banks in many countries to ensure their solidity and a massive amount of liquidity had been provided to them by the European Central Bank at interest rates that reached as low as 1 percent in February 2012.

Notwithstanding everything said so far, as of August 2012 the situation has only translated into a heavy and dangerous credit crunch, inexorably spreading its tentacles globally.

Banks outside the United States have also accumulated the massive amounts of liquidity provided to them by their central banks in form of various "facilities" but as headlines and authoritive sources indicate they are not distributing them in the form of credit to industry, as foreseen—slowing down or halting recovery in some cases. They are all too weary of the cracks in the dam.

The virus has spread, and there are manifestations of it already appearing in places one would think devoid of such problems, shielded, for example, by oil revenues such as the Middle East in unimaginable places such as the Emirates or in Asia in the growing economies such as China.

The double-dip recession has forced many businesses to close, dimming economic forecasts and creating increasing risk aversion strategies by banks—justly or unjustly fearing loss of liquidity or exposure.

The economic policy adopted for the banking system seems to be confined to using different mixes of the same remedy over and over again. It is a vicious cycle that will not break until the number of game-changing agents bearing down on the financial sector shifts the balance.

A growing number of citizens, businesspersons, entrepreneurs, economists, expert analysts, journalists, leading corporations, policy makers, and world leaders have posed some questions: What happened to the original business model of the bank—lending money to their business partners and customers at acceptable rates to drive an economy? What will a bank's business purpose be in the twenty-first century? Who will fill the void originally filled by "pure" banks with a capital B? Will speculative investments become the driving vision for banks? In order to form a perfectly pragmatic and objective answer, one has to consider what some of the key elements in the equation might be:

- First, top executives' salaries and bonuses are linked to short-term profits and returns on investment;
- Second, there is added difficulty in managing and collecting loans, and in general, financing in a recessive economy is very risky and costly;
- Third, incremental costs linked to running business-as-usual operations versus investment-type business models sway the preference from investment in business toward investment in markets.

From the perspective of a bank's top management whose sole mandate is to generate profits from virtual products, why should there be any impediment in the current way of operating? From the unique perspective of a bank, even accountability for systematic failures might not be justified if: (1) people, businesses, and investors search for a profit by buying the products and services offered, (2) customers enter loan and finance agreements freely, (3) financial markets cyclically collapse, and (4) every time financial systems cave in, policy makers become terrorized by two two-word phrases that bankers used successfully in the past—namely "bank rush" and "systemic failure" of the economy—and subside to pressure to use the only instruments used so far each and every time since the 1700s—namely "bailout." This indirectly protects also the customers' interests. If at each meltdown the majority of the institutions involved do get bailed out, why in the world should anyone not be motivated to continue on their path?

From a purely business and pragmatic point of view, in a free market there is no reason there should not be a place for such institutions that have a market demand for what they currently offer.

Does the current economic model have the characteristics to manage new distortive elements? Are current measures working to resolve these very real issues? Will banks and the financial systems, in general, which witnessed cyclical failures, continue to be bailed out on the shoulders of taxpayers? Will the investors, businesses, policy makers, and individuals need to continue to be called upon to pay for future failures of such institutions? Given the virtual nature of money, is there a real need to continue with this self-destructive model?

Are there no other models that could take care of customers' day-to-day transactional needs? Are there no models whose contractual and legal terms cannot be based on more equitable terms, especially during hard times? How do we address and compensate the different needs arising from different perspectives—that of the account holder or depositor, the lending institution, the business, the shareholder, etc.? Is there a model that is adaptable around the evolving economic scenario and real/current needs? One that can coexist with and insulated from more speculative models?

Is there a different approach? One that can produce increased benefits for all involved? Fortunately, there is.

"OUROBOROS"— THE SNAKE-BEAST THAT ATE ITSELF: THE BANKING SECTOR PARADOX

As seen in previous chapters, many people are starting to ask, if money is virtual and is created virtually, why should a bank be allowed to reach alarming failure levels? Why should entrepreneurs, business owners, and employees be prone to closure and repossession while banks obtain bailouts?

Are more banking institutions moving toward a more speculative model or simply financial market-focused? Is this why we witnessed the following in the years leading up to the 2008 near-meltdown?

- bank lobbying to ease regulations;
- a huge push for loan generation at all costs;
- ease of lending to a greater number of persons with increased degree of risk;
- the development of new lending and financial instruments now labeled as toxic, such as mortgage-backed securities (MBSs), collateralized debt obligations (CDOs), and credit default swaps (CDSs);
- decreasing propensity for customer service and quality, especially for base products, such as checking accounts for the masses with increased transaction costs in many cases.

Is the strategic focus of some institutions after the subprime crisis shifting away from loan generation and financing unless given at very high rates, with excessive guarantees, collateral, and requirements? Is instead the focus shifting toward liquidity conservation policies inducing credit crunch and focused on investments in financial markets or, in general, "Virtual Enhancers" (as described later)?

To provide an equidistant and balanced approach, let's try to understand a hypothetical bank's possible perspective. Let's say you were given the post of CEO of a bank in today's economic scenario and your objective was to provide a return on investment given the following set of macroeconomic challenges: increased business closures, increased layoffs/unemployment, delocalization in emerging nations, technological transfer, increasing taxes on business and individuals, etc. Why should a bank faced with today's crisis find the benefit in investing in the real economy or behave according to the classical model (namely, being a fundamental pillar and contributor to the well-being of a country's economy)? Might it is not be more lucrative to focus investments in sophisticated financial instruments, or exploiting the spreads in debt ridden European countries?

The debt levels these countries held was long known. Almost all have a decades-long history of accumulating debt publicly declared and well-known even to the least literate and economically aware person, let alone to most expert financial institutions, operators, and brokers.

Speculation? Conspiracy? The truth might be simpler. For good or bad, all of the above respect what I call the fundamental axiom of money: money goes where money is to be made and has a possibility of being better remunerated. It has always been like this, and no human wall, law, religion, or political system seems to have been able to stop it from achieving this—for long at least. It is the nature of money. Not all is vice, as there are many individuals and entities around the world that will put money to better and more productive uses.

Is it right? Is it wrong? Maybe the real question is whether, given money's intrinsic nature, we can leverage upon this mechanism to reduce its negative impact while improving its positive effect. In an evolved model this will have nothing to do with a choice between electing one of the "isms" of the past.

The single biggest question is, if money is generated virtually through a relatively simple process—in a world where technology has eliminated barriers that once provided the foundations and cornerstones for the current model and the proper functioning of the system—*would a new, evolved modality that achieves more benefits to all stakeholders be possible? Are there evolved models that can guarantee the remuneration, security, solidity, and control requirements needed by the system while addressing the shortcomings of the current system?*

Reasonableness and objectivity are fundamental in both posing and addressing these tough questions.

Undeniably there is a concrete need for an evolution in the current economic model, and the banking system is one of its quintessential elements. Evolution of this system might not be with reference to a possible separation of roles between institutional banks and those that wish to focus on financial markets. In fact, that might not be the central issue at all. In an evolved model, these arguments might not even be as relevant, or they might lose their significance altogether.

The immediate short-term objective should be reducing insecurity in the system, instability in the markets, regeneration of development and economic activity, etc. It should be the challenge to improve on what we have and not create millions of direct or indirect business closures and additional job losses, to see how we can create a better win-win model that benefits our societies, businesses, trades, endeavors, jobs, and possibly a better banking and financial system that can leverage new possibilities.

The existing banking system is a by-product of its time and was founded on assumptions that have been successful in providing healthy and unprecedented levels of growth to human development on a global scale after World War II. But that apparently no longer holds validity, especially since the introduction of new, highly speculative financial instruments.

Additionally the problems are not a product of recent maladies. In the last thirty years, the Savings and Loan crisis of the 1980s, for example, and successive failures have been cyclical and growing in intensity and frequency, becoming chronic and malignant tumors that are spreading to the rest of the economy at large, unless actions are enacted to bring an evolutionary level of change to the existing paradigm.

Are banking and financial institutions the only ones at fault? If we were to leave our legitimate frustrations over the banking system and financial markets aside and analyze the situation with equidistant rigor, we might see a more elaborated picture emerge. According to the January 2011 official findings of the Financial Crisis Inquiry, the following is a list of the primary contributing factors to the financial market crisis:

- collapse/reduction/laxity in government regulations;
- declining roles of government agencies, such as the SEC, in applying oversight;
- lack of control over investment banks and hedge funds in their capacity to produce sophisticated financial instruments and accumulate huge exposure;
- Federal Reserve's failure to stem the tide of toxic assets;

- lack of policy makers' true understanding/appreciation of systemic long-term impacts;
- accountability and governance issues (across the board);
- credit rating agency concurrence;
- allowing non federally chartered housing creditors to write adjustable-rate mortgages;
- international trade imbalances;
- speculator investments;
- housing bubble;
- mortgage holder's full appreciation of loan and payback conditions;
- borrower overextension.

While this in no way is to denote the slightest acceptance, justification, softness, eye closing, etc., with regard to any wrongdoings subject to judicial evaluation, the last three points of the above list concern our society at large—at least anyone who was lured by the sudden attractiveness of the "unbelievably" easy conditions of investing: in real estate, in the market, in funds, or in simply spending beyond real capabilities via credit and debit cards.

A NEW FINANCIAL AND BANKING SYSTEM

No matter how you look at the matter, technological advancement and an evolved model will bring about a new revolution in the banking and financial markets industry, the result of which will be similar to the effect of a big bang for this industry since its inception in the late 1600s and its transformation toward its current model.

The banking system is on the brink of a new step-level evolution, one that will change its connotations, as we know it today, providing greater benefits and new and evolved opportunities (for the market, investments, business, employment, customers, etc.) to many stakeholders and the great majority of individuals—if planned, designed, rolled out, and managed properly. There are already many examples of innovations towards new dimensions. Examples are virtual wallets, Bitcoin and other virtual money phenomena; yet these are just the intial signs of much bigger revolutions.

New enterprises and Financial institutions that jump at the opportunity first will occupy the leadership positions! The rest will need to spend a lot of time and effort in costly swimming before they can catch up or at best become relegated to "me too" paradigms.

The evolutionary enhancement projects to be implemented will enable the financial/banking system to lever on new opportunities available on the new plateau. The progress will be so extensive and profound that it will probably restore much of needed trust in the real banking system in the eyes of the investors, business and households, but what is more important, it will allow real banking to re-occupy a leadership position in creating business opportunities and value creation in areas incalculable till today.

Provided the extent of changes the evolved banking model will bring about, the specific argument could be better elaborated separately with adequate focus, diligence, and conscientiousness, as the first banks to implement these changes will literally evolve the financial system forever, practically overnight and globally!

Banking, financial institutions, personal accounts, savings, financial systems, markets, transactions and their processes, . . . , and anything that has to do with money: how it is generated, exchanged, valued, invested, . . . ; will increasingly shift towards new modes, modalities, and dimensions and change our current ways of doing business forever.

THE GLOBALIZATION FACTOR

As prehistoric man needed to move onto new hunting ground, having depleted resources in his immediate surrounding area, the only way to grow the real economy after the mid-seventies was through a then-new concept called globalization.

The concept of globalization was not new at all. Many civilizations—including the Egyptians, Sumerians, Babylonians, Persians, Hittites, Greeks, Romans, Portuguese, Spanish, and all the way to the Doges of Venice and nineteenth-century European empires—have sought to pursue similar objectives using different terminologies, modalities, approaches, and geographical reach.

In fact, it seems that the concept of globalization has evolved. It has maintained a common trait until World War II, and that is the physical need to forcefully occupy foreign territories. Since the end of World War II, enhancing national economies has been the major focus of most countries. Augmenting international trade has been the imperative goal of a growing number of enterprises and businesses.

However, mounting impediments objectively hampered the flourishing of cross-border business—language and cultural aspects being only two of the elements. The number of barriers covered a wide spectrum of domains, from legislative, to fiscal and monetary policies, or even in some cases the lack of some of these elements.

Many countries were still taking shape as independent states in the 1950s to the 1980s. Predominantly they came from previous colonization and faced decades-long social and political unrest, to say the least, while others had to deal with growing social disparities, dictatorial regimes, revolutions, and wars. The inadequacy of their infrastructure, maturity level of their political and judicial systems, free enterprise models, limited access to education, and financing were the common "fil rouges" that rendered their situations very hard.

Those countries that were able to create stability took the challenge, opted to open themselves to the rest of the world, and enjoyed economic, political, social, and individual growth. In these countries the new form of globalization began.

Soon a first version of modern globalization took shape and became the reference model for doing business abroad. It allowed for international and multinational corporations to grow, investors to find adequate remuneration for their investments, while also providing economic growth, employment, and increased living standards to host countries—without necessarily distracting focus, investments, or jobs in their original home markets/countries.

In its post-World War II version, the diversified objectives of globalization would be achieved no longer through forceful occupation, but driven by facilitating and increasing trade on a global scale. Those graduating in the early eighties know that globalization was *the* mantra and was going to represent the building block of economic growth in the future.

The concepts were based on very simple logic: if a company wanted trade to grow internationally, businesses had to create a local presence, bring expatriate management and key technical expertise, hire and train a local workforce, respect local culture, mitigate challenges, leverage differences, invest locally, etc.

In the initial globalization model, in exchange for access to local markets, job creation, and local business opportunities, central and local governments would provide particular benefits to foreign corporations that wished to invest in that particular area.

These benefits ranged from grants, subsidies, concessions, etc., to repatriation of profits, significant lower tax regimes or exemptions, special financing arrangements for equipment, facilities, and training, custom's clearance, etc. These facilitations came under different names and forms, and they would differ in economic sectors. For example, in the aerospace and defense industry, such exchanges are known as "offsets," where the winner of a bid is given the possibility to sell its military jets if, say, the corporation agrees to localize part of the assembly operations in the country.

Notwithstanding its best efforts, this first version of postwar globalization had its faults and was not immune to questionable practices. One of the first lessons learned was that reducing barriers to entry alone would not suffice to make this effort successful. Lack of adequate legislation or its true enforceability in poorer or less developed nations, for example, led to some of the worst industrial catastrophes ever witnessed. One such example was the Bhopal incident in India, considered to date as one of the world's worst industrial incidents.

Depending on the source of information, the leakage of gas and other chemicals from the plant resulted in anywhere from 8,000 to 25,000 deaths, with a further 500,000 injured from inhalation of or contact with the substances emitted in the air (Chadhury; Eckerman).

On the other hand, globalization was also responsible for fueling the growth of the world economy for at least three decades. Giants such as Procter & Gamble, Colgate-Palmolive, and Arthur Andersen & Co. were examples of this unprecedented international growth providing thousands of jobs internationally in each local market.

So far, so good. Companies would be able to expand and grow their business locally, balancing periodic losses in one market with growing business elsewhere. Investors, executives, management, employees, and communities were seemingly benefiting from a win-win scenario.

As time progressed, foreign governments eased barriers to entry and operations in each country. Although these measures increased opportunities and employment for a certain period of time, they also increased competition and expectations. This soon translated into needing new economies of scales in order to remain profitable in these markets.

It rapidly became apparent that a strategy of synergies had to be implemented. This meant using and leveraging shared facilities and processes. In many instances, production facilities and business processes were either moved to hub-like regional offices to service local business units or sold off to local business partners that were more than happy with the economics. The remnants of the multinationals in these markets became more and more focused on maintaining only sales and distribution offices with lessening degrees of production, administrative, and post-sales maintenance personnel. Expatriates' expertise, which initially formed an essential element, became less necessary as local capability grew.

With the passing of time, no longer needing to be tied to a single brand, local business partners accepted production from other competitors that had similar needs. In many cases this is why today items such as automotive components, appliances or IT hardware from different brands are made by the same manufacturer. As competition grew locally and internationally, pressure on multinationals' financial results led to another twist in the evolution of the paradigm.

The question was whether it made sense any longer to produce in many regional hubs or whether they could just rely on low-cost producers or providers. The answer was simple and formidably logical. A limited set of low-cost producers and providers would be the consequential choice. The ripple effect on the economies of countries where these multinationals were present with local offices did not need long to hit.

Successive waves of layoffs ensued, and they continue to make their effect felt. Today this is compounded by the effects of the double-dip recession and the plethora of new paradigm changing variables discussed earlier.

Another dichotomy is formed. Production is delocalized, and local economies are rendered devoid of economic vitality in producing lasting unemployment. Revenue, remuneration and income sources decrease, and sales and margins drop, forcing many others to delocalize.

Globalization today is at the center of heated debate and a number of legitimate questions. As growing numbers of businesses, individuals, and families lose their sources of income, who will buy products and services in these markets? Is this the end of an era? Will we slip into a long period of depressive economic stall or decline? How long might this take?

WHAT IS HAPPENING TO THE ECONOMY?

It is the opinion of many historians and economists that the post-World War II era is probably the longest period of economic stability and growth the world has ever experienced. We would not venture too far off if we divided the post-World War II era into the following general groupings: an early post-World War II period of booming economies that gained momentum until their apex in the sixties, a downturn in the seventies, a recovery during the first half of the eighties, a period of successive bubble bursts before 9/11, and the period since.

According to the economists and government data in different countries, the current scenario in most of the Western world is a double-dip recession, with the virus spreading globally. It is reasonable to guess that as the economy spirals towards ever lower levels of activity it will at certain stages find new equilibrium levels; a natural tendency for economies to re-adjust to new lower equilibrium levels after new cycles of business closures and job cuts.

These may translate in brief moments of revival and recovery such as those witnessed in the US and UK (Q4, 2013). Fundamentally however can these recoveries be considered structural and systemic in nature and be able to produce lasting results - ceteris paribus?

Growth, in economic terms, can be achieved primarily through two means: non organically through acquisition of a competitor or organically by winning and taking more space in the market, be it in the form of more space on a supermarket shelf, a new customer, or an increased share in a territory. Any space left in a market will be filled by others so long as it provides a return.

A business is usually fueled by the future and the potential for growth. However, this requires critical capabilities, such as riding successive waves of new evolved products and services (P/S) and its capabilities in activating and maintaining an innovation loop. As sales for certain products/services in a portfolio begin to accelerate, the true entrepreneur is already ahead of its competition if he or she is already finding a replacement for them, as demonstrated in the diagram below.

Innovation Cycle Activation Capability for Products or Services (P/S):

Product/Service (A)   Innovative P/S (B)   Innovative P/S (C)

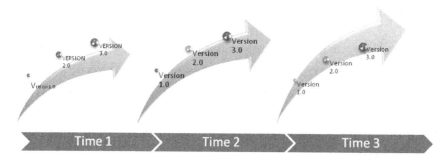

Success and long-term survivability are a fine balancing act in choosing the right moment to invest in innovation and selling off parts of the portfolio. Should the timing be miscalculated, the future of a business is at risk. It is a continuum, a bicycle that needs to be pedaled continuously throughout each cycle. So long as it is done properly, it will increase probabilities for a place among the first few in the introduction of a market-winning idea at each turn.

As humans, it is not hard sometimes to get stuck in self-indulgence. So long as it is not repetitive, some can afford to lose a few minor trains. In another analogy it is somewhat like a boat with a hole in it. One can't afford to let too much water in because the risk is sinking.

The Strategic Success Mix is another element indispensable to survivability. Insufficient leadership, misguided focus, dispersion, entropy, indecision, and lack of strategic vision can contribute to the ultimate dismay of any organization. Many alarms can foretell if a company is on the road to failure.

One of these is simply recognizing that the minute a company becomes more internally oriented and cost-focused, it has reached a pivotal point in its success cycle. If it fails to acknowledge this and jump on a newly forming innovation wave, its surfing time will be over as fast as the wave on which it is currently riding loses energy and momentum unless it is strategically focusing on a successive wave.

One doesn't have to go too far to have real-life examples. The overused sample of the Apple comeback is a perfect case in point. What needs to be emphasized and considered is that this took place in today's economic environment, with the globalization factor, the credit crunch, and the many other challenges facing businesses in this unique recessive period.

To put things into context one must also add that Apple belongs to one of the most competitive industries. Brand names that not long ago made headlines subsided to a company that stood steady in its innovation creed. What made it successful were strategic vision and leadership, among other things.

When economic concerns miss strategic objectives, they start falling into the quicksand of an inevitable cost-centric vortex from which it is exceptionally difficult to rise. This vortex is usually preceded by a set of formal organizational communications that sound very much like mantras anticipating change-management projects. These mantras sometimes can be presented under the following terminology: "shared service centers," "streamlining," "rightsizing," "delocalization," "outsourcing," "redundancy," and "plant closures."

In their essence these concepts are not new. Companies have always been focused on generating profits and returns on investments for their stakeholders, and surely they have always been in search of innovative ways to reduce costs and improve efficiency. What is new is that these phrases exclude or do not necessarily properly convey a very important notion: growing the business!

Incredibly and peculiarly there is little indication, at least not in a relevant manner with respect to development and/or growth in the above words.

Weren't the primary pillars and scope of a going concern and a healthy business also those of growth, profitability, returns on investment, market shares, competitiveness, etc.?

Yet the process is a logical one, under the existing economic model. If data corroborates with the fact that revenue outlooks are dim, the only other variable left to maneuver is cost.

If external factors affecting business persist, how can businesses survive? If these factors persevere, will businesses be facing another unresolvable equation, another dichotomy?

It is an undeniable truth that there was a downturn in business, especially after 9/11, as was the case in the early 1990s. Yet there was still reasonable room for global growth—not on double digit scales as they had become habituated to—but still growth. The absurdity was that, notwithstanding registered (modest) yearly growth in volume of business, multinationals went into a spiral of cutting back on everything from travel expenses to the inevitable—employees, by measures that, in some cases, exceeded the possible real requirements. Sometimes, as we saw in previous chapters, this entailed closing entire regions, countries, and markets. But even more unique is that this behavior was (and still is) activated across the board in every economic sector quite simultaneously.

So was this driven by madness? Some sort of collusion? Objectively and reasonably, probably not. More times than not the answer is more logical. In the last decade or so, increasing numbers of think tanks, economists, universities, and top-ranking strategy consulting firms have been engaged by industry and governments alike to analyze economic outlooks. After much analysis, most came back with similar scenarios:

-   A paradigm of increasing market shares internationally could no longer be sustained;
-   Emerging countries required more and more localized stakes, participation, and independence;
-   More players from emerging countries entered the markets in the globalized world with economies of scale that could not be rivaled easily. In the case of China and India, it would be nearly impossible to replicate their cost base or compete on costs;
-   Market forecasts indicated saturation and stiffening competition;
-   Old paradigms centered around reaching double-digit growth, and returns on investments above a certain percentage were deemed no longer possible;
-   The invention of new technology projected a move away from intensive industrial and physical asset models toward newer ideas.

The need to change horses rapidly was made evident to investors in developed countries. Since change does not happen overnight, there was a need to find a bridge strategy of disengagement. Many large businesses that had access to this wealth of information went into the cost-centric mode, disposing of whole or parts of businesses. The focus became cashing in before sales, profits, and share prices started to be affected.

Were the observations of the think tanks wrong? Though it is hard to predict the future, the projections are logical. But was the strategic reaction correct?

Though it is easy to understand how boardroom decisions were similarly influenced by short-term logic and why no one might have wished to stand out as going against the general flow of the tide, it is more difficult to understand how the overall impact on national economies of such parceled decision making failed to become a geo-political issue at least one that addressed this before allowing things to reach the stage they have reached.

While businesses need to be free to execute the strategy they deem best for their organizations and stakeholders should not someone assess the overall impact on the general economies, how this effects geopolitical balances, and provide a general direction to avoid or at least mitigate the occurrence of scenarios with extreme economic impact?

While it is reasonably credible and highly plausible that many steps were taken, it may be equally plausible that many remained unheard voices or botched tentatives.

Everyone jumping ship without necessarily needing to do so at the same time from a single ship is one grave event. If everyone jumped ship on all of the US Pacific Fleet's ships on the days preceding the naval battle of the midways as US code-breakers caught the first glimpse of the monstrous disadvantage in forces they were going to be dealing with, that is a totally different affair, one of formidable consequences, devastating leadership failure and unknown historical repercussions.

The reason the US Pacific Fleet was able to come out victorious is that they came up with a winning strategy against enormous odds.

To be fair; to put things back on track is exponentially more difficult for today's leadership, if it does not start to think beyond the current reference models for a winning strategy.

Corporations that still survive in developed nations now face the heavy burdens of austerity measures and increased taxes, forcing them to engage in self-consuming vortices to obtain so-called synergies, economies of scale, cost reductions, streamlining, reorganizations, shared service centralizations, enterprise change, enterprise turnarounds, etc. In some instances this is the strategy of last resort—just to become attractive to prospective buyers, not unusually a foreign investor or investment funds.

Another set of dichotomies? Does this convey it is too late for anything else? What is the compound effect on an economy and corporations if the primary focus becomes a cost-centricity vortex in which, at each downward turn in the spiral, an ever-increasing amount of investments, businesses, jobs, markets, and customers are lost in the process?

Are there other effects on the economy and in geopolitical terms? Unfortunately, yes. The following is a possible sample:

- loss of strategic competitiveness
- increased dependence on others
- loss of leadership
- loss of freedom of movement
- loss of strategic advantage
- loss of momentum

- loss of resilience
- loss of credibility and gravitas
- loss of relative weight in international fora
- loss of influencing capacity
- loss of representativeness
- loss of economic returns
- loss of leverage capability
- loss of critical decision-making possibilities
- forced subservience to others
- decreasing levels of freedom, choice, and alternatives.

But what might be least apparent is the potentially enormous impact on devaluation of shareholder value, devaluation of stock prices, consequential economic loss, and initiation of another self-consuming loop.

Unfortunately, so long as the reference economic models remain the same, decisions undertaken by boards, investors, executives, and businesspeople cannot but be justified, as they have very little maneuvering ground.

WHAT ABOUT CUSTOMERS, SUPPLIERS, AND JOBS?

Unless we are dealing with machination and plot theories (cynical or rhetorical), many business leaders, policy makers, economists, and persons in general seem to genuinely care about the future, especially in finding a possible solution for the immediate future.

In this chapter we will try to understand the impact of the current crisis and cost-centric focus from both the customers' and the suppliers' points of view. From the customers' point of view—be it a business or an individual—another key item is the association between brand/product and perceived value/quality that has become difficult to appreciate. Ever more frequently we hear sales reps tell us that essentially brand x, y, and z, which were historically associated with different manufacturers and quality levels, are now being produced by the same manufacturer overseas hence, the demarcation line between them is becoming very difficult to assess.

An increasing number of business concerns are de facto distancing themselves from their customers and suppliers, rubber-walling their interaction, reducing contact possibilities, call-centering without truly addressing customer requirements or automating interaction via no-reply e-mails and text messages—exasperating, and frustrating customers, and increasingly reducing contact references on all media.

In a cost-sensitive economic spiral, the destructive effects of this self-consuming paradigm appear even more evident in a business-to-business scenario. As parts of businesses are sold or

163

outsourced, ever-larger numbers of corporations and businesses remain increasingly devoid of the products and services and quality levels they once were renowned for.

In this environment one of the remaining survival strategies, for example, is positioning the business in the crowded space known as the "prime contractor" space or the system integrator (not necessarily the one making most of the money but simply the one on top of the pyramid). In this particular economic sector, primes and integrators become collectors and coordinators of layers of subcontractors below them, each of which in turn seeks to create their own pyramid under them.

Take the example of large businesses that are faced with a Damocles Spear paradox. A critical capital investment decision needs to be made, but the company is faced with a constraint on low budgets and pressures from stakeholders. To cut costs these organizations develop improbable tenders.

Tenders are launched, requiring best-in-class products and best performance, for lowest price shifting the problem to the bidders. In a growing number of cases, the lowest bidder wins the deal, many times "dumping" with the hope of recuperating costs somewhere down the line.

Dumping is the act of selling at the lowest price, many times below cost, in the expectation of recuperating either through more sales to the same customer or through future business deriving from after-sales services such as maintenance, for example, just to win a bid. In this scenario the suppliers' objective becomes positioning itself at the top of its supply chain, trying to win large contracts, and then filling the offering basket with a plethora of products and services mainly provided by other subcontractors, who, in turn, turn to other subcontractors.

This practice leaves declining chunks of real in-house business for each company in the supply chain, virtualizing their value added and forcing the same logic down the chain in order to remain in business. Ultimately this reactivates the cost-centric vortex of "streamlining," "rightsizing," "delocalization," "outsourcing," "merging," "redundancy," "plant closures," and "job losses."

What's more, in today's economic scenario of lowering budgets, dumping with the hope of recuperating later with additional business might simply be a chimera in a growing number of cases.

This self-consuming cycle has increased in the last years and has deteriorated the fundamental blocks of the real economy since the financial crisis began. Trickled access to financing, higher taxation, and stringent austerity measures only adds to the problem and suffocates any leftover business. Even more importantly, after a cost-cutting spiral, the amount of money left to invest in R&D and in general innovation is reduced.

Programs on which millions had been spent to- date are dumped, frozen, or halted, as it simply becomes easier and less costly to put someone else's product in the bundle offering for the customer or, in a best-case scenario, buy the company that supplies the specific product or service.

Programs, ideas, and licenses that once formed the lifeblood for future business growth become objects to sell off to the highest bidder. In many cases this forces businesses to lose their competitive edge, which will require much time and cost just to recuperate.

Acquisitions become another means of survival. Competitors are bought, hopefully for their market share, so that the sum of the two companies will create enough synergy and complementarity to bring about the so-called $1 + 1 \geq 3$ paradigm. The sum of the two should yield an organization that will produce, not twice the business volume, but something in the order of more than or equal to three times this.

Many mergers and acquisitions (M&A) analysts, investment banking firms, consulting firms, and executives know all too well that although this particular objective is theoretically achievable and has in some cases been achieved, in many cases, this does not materialize, especially in economically difficult times. Any readily available website dealing with M&As will provide ample insight into the very low success rate of corporate marriages (sometimes in excess of 70 percent fail to integrate). The few examples that are successful are due to particular factors. One such factor is when an acquiring company invests in a post-merger/acquisition program and sticks to it meticulously. This requires a lot of money, time, and resources, but mostly capable and confident leadership.

After consolidation, the resulting company is usually a much bigger concern, with access to complementary products, services, markets, and a larger customer base. On the other tip of the scale, the new larger entity ends up dealing with at least a subset of the following challenges: redundancy, duplication of jobs (staff and line), and different methodologies, approaches to customers, procedures, systems, production facilities, offices, organizations, corporate cultures, strategies, etc.

Cost becomes the immediate concern for both shareholders and management alike, and the natural end result is an internal focus and months, if not years, spent in cyclical reorganizations, culture change initiatives, a vortex of expense reductions, and program and job cuts. The organization impedes itself in being effective in the marketplace while competitors fill the void that is created as a result of the introspective focus.

In this period of time, the new entity becomes inwardly focused. Albeit officially declared objectives, the organization's primary focus naturally shifts toward self-preservation. Who will remain with a job? What curtailment of responsibilities will one face? In which organizational unit will he end up? Or what new opportunities might be available? These will be the predominant issues for the persons who make up that organization.

As organizations are reviewed cyclically to realign them with new cost-centric objectives, more resources are shed. In very large companies, due to the sheer numbers of persons involved, this process of downsizing commences with the most costly persons on the payroll in many cases independently of utility to the companies' well-being.

The extent of damage this exercise creates is not known until it is too late, as valuable expertise, management capability, and established networks (both results of costly experience) are lost, generating increasing levels of entropy, insecurity, and knowledge loss, which no knowledge-sharing tool can, at least for now, replace. Valuable employees will jump ship as soon as they can in order to not be laid off.

In any merger, the buyer will (independently of the contractual clauses stipulated to protect key high-level management figures from being fired for a certain time frame) dispose of the bought-out executive team through different means.

After the dust settles, top executives or key figures of the bought company, for example, could be assigned to dead-end projects. Those that find jobs elsewhere leave as soon as they can, because, with the exception of a few cases, the next step is usually the disposal of many of the top team members of the previous organization. The new consolidated company soon finds itself with a gargantuan gap in the understanding of how the other half of the company works and ticks.

Offices that once acted as central locations become of secondary or tertiary importance and left—basically to their own.

The larger the companies involved, the more frequently employees will refer to themselves with the old company name. "In X we used to do it this other way, which was much better. I am an ex-X employee . . ."

In some cases, even after years of the consolidation, especially internationally, it is not uncommon to witness contractual terms and payroll slips that still have remuneration voices that belonged to the former employer, creating organizational nightmare scenarios throughout the company. Friction is added as two persons performing the same tasks are remunerated differently (not based on performance). Additional entropy and motivational alienation are generated.

When resizing, outsourcing, selling to third parties, and performing mass layoffs, the focus is cost. Although some consideration is given to people with very specific know-how, this remains subservient to the overall cost objective. In many instances, entire layers of middle management and key staff are laid off in the process.

The inevitable results of these cyclical cuts are surely less populated organizations. Note that the term "lean" was not used, since this suggests that an organization embodying this adjective is healthy. What is hidden from the official income statements and balance sheets are time bomb-like liabilities with long-lasting destructive effects. Organizations might be left with a mix of the following killer viruses detrimental to human establishments of any type: reduced resilience; reduced innovation and renovation capability; reduced motivation; entropy; lack of clarity and direction even in day-to-day activities; reduced confidence in strategy and management; immunity toward yet the next round of costly change management programs; indifference; cynicism; and a reduced sense of belonging, usefulness, pride, and ownership.

It would be curious to assess the real cost of these factors to an organization and determine the true net cost savings, or loss of opportunities of mass layoffs over a medium-term period, not only for existing shareholders but also future prospect buyers—including the effect of these on new concepts (that could be christened with the following names), such as "true net capabilities left" (to understand if an organization is left with the capabilities it needs to survive), "resilience ratio" (an organization's capability to react), "organizations' post-cure survivability ratio" (organizations' probability of survival). These are all new notions and will need to be elaborated in a separate book. The problem is that, given the market pressures to achieve numeric results in very short terms, the true net cost might never become visible or of relevance to market analysts or investors, leaving a potential disaster waiting to happen out of sight.

Pressured to achieve even more growth results with less could entail objectives such as budgets, targets, and timelines becoming unrealistic to achieve. More often than not—with mass layoffs—few individuals within certain functions become focal points for the organization and are overwhelmed with work and go into overdrive working conditions, laboring for extremely long hours while many within the same organization are left with barely any chores.

Segments of key processes become dangerously understaffed and under managed, for the most part, in emergency or patch mode by a few willing individuals with an enormous sense of responsibility, whose concerns remain unheard. Each emergency is patched away, and things are forgotten again as the organization changes once more. Each emergency becomes a potential time bomb, waiting to explode. Most issues remain within the confines of the four walls of the organizations until these have impact on customers or translate into catastrophic events, such as the oil spill in the Gulf of Mexico, with severe and dire consequences that can no longer be contained beyond the inner walls of the company.

Some companies that have seen this movie before mitigate such risk eventualities using for example outsourcing strategies. Those that need to know are, at least for the initial period, mostly aware of the risks involved. Unfortunately, their hands are tied by perverse cost logic that sometimes induces corner cutting even in routine activities—all you need for disaster after that is the occurrence of one unfortunate set of circumstances or event.

As jobs are shed, effective hierarchical interactions lessen; even the largest organizations de facto become more flat while processes and protocols remain attached to previous logic, and unless the systems are updated (at currently unaffordable costs), these could become difficult to manage. It is common to see top management interact directly with whomever they feel is necessary to perform a task at hand, short-circuiting once-vital processes, creating among other things further disarray and confusion.

Especially in larger organizations it is not hard to find situations where the left hand is unaware of what the right hand is doing—and sometimes at a greater final cost to the customer, the stakeholders, and the organization itself. How many times does it happen, for example, that bid teams inadvertently or in good faith, pressured by improbable deadlines, revert to a subcontractor, not knowing that the specific service is produced by a division of their own organization or vice versa? How many times does the sales force of the same corporation call on the same customer? How many times do procurement departments of the same company call on the same suppliers and have separate contracts with them for the same products at different prices? Contracts with hotel chains and car rental companies are the greatest examples.

In relatively short amounts of time, cost-centric logic permeates everything and everyone till it becomes a self-consuming paradox, blocking an organization. Travel expenses are cut across the board, while at the same time sales quotas rise. R&D is cut while innovation could be exactly what the company needs to take it out of the dire straits it finds itself in, suffocating its future.

Forced by an inward-looking logic, organizations nowadays dream of becoming flat, as if dealing with obesity rather than becoming winners, the only difference being that reducing weight in an organization sometimes equates to not necessarily losing the fat but parts of vital organs, such as brain tissue, eyes, kidneys, liver, and ears.

Finally, a cost-effective organization per se is not by any means synonymous with a winning organization and one with a future. Reduced human capital does not necessarily equate with a winner (nor its inverse for equidistance). An organization is like a body. Repetitious crash diets reduce natural defenses and induce maladies. Sooner or later the stakeholders in a company end up with an organization that will not be able to sustain itself for long. Each organ and cell play a vital role in the health of an organizational body, and if the slimming cure inflicts damage to any of these, that organizational body will most likely not perform as it should. Eliminating successive groupings of synapses (e.g. expertise, coordination, and management) in different areas means affecting the brain of the organization permanently.

Losing entire levels of expertise based on years of experience is like expecting a patient to lose parts of its brain or vital organs and still remain lucid and healthy. Inner focus over time brings loss of customers, business opportunities, and markets, taking the organization a further step down the self-consuming vortex.

Multiply this effect across an entire economy, and the result is a self-destructive economy. So what is the sense of all of this?

De facto there seems to be a trend developing in major brick-and-mortar corporations, one that denotes an ever-increasing pressure on top-level management to resort to bringing results through financial transactions—buying and selling assets or deriving profits from stock market-related activities, acquisition, disposal and or sale of parts of the company, patents, shutting down otherwise profitable subsidiaries. etc.

This vicious cycle also forces brick-and-mortar concerns to add fuel to the transfer of echnology and production to more "cost-efficient" countries or regions of the world, leaving a greater void in the countries of origin—and I am not talking about only the Western world. Even countries such as India and China are now moving their production facilities to regions such as the African subcontinent.

More cuts, more jobs, and more technologies lost create another dichotomy. But what is the effect of all of this?

CHINA, INDIA, AND EMERGING NATIONS: A NEW PARADOX— FEAR OR OPPORTUNITY?

Equidistance and objectivity—the following chapters are not against or for China, India or any other emerging nation, nor is it against any of their very hardworking and respectable societies and individual citizens. This is not about east or west but about the paradox these countries will probably be facing in the not-so-distant future.

This is neither about xenophobia nor the promotion of any such feelings. Apart from the brief moment of glory that emerging nations are currently enjoying, unless the model changes, there is a very high probability that these will end up in similar if not worst boats and share a similar fate but one of exponentially higher consequences.

Though some of the hyped headlines every now and then might induce many to fear the seemingly unstoppable growth in BRIC (Brazil, Russia, India, China) countries or other emerging countries, this is not as apparent or justified if more data is analyzed in greater depth and positioned in the context of historical cycles.

Take, for example, factual data regarding a single indicator such as gross domestic product (GDP), real growth as presented in the 2011 CIA World Fact Book.

In this report the GDP indicators for China (+9.2 percent) and India (+7.8 percent) are growing at very high rates. Yet, if one steps away from these two elements and asks, "relative to whom or what?" a different picture starts to emerge. Note, these numbers have been downgraded since the report by others from such authoritative sources as the IMF.

In fact, according to the same source, China and India are growing less than many other countries. The following is an excerpt from the CIA World Fact Book GDP, showing how each country ranks in percentage of annual growth. It indicates those that grow faster on top and those with less growth as you go down toward the bottom. To say the least, it is an eye-opener (to reduce a very long list, some countries within the ranking have been taken out):

Rank	Country	GDP Real Annual Growth (%)
1	Qatar	18.70
2	Mongolia	17.30
3	Ghana	13.50
4	Panama	10.60
5	Turkmenistan	9.90
6	Iraq	9.60
7	**China**	9.20
8	Papua New Guinea	9.00
9	Laos	8.30
12	Sri Lanka	8.00
13	Argentina	8.00
14	Estonia	7.90
15	**India**	7.80
16	Kazakhstan	7.50
17	Ethiopia	7.50
19	Mozambique	7.20
20	Afghanistan	7.10
21	Uzbekistan	7.10
22	Equatorial Guinea	7.10
23	West Bank	7.00

24	Rwanda	7.00
26	Nigeria	6.90
27	Peru	6.90
28	Georgia	6.80
29	Zambia	6.70
31	Ecuador	6.50
32	Congo	6.50
33	Chile	6.50
34	Maldives	6.50
35	Saudi Arabia	6.50
36	Uganda	6.40
37	Indonesia	6.40
38	Paraguay	6.40
39	Bangladesh	6.30
41	Botswana	6.20
42	Tanzania	6.10
43	Haiti	6.10
44	Gibraltar	6.00
45	Zimbabwe	6.00
46	Uruguay	6.00
49	Lithuania	5.80
50	Vietnam	5.80
51	Kyrgyzstan	5.70
52	Kuwait	5.70
53	Colombia	5.70
56	Gabon	5.60
57	Niger	5.50
58	Burma	5.50
59	Gambia	5.50
60	Belarus	5.30
61	Mali	5.30
62	Malaysia	5.20
63	**Taiwan**	5.20

64	Isle of Man	5.20
65	Lesotho	5.20
66	Ukraine	5.20
67	Mauritania	5.10
68	Bolivia	5.10
73	São Tomé and Príncipe	5.00
74	**Hong Kong**	5.00
75	Congo	5.00
76	Turks and Caicos	4.90
77	Burkina Faso	4.90
78	**Singapore**	4.90
79	Djibouti	4.80
80	Israel	4.80
81	Guinea-Bissau	4.80
82	Armenia	4.60
83	Bermuda	4.60
84	Turkey	4.60
85	Morocco	4.60
86	Malawi	4.60
87	Dominican Republic	4.50
88	Sweden	4.40
89	Oman	4.40
90	Kenya	4.30
91	**Russia**	4.30
92	Mauritius	4.20
93	Burundi	4.20
94	Venezuela	4.20
95	Central African Republic	4.10
96	Guinea	4.00
97	Costa Rica	4.00
101	**North Korea**	4.00
102	Nicaragua	4.00
105	Poland	3.80

107	Cameroon	3.80
108	Mexico	3.80
109	Guatemala	3.80
111	Philippines	3.70
112	Namibia	3.60
113	**South Korea**	3.60
114	Luxembourg	3.60
115	Honduras	3.50
118	**South Africa**	3.40
119	Austria	3.30
120	Slovakia	3.30
121	Macedonia	3.30
122	**United Arab Emirates**	3.30
126	Greenland	3.00
127	Algeria	2.90
129	Brunei	2.80
130	**Brazil**	2.70
131	French Polynesia	2.70
132	**Germany**	2.70
133	Finland	2.70
134	Somalia	2.60
135	Jordan	2.50
136	Chad	2.50
137	Iran	2.50
138	Belize	2.50
141	Albania	2.50
142	Aruba	2.40
143	Pakistan	2.40
144	Iceland	2.40
145	Bosnia and Herzegovina	2.20
147	Bulgaria	2.20
148	Canada	2.20
149	Switzerland	2.10

151	Serbia	2.00
152	El Salvador	2.00
158	New Zealand	2.00
159	Australia	1.80
160	Barbados	1.80
161	Czech Republic	1.80
162	Montenegro	1.80
163	**France**	1.70
164	Norway	1.70
165	Netherlands	1.60
169	Romania	1.50
170	Lebanon	1.50
171	Bahrain	1.50
172	**United States**	1.50
173	Jamaica	1.50
175	Cuba	1.50
176	Tonga	1.40
177	Hungary	1.40
178	Egypt	1.20
179	Slovenia	1.10
180	Cayman Islands	1.10
181	**United Kingdom**	1.10
186	Ireland	1.00
187	Madagascar	1.00
190	Spain	0.80
191	Croatia	0.70
192	**Italy**	0.40
193	Micronesia	0.30
194	Azerbaijan	0.20
195	Thailand	0.10
196	Cook Islands	0.10
197	Tunisia	0.00
198	Cyprus	0.00

199	Sudan	−0.20
202	**Japan**	−0.50
203	Liechtenstein	−0.50
205	Montserrat	−1.00
206	Trinidad and Tobago	−1.40
207	Andorra	−1.80
208	Syria	−2.00
209	Swaziland	−2.10
210	Portugal	−2.20
211	Yemen	−2.50
212	Puerto Rico	−5.80
213	Côte d'Ivoire	−5.80
214	Greece	−6.00
215	Anguilla	−8.50

Just comparing a single indicator, such as the real GDP percentage growth, has provided additional insight into China's and India's growth scenario and rebalanced growth perceptions of many nations. Growing at a faster rate is extremely misleading.

Take, for example, war-torn countries such as Eritrea, Ethiopia, and Afghanistan, which have growth rates that position them amongst the highest on the first twenty on the list. It is more than plausible that after many years of devastation they currently benefit from growth, as everything needs to be rebuilt. The total economic value that is involved though is surely very far from even the smallest realities of developed countries.

To illustrate this better, see the following chart. It represents a projection of a sample of faster growing economies versus slower ones using only the percentage GDP growth as its single means of performance metric (the underlying data is made of estimates hence subject to continuous update).

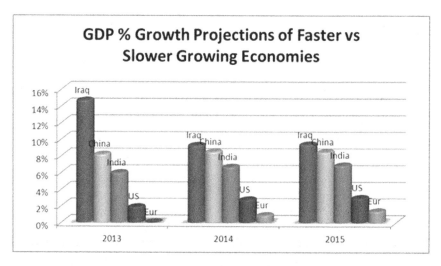

Source: Raw data from The World Bank. 2013. Global Economic Prospects, Volume 6, Jan 2013. Washington, DC; IMF. 2005 PPP weight. Europe Area defined as Eur.

To be useful one should look at the above numbers within the context of other data and sources. The GDP real growth as a percentage does not tell us, for example, the amounts involved. For instance, a nation might be growing at tremendous rates, but if the entire GDP of that country is a few billion or million dollars a year, the "so what" element of the argument loses all relevance.

Without the need to list all countries, we will evaluate the Chinese-Indian paradox in the following diagrams. In the diagram below (GDP in Current US$), we see the GDP of China and India and how they compare with the other reference countries.

GDP Current US$

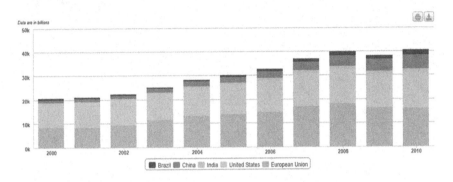

Source: The World Bank (The World Bank DataBank)—in order of appearance from top layer Brazil, China, India, US, EU.

The preceding graph suggests China's and India's GDP, although growing fast, is still a fraction of that produced by the United States and European Union countries. What it also fails to denote is that the European Union is still de facto made up of its member countries, each with distinct capabilities and share of the data.

The following graph, using the same data via a different format, provides an additional viewpoint and extra information about the dynamics that are not as apparent as in the preceding graph.

GDP Current USD

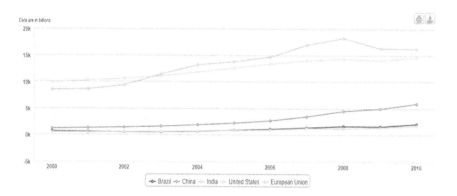

Source: The World Bank (The World Bank DataBank)

In the preceding graph, the GDP of the EU ranks first, the United States second, China third, and Brazil and India fourth and fifth. In this graph, the only thing that has changed is the way data is represented. It suggests that Brazil's GDP, for example, is at nearly the same level as that of India with a fraction of that country's population, but it is also growing at a higher rate. Additionally it shows that the United States has been falling slightly behind the European Union since 2003.

This data however fails to convey that the European Union is (notwithstanding incredible efforts) objectively far from being a truly cohesive entity. The reality is that the number represented here is only the mere algebraic sum of distinct countries making up the union.

The following graph instead provides us with an idea of the ranking of the major economies in terms of GDP in USD as they pan out over 2013-2015 allowing another window on perception to be opened (this data is continuously updated hence subject to change).

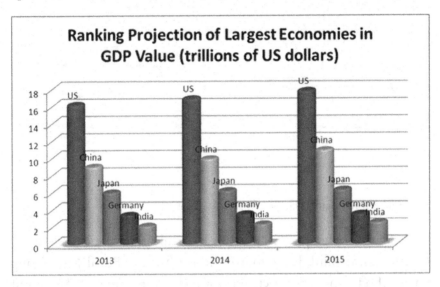

Source: Raw data from IMF, World Economic Outlook.

Enriching the analysis even further, we obtain an additional perspective. Many economists, the CIA World Fact Book together with other authoritative sources such as the World Bank and the IMF, for example, state that the exchange rate measures of GDP do not provide an accurate measure for output. They in fact suggest using other GDP indicators such as the Purchasing Power Parity (PPP) to provide a better basis for comparison with other countries valued at prices prevailing in the United States in a specific year.

GDP PPP Current International $

To provide an example of this additional view, the following graph has been produced using the World Bank data.

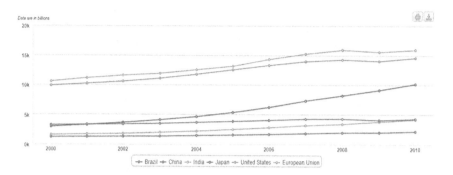

Source: The World Bank (The World Bank DataBank)

In the above graph (GDP PPP), EU ranks first, the United States second, China third, Japan fourth, India fifth, and Brazil sixth. Using this method, a new perspective is formed. China grows at faster and at a steeper rate than the preceding data suggested, India is growing faster than Brazil, and India is reaching Japanese GDP using PPP.

At the same time, other economists would prefer using alternative indicators, such as gross national income—again, differing in their opinion as to whether it should be at current USD, PPP at international USD, or a variety of other indexes to provide a better measure of output.

As one can begin to perceive, the most important point here is what each bit adds to the general picture, bearing in mind that economists have differing views—each respectable in its own right.

So far all the information we have seen has been relative to absolute terms (i.e., the total sum of national output expressed in dollars or as percentage points, with no indication as to how this output is distributed among the citizens of each country).

Even here there are many ways to go about this. We know that the data does not equate to the real distribution of GDP among each individual in a nation. Yet in order to have a better appreciation for the broader picture, this data is necessary.

Factoring in data regarding the Chinese and Indian population and how it is split among different age groups and percentages of those living in urban settings, the following picture starts to form:

Estimated Tot Population	% of Pop in the 0-14 Age Group	% of Pop in the 15-65 Age Group	% of Pop Living in Urban Settings
• China 1.3 Billion	17.6%	73.6%	47%
• India 1.2 Billion	29.7%	64.9%	30%

Source: 2011 CIA World Fact Book

IMPLICATIONS—so what? The above data suggests that

- in China 950 million persons (more than the combined number of citizens in North America and the European Union) are in the productive age bracket;
- in India 774 million persons are in the same category;
- in China 611 million people live in large cities (this rate is growing alarmingly), exerting unparalleled pressures on the most elementary life support services (e.g., food and water supply, sewage, waste management, pollution control, health and epidemic control);
- in India 360 million people (more than the United States' total population in 2012) are in the same condition (while growing at an even faster rate); and
- China and India account for 35.7 percent of the world's total population with a growing life expectancy, meaning a tsunami

of persons unprecedented in scale who will need pensions, growing medical assistance, jobs, etc.

This also means a gargantuan stress on the backbone structures of these countries. Should everything else remain the same in the not-so-distant future, this demographic pressure will most likely exert the same burdens on their respective economic systems as those faced in developed countries—but at exponentially greater levels, with the scale of the remedies titanic compared to the ones currently faced by developed countries.

These economies of scales are unprecedented in human history; therefore, it is difficult for anyone to foresee systemic breaking points, due to the sheer number of persons involved. We do not know, for instance, if there might be health considerations once a certain limit in human concentration is reached. We do not know if there are critical mass issues that emanate from waste management, the distribution of electrical power, or an inundation of lethal concentrations of electromagnetic waves emitted by wideband and cell-phone broadcasters and users of human carbon dioxide production.

With this in mind, for those who might have thought it this way, is it still better to be in the shoes of China or India? *Better yet, instead of wishing to be in someone else's shoes, what can we do to activate growth in our economies?*

Total Labor Force

The following adds another set of elements in evaluating the general situation of China and India.

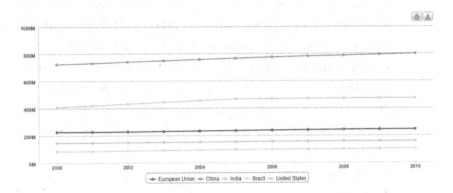

Source: The World Bank (The World Bank DataBank)
Ranking from highest to lowest in terms of labor force: China, India, EU, United States, and Brazil

The World Bank 2011 data suggests that, with a total of approximately 800 million persons, China has by far the largest available working force in the world, followed in second place by India, with 487 million, the European Union with approximately 228 million, and the United States with 153 million. Indonesia and Brazil follow with approximately 100 million souls each.

The data might also imply the following: China's workforce is nearly equivalent to the sum of the combined workforces of India, the European Union, and the United States! This infers that: It theoretically has access to an unlimited source of continuously replaceable cheap labor rendering the model impossible to replicate, but also that as a consequence it has the biggest potential for social disaster in case of: economic slowdown, requests for social rights etc.

Granted, the definition of poverty line is subjective and each country uses its own definitions. The following data, however, is what seems to be declared by each country (World Bank and *CIA Fact Book*):

- *Twenty-five percent of the Indian population, or 300 million persons, lives below the poverty line. This is nearly the total population of the United States or approximately the combined workforce of the United States and the European Union!;*
- Living under the poverty line is 13.4 percent of the Chinese population. This is a new level set by the government in 2011. *Hence, under this definition there are approximately 128 million persons (c. half of the US population) living under the official poverty line;*
- Twenty-six percent of all Brazilians live below that country's defined poverty line.

The absence of a universally unequivocal, uniform definition, modality, identification, and accounting for who can be considered below poverty line is subject to debate. The crude reality is that the number of poor persons is likely to be different from, and probably much higher than, the official data.

Differences in perceptions derive from one's cultural origins and upbringing. Nonetheless it is hard to think that the vast majority of persons living in unhealthy slums or shantytowns, in all honesty, can be considered well-off by any human standard. Otherwise, it is not clear why as soon as the mere chance of moving out of such places becomes possible, most persons living in them flee from these horrendous situations.

It is a well-documented fact that globalization, access to the Internet, mobile technology, satellite television, international travel and immigration, growing interaction with foreigners, and even the mere possibility of seeing different lifestyles produce an increased desire to experiment with new ideas, freedoms, and ways of life (positive or negative), especially in younger generations in less developed countries.

Many sociologists and economists agree that recent Arab Spring revolts, events such as those that spurred Tiananmen Square movements, and growing momentum in politically conscious movements in India (with periodic reactionary, terrorist, and extremist actions) and most southwestern Asian countries are all indications of heat being generated in the social caldera (a volcano's magma chamber) of these countries. The greater the perceived social disparity, the greater the pressures accumulating.

Social inequality and reduced individual freedoms have well-confirmed sociological interconnections. Although democracy and political liberties can diminish the chances of explosive, implosive, or runaway social revolts, there is a natural breaking point for everything.

If the exemplary high growth rates experienced in some developing countries still yield the impressive unemployment in absolute terms and the number of persons living under the poverty line (both according to purely subjective data), what will happen the minute the internal bubbles (i.e., investment, housing, stock market) burst, especially for those segments of society that have tasted new freedoms and living standards or those on the complete opposite end of the scale?

Would this not also be valid for developed countries faced with unpredictable external forces—for example, a sustained economic recession or the effect of the deepening of Eurozone crisis? In some European countries, for example, the employment rate among the young has reached the alarming level of +37 percent 15th Feb. 2013) Let us be reminded that the young represent everyone's future.

Considering the high growth rates reported by countries such as China, India, and Brazil, the unemployment and poverty rates are substantial indications of potential viruses brewing within these economic realities. The data below represents the estimated unemployment rate in these countries.

2011 Estimate
Unemployment Rate

China	6.5%	
India	9.8%	
US	9.1%	
European Union		9.3%
Brazil	6.0%	
Japan	4.8%	

Source: CIA World Fact Book

This might suggest that some 84 million persons in China are officially unemployed, that 117 million individuals are unemployed in India according to those countries' official data. And this excludes the staggering number of underemployed of unofficially unemployed persons.

If we examine GDP and gross domestic income per capita using two different methods (among many others), we obtain the following two charts:

GDP Per Capita Current USD

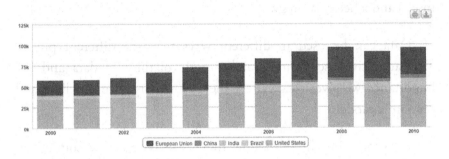

Source: The World Bank
Ranking: United States first, EU second, Brazil third, and China and India last

GNI Per Capita Atlas Method Current USD

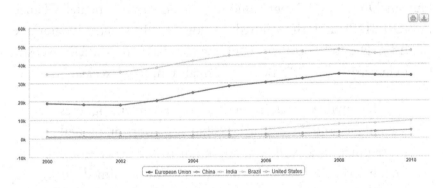

Source: The World Bank (The World Bank DataBank)
Same ranking as previous graph but with China slightly higher on the bottom level of the scale

Independent of the method used, the above graphs denote the overwhelming difference between income per capita among developed and emerging countries. Of these, only Brazil seems to be growing at a faster rate than China and India. Size in numbers seems to have its negative effects after all. Producing the groundwork for better wealth distribution, for example, is not as easy as it might sound. The other important information this might suggest is that there is no pragmatic or realistic way for developed countries to match the cost of labor of emerging countries unless it is through the adoption of a different model and a better strategy.

Data can be used in different ways to make different points. The subjective use, opinion-ability and volatility of data and the importance we give it can affect the way we organize our lives and economic models.

Additional insight as to how much can be done in coming up with new definitions, models, perspectives, and ways of accounting for things comes from a recent document produced by the United Nations in the Inclusive Wealth Report 2012 (IWR), a joint initiative launched at Rio+20 by the United Nations University's International Human Dimensions Programme on Global Environmental Change (UNU-IHDP) and the United Nations Environment Programme (UNEP). The full document is publicly available on the UN website (UN University; UNEP). Below is a small summary excerpt.

> The world's fixation on economic growth ignores a rapid and mostly irreversible depletion of natural resources that will seriously harm future generations. The report unveiled a new indicator aimed at encouraging sustainability—the Inclusive Wealth Index (IWI).
>
> The IWI looks beyond the traditional economic and development yardsticks of GDP and the Human Development Index (HDI) to include a full range of assets such as manufactured, human and natural

capital, shows governments the true state of their nation's wealth and the sustainability of its growth.

"Gross Domestic Product (GDP) . . . is far too silent on major measures of human well-being namely many social issues and the state of a nation's natural resources," said UN Under-Secretary General and UNEP Executive Director Achim Steiner.

"The IWR stands for a crucial first step in changing the global economic paradigm by forcing us to reassess our needs and goals as a society," said Professor Anantha Duraiappah, Report Director of the IWR and Executive Director at UNU-IHDP.

Governments and international organizations should establish research programs to value key components of natural capital, in particular ecosystems.

CHINA AND INDIA: THE NEXT SUPERPOWERS?

The focus of the previous chapter was on internal issues that contribute to the paradox effects within growing economies such as China and India. Yet, not losing track of outwardly-looking facets is as important, as they could heavily contribute to increasing the paradox effects for these countries.

Many analysts suggest that China and India are growing their presence and influence internationally. The argument is that it is not only about markets but also about access to vital resources and projection of political influence in two distinctly different ways. They suggest that The People's Republic of China (PRC) and India, on the face of it, differ substantially in their apparent approach to international growth.

Historians mention that India boasts one of the oldest known civilizations in the world, dating back to 2,000-3,000 BC. Tribes from the northwest merged with the indigenous Dravidians, giving birth to the Maurya Empire. The largest extension the Indian Empire reached is said to have enclosed many of its current neighbors, with the exclusion of China. How far off or limited these historical lines might have been is of little relevance here. Today India is the seventh largest country in the world in terms of territorial extension.

India comes from decades of democratic rule and is led by a democratically elected government—it is known to be the largest democratic state in the world in terms of population. So far, there are diverging opinions on India's international aspirations there are analysts which see India to be moving more via leverage on individual entrepreneurial initiatives primarily focused on building and developing the national economy with priority given to services industry rather than cheap labor-based manufacturing for export purposes.

Whilst others suggest that India has expansionary aspirations that go beyond commercial ones, especially when it comes to immediately confining states such as Sri Lanka, Maldives, Bhutan, Myanmar, and Pakistan.

Many however seem to agree that India already faces many challenges with long-standing disputes over borders with Pakistan, with reference to not only the Kashmir region but also China and other neighbors, in addition to several separatist and insurgency movements both along these borders and internally. Its rugged land borders represented by the Himalayan range are some of the most highly militarized in the world, draining substantial resources from the state's annual budget.

Though no one can predict the future, should there be international ambition in any outward direction, it might be one most probably led by trade and economic motives. Successful Indian entrepreneurs, both in India and abroad, seek to grow their enterprises, business relations, and networks internationally. Invading poor and resource-less neighboring countries might be a possibility among many others but reasonably a strategically senseless one (everything else remaining the same).

India does suffer from many endemic, ideologically inspired movements, which have in the past resorted to pockets of reoccurring violent confrontation, which have the potential of provoking not only internal problems but international disputes (CIA World Fact Book).

China (People's Republic of China or PRC) is also among the oldest known civilization in the world and one that for centuries contributed to mankind's advancement through innovation, science, the arts, philosophy, commerce, and trade. In terms of landmass, China today is the fourth-largest country in the world. Like India it has remained mostly within the same general physiological area protected and demarcated by natural barriers (e.g., mountains, large deserts) on its borders.

China, on the other hand, led by a centralized government, to the eyes of a growing number of analysts, seems to adopt a coordinated approach in achieving strategic objectives through what might be perceived as a true international expansion strategy—actively implementing projects; pushing and promoting diplomatic, economic, and military ties with many foreign countries, and leveraging a growing number of influential locally naturalized Chinese.

Many expert analysts, reports, specialized articles suggest that the PRC backs this strategy also with financial assistance through some of the country's most important financial institutions.

Given the incredible growth in the economic power of China, many theories are developing to explain how China is projecting its power internationally. Each of these produces a wealth of information and different perspectives. The purpose here is not to promote or demote any of these ideas but to go beyond. For example, as seen in earlier chapters, China has grown its GDP *tenfold* since 1978 (CIA World Fact Book). It has become the second-largest economy in terms of GDP. It is increasing its presence on a worldwide scale and growing economically.

Hence, for all practical purposes it might already be superpower. China is already a mighty and formidable reality! Given that projections are very important, analysts are at odds if we need to wait for these to happen to address important, impelling geo-strategic issues appropriately.

An article in *The Economist*, making reference to Stefan Halper's book, says "Party Rule (in China) depends on Economic Growth, which in turn depends on resources supplied by unsavory countries. Politicians in Africa in fact rarely talk about following a Beijing Consensus. But they love the flow of aid from China that comes without Western lectures about governance and human rights" (The Economist; Stefan Halper).

According to its authors, the PRC operates in the international arena with a model for its projection of power. One of these is called the "Beijing Consensus." The Beijing Consensus seems to build its foundations on the Chinese model of development, which might be summarized in three strategic priorities:

1. Focus on infrastructure development;
2. Produce economic reform;
3. Evaluate implementation of civic reform. In other words, instead of being pressured to create reforms, provide economic possibilities and let the people adhere and adapt to the existing system. This substantially frees China from many external pressures deriving from international organizations and nations, allowing it to write its own book—in a we-can-do-it-using-our-own-model type of context (Foreign Policy Centre; Joshua Cooper Ramo).

The Beijing Consensus seems to encapsulate the essence of the approach used by China in developing international relations and trade.

According to these sources, the cornerstones of the Beijing Consensus seem to be centered primarily around the following elements:

1. Use of the Chinese model of development;
2. Structural development: Interested in large-scale infrastructure projects that can improve productivity, China can provide both the means and manpower at low costs to roll out these projects. The reasoning here is that if you do not have dams, electricity, roads, ports, etc., you cannot produce anything effectively and efficiently;
3. Noninterference: The PRC is interested in trade with no strings attached. If the two nations find a common ground, no concern is given to other factors, such as respect for human rights and democratic rule;
4. Friendship and respect: The PRC respects standing rulers and their followers and sees reciprocal respect as a long-term key success factor.

So how might this pan out in the real world? How might the PRC implement this international strategy? Is it already being implemented? Is it already happening?

The deal is simple: the creation, expansion, or renewal of infrastructure in exchange for a space to do business with substantial preferential treatment. On the face of it, it all seems to be limited to the possibility of promoting trade. In reality, analysts believe the influence appears to go beyond mere commercial issues. China obtains access to resources important to its growth and local markets for its cheaper products in countries where equivalent western products have usually been beyond the purchase possibilities of locals.

Large-scale infrastructure projects in some cases foresee a substantial stake in the development activities due to a lack of local expertise.

The same sources cited put increasing concern on the presence power projection and influence into the context of a much broader global and geopolitical picture in order to fully appreciate its consequences. The growing presence of the neo-economic giants might not be limited to supermarket shelves, jobs, and local economies.

In the Caribbean, only a few hundred miles off the coast of the United States and all of northern Latin America, interestingly close to the largest subsea oil fields of the region, the same phenomenon is happening.

The void created by budget cuts that led to substantial withdrawal of developed countries is being naturally filled in many parts of the world by the BRIC countries. This influence is growing in Venezuela, Colombia, Ecuador, Peru, Bolivia, Uruguay, and Paraguay—namely, most of the South American subcontinent.

The *Business Journal's* report titled "China's Growing Investment in the Caribbean" from June 28, 2011, cited a recent report released by the UN Economic Commission for Latin America and the Caribbean. It provided the following data: Chinese foreign direct investments in the Caribbean and Latin America in 2010 were nearly $15 billion compared to $7 billion in 2009 and were primarily focused on major infrastructure projects: Dominica (cricket stadium, $17 million), Anguilla (hospital and stadium), Trinidad and Tobago (aluminum project, prime minister's official residence, and national academy for the arts, $3 billion), and Dominican Republic (resort).

In Latin America, over 90 percent of the investments were focused on mineral extractions. According to the UN report, diversification is also taking place, with foreign direct investments targeting also manufacturing and service (including tourism) and agriculture projects in Mexico, Central America, and the Caribbean.

A Reuters report by Linda Hutchinson-Jafar stated that, notwithstanding the heavy load of loans on some Caribbean states such as Jamaica, Barbados, and the Bahamas, China is stepping up and breaking ground with projects such as the Baha Mar tourism development in the Bahamas worth $2.6 billion, while Jamaica will be receiving $1 billion worth in ports, a conference center, and highway projects.

In Cuba, the report continued, "stores are filled with Chinese goods while Chinese built cars and buses are becoming common sight." This is over and above the $6 billion investment in one of Cuba's oil refineries and the construction of a natural gas terminal in exchange for sugar and nickel, while contemplating the joint production of pharmaceuticals.

An article in the March 2012 *Economist* ("The Caribbean a Chinese Beachhead") reported on the national stadium in the Bahamas, designed and paid for by China and built mainly by migrant Chinese laborers.

Moving on to the African continent, most African countries (i.e., Congo, Sudan, Angola, Uganda, Nigeria, Egypt, Ethiopia), which make up the biggest chunks of Africa's territory, are beneficiaries of very large infrastructure projects from China, for example.

An OECD paper by Dr. Martin Davies on "How China is Influencing Africa's Development" citing other studies by *Deloitte* (mergermarket: the emergence of China), *PricewaterhouseCoopers*, and

McKinsey Quarterly on state capitalism suggest that since the first half of 2009, while the developed world was at grips with the financial crisis, China's investments in the African continent "had increased an impressive 81% compared to the same period the previous year" and provide valuable insight as to the other side of the coin, namely the failure rates of some of these enterprises, especially in small mining activities (PriceWaterhouseCoopers, Feb 2009), together with the impact that the PRC might have in Africa's Development. The paper also states that at the 2007 World Economic Forum, Mr. Li Ruogu, EXIM Bank's CEO, said that "as much as 40% of the Bank's loan-book is now held in Africa." (OECD, Davis, & et al). The same source states that at the FOCAC meeting held in Sharm El Sheik on Nov 9, 2009 Premier Wen Jiabao stated ". . . China would provide 10 billion US dollars" of investments in this continent in the next years.

The following is a brief sample some of the major projects financed by the PRC in Africa and nearby island states in the Indian ocean (Frontier Advisory Analysis; The World Bank, IMF, CIA World Fact Book):

- Sudan: CNPC acquisition of 40 percent of the Greater Nile Petroleum Operating Company; China owns most of the oil fields in South Darfur; pipeline to Port Sudan; 60 percent of Sudan's oil production goes to China;
- Nigeria: CNPC bought an oil block (six by 2005) in exchange for hydroelectric power; Lagos Kano Railway;
- Angola: $5 billion loan for oil and national infrastructure-related products to be paid back in oil;
- Tanzania and Zambia: railroad;
- Zambia: copper-related industry;
- Mauritius: manufacturing, trade, tourism, hospitals, and stadiums;
- Ethiopia: electrical machinery, construction material, and steel industries;

- Egypt: petroleum equipment, electrical appliances, textiles, and automotive industry;
- Algeria: highway project;
- Guinea: Souapiti Dam, bauxite, and aluminum mining;
- Congo: Congo River dam for oil;
- Ghana: Bui Dam and cocoa;
- Gabon: key infrastructure for iron ore;
- Madagascar: nickel mining;
- Zimbabwe: coal mines and thermal power plant for chrome;
- Mozambique: coal;
- Democratic Rep of Congo: roads, rail, copper, and cobalt;
- Others: timber, gold, diamonds, and minerals.

According to multiple sources, the billions involved in these exchanges are from officially released numbers and might not necessarily coincide with true amounts, especially when it comes to armament sales.

Arms and armaments, for example, are also economically cheaper than their counterparts, and many poor countries or rebel groups can afford machetes, low-priced rifles, and grenade launchers. When distributed on large scales, these can inflict more damage than arms of mass destruction, as was the case in the 1994 Rwandan Genocide. Detailed accounts of the events can be also found on the UN websites.

Moving farther east toward the Middle East, most Arab states and non-Arab states, such as Iran, have more than two millennia of trade experiences with China. Historically, they have preferred not to have long-term initiatives that create too much of a close-knit rapport with China, mutually avoiding the reciprocal "strangling noose" effect. Doing business at arm's length and maintaining parity in rapport have been essential elements that historically made trade successful among these nations. But is this still true?

Notwithstanding the actual political boundaries of the Middle East and their deeply rooted historical arm's-length trade strategies, currently unparalleled sums are being invested by China in this part of the world (e.g., billion-dollar joint petroleum project in Iran). They cover just about all countries in this region, including Iraq, the United Arab Emirates, Syria, Yemen, the Kingdom of Saudi Arabia, Jordan, and Lebanon.

Moving over to Asia, notwithstanding cultural issues dating back centuries, the economies of entire states in Southeast Asia are heavily influenced by large investments, while others are influenced by the added physical presence of large now-indigenous Indian and Chinese communities, to the point that they have created a counterbalance of "real" influence and power with respect to the indigenous populations, which still represents the majority in terms of population. This can be noticed in countries such as Mauritius, Indonesia, and Malaysia.

Indian and Pacific Ocean islands are ever-more (willingly or not) pulled into the sphere of influence of China and India. Most of the countries in these regions have the same characteristics. They are either rich in mineral resources or strategically positioned, denoting a factual need toward projection of power.

In his paper Dr. Davies suggests that State capitalism allows state-owned firms through state owned banks financing to permit these companies, which would otherwise not be able to invest in these times, to fill the void by riding economic growth "counter-cyclically" with respect to the rest of the world "manipulating market outcomes for political purposes" (Bremmer, 2009) that is now facing the economic crisis.

Additionally aiding such a policy is a different capital risk model used by Chinese state-owned banks that, as some analysts suggest, might not need to be fully accountable to private stakeholders but political interests. This creates a totally different set of premises and operational platforms—rendering what is considered risky not viable for the developed world—as possible for China. Some might see in this the possibility of playing with an additional and or different set of cards.

Moreover, soft loans and preferential financing conditions do not only go to governments but also to state-owned enterprises that act as the key implementers of the large infrastructure projects.

Some of the sources cited so far confirm that China's strategic plan, an integral part of the PRC's eleventh five-year plan, has designated priority zones that include Cambodia, Egypt, Mauritius, Nigeria, Pakistan, Russia, Tanzania, Thailand, and Zambia. If you include other countries of special interest to the PRC and look at where they are positioned geographically, it is not hard to notice the resemblance it has with the semicircle around the southern part of the North American continent. The only difference here is that it encloses nearly all of the countries that face the Indian Ocean in its entirety and all of Southeast Asia.

Furthermore, the reports suggest that the PRC uses these economic zones, such as the one in Egypt's Suez region, to penetrate adjacent markets—in this case, the Middle East and North African countries with "Made in Egypt" products so as to avoid the growing psychological effect sometimes associated with the "Made in China" branding. Market development is one of the key objectives here. Other objectives, as discussed by Davies, include access to resources and political influence. Aid is another tool used to help the PRC's localized consolidation—in symbolic gestures that generates acquiescence in the masses.

To sum up the geographical extension of the PRC's activities around the world, the above areas cover circa 50 percent of the world's emerged lands and have a real presence in over 75 percent of the world in absolute terms, including seas and oceans.

This is becoming a matter of concern for many analysts, policy makers and businesses but to maintain equidistance we need to mention that though it can be seen as an unprecedented level of potential global reach in human history, it is not. To shed some tranquility, the United States has reached a significantly higher level. If one factors in historical time frames and the strategic importance nations played, Britain came close in its period of maximum splendor.

This, however, by no means suggests the need not to be fully aware of the geopolitical implications and ramifications of this phenomenon.

Assessing wether or not there is a power projection strategy, the detailed accuracy of its parameters, the accuracy of the viewpoints presented, and to what extent—these are not the objectives of this book—rather to convey that many variables are at play here exerting additional pressure and that induced imbalances add considerable complexity to existing models. One needs to constantly be reminded that, with all their shortcomings, the civilization, prosperity, freedoms, and fundamental rights we so much give for granted in the developed world are, in many cases, not fully available to the billions who wish for these in their own countries.

At the end of the day, BRIC's will probably do what is deemed best for them and try to reduce a competitor's superiority as natural strategy. The current state of affairs seems to be still led by and fuelled by a positive economic exchange between nations. Ideally, the objective should remain exactly that—creating the premises for collaboration, trade and the free movement of persons and ideas.

The development and protection of free societies, a healthy geopolitical balance and strategy, multi-polarity, and stability, are key to future prosperity, development, and peace internationally. Seen from a different prospective, as will be self-evident later, BRIC's can be an opportunity for a much more remunerating multilateral economic growth.

The wealth of a society or a nation is linked in its ability to successfully lever and enhance uniqueness and diversity. These have provided and will continue providing one of mankind's most successful survival strategies and the base of development, knowledge, trade and the advancement civilizations.

It is the treasure each society produces, and as will become more evident later, this distinctiveness encases a part of the solution.

Building this wealth on the foundations of fundamental rights and freedoms while respecting others—will allow an ascent towards ever greater levels of civilization—constituting the cornerstones for prolonged economic development and prosperity.

Ultimately, the only real lever for lasting peace is economic development and environment where people can prosper and focus on themselves and their loved one's wellbeing in a geopolitically, continuously balanced, context.

A WINNING ALTERNATIVE
IS A BETTER STRATEGY
AND VICE VERSA

In a head-to-head confrontation, everyone loses something. An effective and lasting alternative might simply be a better strategy that promotes long-term economic prosperity and hope and one that turns the table around again or at least provides adequate possibilities. This must include seeking innovations that allow valid alternative solutions to tackle the shortage/depletion of natural resources and energy sources.

Although some signs might indicate differently, the fate of nations with very large ambitions that enact fast expansionary policies is historically well documented. From Alexander the Great to Napoleon, to Hitler—they all failed. All colorization attempts have failed! All ideologically driven internationalizations have botched.

Yet many will argue that their epitaph was the mere endings of entire films. Some might be more than glad to live out parts of the movie and jump ship before the film ends! Otherwise we cannot explain all the wars that have taken place to date.

Nevertheless, although in the short run there might be wins, the challenges the neo-economic giants face are probably even greater than those faced by the more developed counterparts, if not for anything else but their sheer population! Some of the factors that have failed fast expansionary policies include:

- sustainability of complex models

- overextension beyond control
- limit of resources and capability
- congestion of priorities
- overlooking small fires that can become uncontrollable
- inexorably arriving at one-size-fits-all policies that backfire
- energy-draining governance loops (controlling the controllers)
- runaway scenarios (appointed leaders on the outskirts that do as they please and fuel dissidence among locals, absorbing greater levels of energy)
- overlapping powers and conflict of interests
- internal conflicts
- power hunger of emerging rich and middle classes
- energy-absorbing cultural aspects
- unsustainable economies of scale
- inability to sustain win-wins across the board, creating waves of growing dissatisfaction
- failure rate factor (as news of failure of initiatives spread)
- too many compromises, many creating sharp contrasts.

Additionally, internally the neo-economic giants might also have to deal with social divaricators; corruption; legislative deficiencies; civil liberties; property rights; infrastructure, resource, and energetic deficiencies; unemployment; poverty; thirst for political and individual freedoms; inflation; bubble burst potential in local real markets; and control of richer and influential groups (e.g., religious, sectarian, political dissidence, minorities). In many ways, possibly some of the very same variables developed nations had to affront in their evolutionary path.

A recent article in *The Economist* pointed to growing concerns over India's trade deficit with China (India imports nearly three times more than it exports to China). In June 2012, this equated to circa $40 billion, representing nearly half of India's overall trade deficit with the world if oil imports are excluded. This has translated into a devaluation of the rupee by a fifth in the past year.

On the other hand, other articles on China and India state that economic growth in these countries is not affected by the economic crisis enveloping the developed world, as the sheer number of persons forming their respective economies is big enough to sustain such growth for some time.

Though there is room for debate on every single issue, there are at least three certainties:

1. It is hard to foresee the future;
2. Historical data tends to convey that extremely generous growth periods are, at best, cyclical events. Historical data only confirms that the above factors inevitably lead to social unrest (nationally and/or internationally);
3. Globalization and the economic crisis in developed countries will affect demand from developing nations.

If nothing is done, the current economic virus might only linger longer, produce more damage, especially in the developed world, for an even longer time, and affecting larger numbers of persons, families, businesses, enterprises, governments, nations, and continents. The effect on the neo-economic giants, however, though similar in nature, might probably need to deal with forces exponentially larger than the ones faced by the rest of the globe.

Fundamentally, if the model does not work any longer, this is valid for everyone, including BRIC and developing countries. We may have a choice though, a way to turn this paradigm around to find a better alternative, a better strategy for the future.

All of this argumentation excludes the effects of paradigm-changing variables, such as Mobint, advancement, innovation, and Web inclusivity.

Should there be a willingness on behalf of those seeking a winning strategy, to set aside or substantially reduce the axiom of fear as the underlying, or one of the predominant geopolitical strategies (different from achieving sound geopolitical balance)— the opportunities to revive economies in those nations that elect a winning strategy, are limited only by their strategic thought processes and convictions in devising and enacting policy.

This however also entails being able to evaluate matters from different perspectives and avoid model fixation.

In reality the number of possibilities and opportunities has never been so vast!

Adopting a winning strategy is at the base of prolonged economic development—globally; it is what has taken man out of the darkest and most hopeless scenarios, allowed it to prosper and achieve what no other known specie has been able to achieve.

A policy of positive willingness to improve and strategic vision might help develop resilience, hope, solutions, and form the foundations of new levels of civilization and renewed prolonged eras of prosperity.

IMMIGRATION: IS THERE AN INVASION? EMIGRATION: IS THERE A PLIGHT?

The book does not convey a preference for or against immigration/emigration, but it looks at facts and challenges we currently face.

Not long ago Emma Lazarus said, "Give me your tired, your poor, your huddled masses yearning to breathe free . . ." Those that no one wanted made America's success. Undeniably, America would have never been America without immigration.

Similarly, the history of many families in most countries is made up of stories of immigration and emigration. The new lands of opportunity are created by immigration of the best and the poorest of the poor. See the internal mass immigration movements in India and China, and external emigration from Pakistan, Afghanistan, and Sri Lanka to the new lands of opportunity, such as the United Arab Emirates, Saudi Arabia, Malaysia, and Brazil. The numbers are staggering by any scale.

Mass immigration also has its challenges:

- intolerance
- added pressures to hosting societies
- added challenges (e.g., poverty, schooling, public safety, health, national security, national debt)
- pressures on labor markets and wages
- inequalities

- cultural aspects
- integration.

But is immigration only from poor to rich? Or is it more from stalled economies (economics that do not offer jobs or whose job markets are saturated with only those that at best are at odds with survival) to active economies?

Demographic data from the United States, European governments, and the United Nations suggests that emigration nowadays is made up of millions of laureates, high school graduates, highly skilled workers, and professionals that are moving from hard-hit European countries and the United States to more active economies around the world.

Sometimes it is not for jobs that they have studied for or invested years in acquiring valuable expertise in, but to humble, low-paying employment. In the majority of cases, it is for precarious jobs. Millions face this excruciating dilemma, but it is a fact that involves an ever-growing number of persons and families around the world, a diaspora of gigantic proportions, one that needs to be addressed before its repercussions add yet other layers of complexity and dichotomies.

The world of small regions being mostly populated by small homogenous indigenously born persons is changed for good. This book is not about whether immigration/emigration is good or bad. As with anything, one will find arguments for or against it based on the point they want to make in that particular moment in time. The approach for this book is more humble. It is to start with a fact—the immigration/emigration phenomenon exists. It is a reality. The question is how to manage it better and leverage whatever is possible to make it produce better results for all.

Given the sensitivity around this subject, objectivity and caution should be used in analyzing this topic. As in all cases, one can see this phenomenon from different angles, perspectives, or filters, some of which lead only to damaging and unjustified xenophobic feelings. It is necessary to put all viewpoints in the equation in order to address them so as to arrive at a viable solution. The following is a list of some of the possible thought processes (the fact that they are mentioned here does not convey any shared vision or acceptance):

- Extreme conspiracy theorists might claim that for the first time in history, at least theoretically and in an unprecedented manner, nations such as China and India would have access to potential large communities that could act as eventual troops on the ground in every angle of the world, providing these countries with the possibility to take down critical national infrastructures before a physical invasion. The reality is that there are as many US, European, and non-BRIC citizens trying to live their lives and make a living in just as many places. Equally true is the fact that many of these communities have deeply rooted histories and have been citizens of these countries for generations—just like German Americans, Italian Americans, and Americans of African ancestry;
- The physical or virtual protectionist might deem viable alternatives curbing or stopping immigration by building walls or spending billions on electronic defenses;
- "Cost only"-driven globalization viewpoints might prefer lax policies to allow for better exploitation of low-cost labor based on fluctuations in market demand for use in their businesses. This viewpoint could incorporate diametrically different logic, such as temporary labor importation and adopting outsourcing, delocalization, business process, knowledge, and industrial transfer strategies;
- Technocrats might prefer resorting to a mix of formal instruments (such as point-based immigration and visa requirements) to address different national needs and opt for

affecting policies via official international diplomatic actions or through international for a, such as the WTO and UN agencies;

- The unscrupulous businessperson, though publicly against immigration and formally shames any type of immigration, hires illegal immigrant workers to match competition;
- Speculators (of any origin) see immigration as a highly remunerative economic opportunity—be it in the form of human trafficking or any other activity that could leverage clandestine immigration and other heinous uses (e.g., organ removal for transplants, illegal adoption);
- In the formal corporate view, diversity is promoted as the best form of human capital leverage;
- Jobless persons see emigration as an opportunity to relocate to the new lands of opportunity;
- Disaster-affected persons who have suffered catastrophic natural disasters, war, persecution, genocide, famine, or health-related plagues might be forced to leave their loved ones, probably knowing they will never see them again, bestowing their lives, destinies, and earthly and monetary belongings in the hands of human traffickers that shove them into boats simply to seek better survival possibilities;
- A sizable group that could encompass the silent majority might wait and hope that their elected government officials find a viable solution to this growingly unparalleled phenomenon;
- The cultural catastrophists see immigration as a threat to the annihilation of the local values;
- Some welcome it;
- And some fear it;
- Millions suffer from it, either enduring it and its humiliations or seeing their loved ones need to leave;
- Some see it as their only solution for continuance.

Are any of these, taken singularly, the right viewpoint? Might each person in the privacy of his own thoughts change perceptions about immigration/emigration many times over even during the same day? Is the origin of the frustration more over the prolonged effects of a disastrous crisis? Or the skin color of our neighbor whose friendship we appreciated until not so long ago?

If we were able to magically change the color of our pigmentation, learn a new language instantly, or change cultures at will—just with the power of our thoughts—and all became the same color, speak the same language, uphold the same values and behave in the same manner, would you think that we would still not be frustrated or see immigration under a different light?

Does it only have to do with a person's origin or differences in the way we appear, talk, and behave? Or has it more to do with primordial fears? Are our fears more tied to anxiety derived from a possible scarcity (e.g., job, business opportunity)?

What if we were confident or objective? Could we manage or at least address this phenomenon in a better way? Would we not be more rational when we do not face fear or anxiety? When things go well (economically or otherwise), do we not see these same issues under a totally different light?

Let us then start from this rational point of view.

1. Is immigration/emigration a natural phenomenon that always existed and will continue existing?
2. Do we wish to be free to move where we choose in order to seek new opportunities, jobs, or simply perspectives?
3. Is immigration a cause, a consequence, or a natural necessity?
4. Has any entity, person, government, or empire (that had no limit in the exercise of brutal force to inflict death at will)

ever been able to stop, curb, or limit this phenomenon in the history of mankind?

5. Except for a very few indigenous persons left in faraway corners, are we not a by-product of generations of families that have emigrated, mixed, and re-emigrated multiple times?

6. Are we heading toward a more open world, or do we wish to have a more restrictive one? Or better yet, what is the world that we wish to see? Would it be a world where we could have the potential to choose to live in parts of the world be it within the confines of a nation or internationally—in France one year for a job opportunity, in Sedona the next, and maybe South Africa because it is where we will feel more at home? Or would we prefer a world made of layers of walls (electronic, physical, or virtual)?

I will leave each reader to answer these questions on their own, because the answers you give might be more important than what I could ever suggest. The fundamental question is how to arrive at a viable solution, one that could improve the level of positive immigration/emigration while addressing the impelling needs stemming from unemployment, business closures, poverty, famine, man-made or natural disasters, war, and sickness.

The fundamental premise for positive immigration is one that generates prosperity and general well-being to hosting societies and immigrants, while the fundamental premise for managing migration over the long run is creating environments that offer acceptable/favorable living possibilities, opportunities, and prosperity locally.

It is important to highlight that migration does not necessarily involve a move from bad situations to good it seems instead to be multi-directional. In the current socioeconomic scenario, there will also be an emigration stemming from persons seeking to move to more rural environments, to disastrous urban favelas, or to the best of two very bad alternatives, fueled probably by desperation, fear, and a search for a relatively more secure environment. This will logically add pressures and challenges on host societies and individuals impacted by this phenomenon.

The approach to the management of mass migratory phenomenon must evolve from its current state of affairs if we seek ways to address it according to the needs of each society. We must remember that the dimensions of the problem will be exponentially higher as time progresses and an economic crisis of planetary dimensions will not help, will they?

Has time come to evaluate new avenues?

REFOCUS AND OBSERVE

Glimpse and you will get—but a bare flicker—of a picture,
Look and you will see a vivid frame of the same,
Observe and growing numbers of awe inspiring
worlds in motion might open before your eyes!

For the first time in human history, we are witnessing something unique. Young and living generations potentially are prone to be left without any reference points going forward, hardly any legacy, something that previous generations instead were provided with. For previous generations the models and frameworks left behind still continued to serve their purpose, and evolution took place over longer periods of time.

Provided the enormous step-level transformations and paradigm-changing innovations that we face, can the existing economic models still act as reference points going forward?

Better yet, though perfectly conscious of the many transformations taking place, are we sure we are not forcing ourselves to see these impelling step-level evolutionary requirements for change through the prisms and filters of our existing economic models?

Is the real reference model that is shaping all around us developing on a very different level (plateau)? Are we continuing to look at our existing economic model, staying in the cocoon of our comfort zone whilst being drawn into a black hole by the force of growing implosionary forces? Or do we wish to move on and leverage the opportunities that lie ahead should we wish to take the paces toward the step-level evolutionary changes that *we* have produced?

Man has evolved from nomadic creatures that lived on the sidelines of nature, literally trying to survive on a daily basis, leveraging sheer brute force and finding strength in belonging to small groups of hunters and gatherers, to a complex interwoven society on a global scale that has wandered beyond earth, achieved linking human beings in different parts of the planet at the push of a button, and developing an appreciation for sciences, art, intellect, and spirituality—in just a few thousand years. Yet today we seem incredibly powerless in managing what is, at the end of the day, a man-made reality.

In the following chapters we will look at some of the main elements and domains forming the existing economic model and examples of a few elements that affect it, in order to better appreciate what is happening in each in terms of systemic dichotomies and blocks should we wish to insist on existing models to resolve and address important issues.

WHAT IS PUBLIC DEBT?

In an economy stricken by recession, the more that goes to government, the less is left over for business, employment, and everything else.

In a televised talk show, a young woman posed a dilemma to the invited guests who happened to be a democratically elected government officials. She said something along these lines: "You talk about public debt. The nation's deficit you define as being our debt. You mention the fact that we, the tax contributors, need to collectively resolve the situation since it's long overdue, the fact that the markets demand it. I am just twenty-two, and I fail to understand whom I'm indebted to, why I find myself with this debt, who contracted this debt on my behalf, and with what legitimacy. Should I even come to appreciate your discourse and accept its reasons, how in the world am I ever going to pay back the debt you are mentioning if there isn't the slightest hope of a proper job in sight? Who are these so-called markets to which we all have to be subservient and subjugated?"

Following her logic, it is not hard to think she could have also asked the following questions: What makes the market needs more justified than mine? Should not my life's prerogatives come first and then your so-called debt or that of the markets? If I can't help myself, how can I be expected to chip in my share for the well-being of this society?

Although some of these questions might appear rhetorical, they are objectively legitimate, especially when posed by younger generations. These questions push us to look beyond the boxes, the things we have come accustomed to as the norm and accepted as truths, beyond the obvious, beyond those things that make perfect sense in their current framework but that might cease to be logical, as soon as one looks beyond. This is exactly the type of paradox in which we live.

What is a country's debt made of? Are we sure the way it is calculated is relevant to the reality we live in today? To the challenges we will be facing? To the technological breakthroughs we will be producing? Who can insist on public debt to be defined and calculated the way we find it done today? To what avail?

Though a country's debt calculation has evolved over the centuries with the contribution of many economists and other persons, and notwithstanding all the progress made, are its shortcomings not questionable? This is especially true when we factor in other elements. Though there are some generally accepted guidelines that most nations adhere to, what constitutes public debt for one country does not necessarily hold true for another.

For example, the European Union states adopted a common framework of representing debt of its member countries in 2010 with the approval of the Stability and Growth Act (ironically this same pact has become part of the problem in the current Eurozone crisis)—for the first time using the same captions and methodology in explicitly reporting debts that were previously "handled" differently by each state within the union. To be fair, this might have had good intentions, but as senior economists and politicians acknowledge now it is in many cases only acting as a straitjacket for many of the states within the union—a noose, according to some, that might be getting tighter around each member's neck by the day. In fact, part of the tremendous difficulties policy makers have is finding a viable solution to something that was ratified only a few of years ago.

Some items can be excluded as a conformant to each country's law and public policy. In the US example, calculations of debt of economically relevant amounts pertaining to the following items are excluded (US Department of Treasury):

- Fannie Mae and Freddie Mac: They represent the obligations of both these government-sponsored enterprises worth circa $5 trillion, primarily made up of mortgage payment guarantees;
- Temporary Liquidity Guarantee Program, Exchange Stabilization Funds, and the like: These consist of federal government guarantees, such as the TARP, for mutual funds, banks, and corporations designed to deal with the problems arising from the late 2000 financial crisis;
- Future impact of unfunded obligations, such as social security, Medicare, and Medicaid, for a total of $46 trillion, that will need to be distributed over the next decades through to the year 2084.

At the end of fiscal year 2011, the total federal debt of the United States was a staggering $14.8 trillion. According to the monthly statement of May 2012, the amount is $15,437,987,849,460. (This will surely change by the time this book gets printed). This amount exceeds the current GDP of the United States. (US Treasury Direct).

Princeton's wordnet defines public debt as "the total of the nation's debts: debts of local, state and national governments; an indicator of how much public spending is financed by borrowing instead of taxation".

The US Treasury Department instead uses the following definition to describe public debt (US Department of Treasury website):

"The U.S. Government is just like a business. The Government has to provide services for the people of the United States such as military protection, education and health programs, the space program, and social services programs. It also needs money to buy supplies and equipment.

The government's main source of money is the taxes it collects from individuals and businesses. There are different kinds of taxes. Here are some examples:

- Income tax: money people pay to the government based on how much they earn from their jobs;
- Sales and excise tax: money people pay to the government when they buy things;
- Corporate tax: money businesses pay to the government based on their earnings.

However, the amount of money the government spends for the services it provides is often more than the taxes it collects. To make up the difference, the government borrows money. In other words, it goes into debt.

When the government borrows money, it doesn't go to the bank and apply for a loan. It "issues debt." This means the government sells Treasury marketable securities, such as Treasury bills, notes, bonds, and Treasury inflation-protected securities (TIPS) to other federal government agencies, individuals, businesses, state and local governments, as well as those from other countries. Savings bonds are sold to individuals, corporations, associations, public and private organizations, fiduciaries, and other entities.

Here is how Treasury securities, such as savings bonds, generally work. People lend money to the government so it can pay its bills.

Over time, the government gives that money, plus a bit extra, back to those people as payment for using the borrowed money. That extra money is interest.

This is how the US system of debt works. The US Treasury issues or creates the debt. The Bureau of the Public Debt manages the government's debt. That means it keeps records, takes care of selling the debt, and handles paying back people who loaned the government money. The US Treasury and the Bureau of the Public Debt do not decide how the money is spent. The legislative branch of government (Congress) decides how the money is spent. There is a maximum amount of debt the government can have. This is known as the "debt ceiling." To raise that amount, the US Treasury must get Congress to approve a new and higher limit."

What Is the Makeup of the US Federal Government Debt?

According to the Government Accountability Office (GAO), the total US debt is divided into two primary components: government accounts (which for 2011was $4.7 trillion) and public debt (which for 2011 was $10.1 trillion).

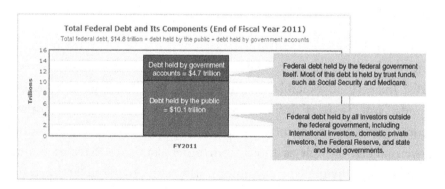

Source: US Government Accountability Office, Department of the Treasury

Debt Held by Government Accounts

According to the GOA, debt held by government accounts is balanced primarily in trust funds held by the federal government that accumulate surpluses. Trust funds are defined as "accounting mechanisms" used to link receipts with the expenditures of those receipts. Examples of such trust funds include social security, Medicare, military retirement and health care, civil service retirement and disability, etc., as evidenced by the following diagram (US Government Accountability Office).

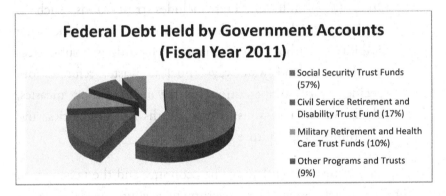

Federal Debt Held by Government Accounts (Fiscal Year 2011)

- ■ Social Security Trust Funds (57%)
- ■ Civil Service Retirement and Disability Trust Fund (17%)
- ■ Military Retirement and Health Care Trust Funds (10%)
- ■ Other Programs and Trusts (9%)

According to the same document, this is a more detailed composition of debt held in government accounts:

- Airport and Airway Trust Fund, worth $10 billion (taxes received from jet fuel, passenger tickets, airport taxes, etc., less outlays in what is needed to fund the FAA, to carry out airport and airways programs, grants in aid, and subsidies to airlines, R&D engineering, and development)
- Deposit Insurance Fund ($32 billion)
- Employee Life Insurance Fund ($40 billion)
- Exchange Stabilization Fund ($23 billion)
- Federal Disability Insurance Trust Fund ($154 billion)
- Federal Employee Retirement System ($819 billion)
- Federal Hospital Insurance Trust Fund/Medicare ($244 billion)

- Federal Housing Administration ($5 billion)
- Federal Old-Age and Survivors Trust Fund ($2.4 trillion)
- Federal Savings and Loan Corporation Resolution Fund ($3 billion)
- Federal Medical Insurance Trust Fund ($80 billion)
- Highway Trust Fund ($14 billion)
- National Service Life Insurance Fund ($7.5 billion)
- Postal Service Fund ($0.5 billion)
- Railroad Retirement Account ($0.3 billion)
- Unemployment Trust Fund ($15 billion)
- Other ($939 billion). This includes trust funds, such as uranium enrichment and decommissioning, black lung disability, harbor maintenance, hazardous substances superfund, inland waterways, nuclear waste, reforestation, vaccine injury compensation for trivalent mumps, measles, rubella, varicella, tetanus, related deaths and disabilities, and such things as agriculture disaster relief.

This debt reflects a burden on the economy and the taxpayers in the future. In fact, whenever a government account needs to spend more than it receives from the public, the government must obtain this amount by increasing taxes, cutting spending, or borrowing more. The GOA goes on to say that debt held by trust funds, such as social security and Medicare, is not equal to the future benefit costs implied by the current design of the programs and, therefore, does not fully capture the government's total future commitment to these programs.

Debt Held by the Public

Debt held by the public (worth more than $10 trillion) is the amount the federal government has borrowed to finance the cumulative cash deficit. It is the value of all securities sold to the public, which can be made up of any investor outside the federal government. This creates a debt toward a wide variety of investors, including private domestic international investors, the Federal Reserve, and state and local governments, as seen better in the following diagram.

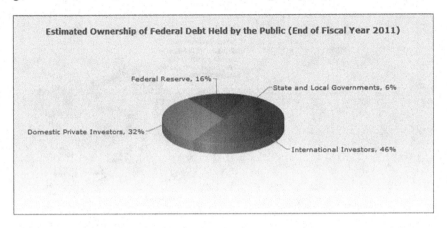

Source: (US Federal Reserve—Flow of Funds Accounts of tjhe US—Etimate Ownership of Debt Held by Public)

The more than $10 trillion is divided into two parts, namely marketable securities ($9.9 trillion) and nonmarketable securities ($0.5 trillion), holding things such as:

Marketable securities:

- o bills ($1.5 trillion)
- o notes ($6.5 trillion)
- o bonds ($1 trillion)
- o treasury inflation-protected securities ($0.7 trillion).

Nonmarketable securities worth the remaining $0.5 trillion:

- o US Savings Securities
- o Foreign Series
- o Government Account Series
- o Domestic Series
- o other.

In 2011, more than 40 percent of the publicly held debt of $10 trillion was owned by foreign investors of the following countries:

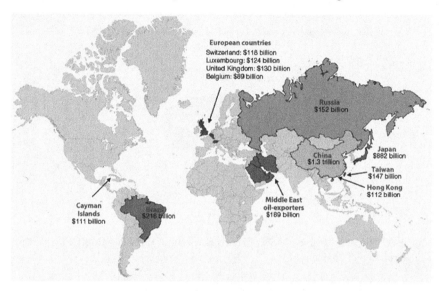

Source: Department of the Treasury, Federal Reserve Bank of New York and the Board of Governors of the Federal Reserve System. Countries shown on map represent 75 percent of foreign-held Treasury securities. Data from Report on Foreign Portfolio Holdings of U.S. Securities as of June 30, 2011. Map from Map Resources. China refers to Mainland China and not Hong Kong, Macau, or Taiwan. Middle East oil exporters are Bahrain, Iran, Iraq, Kuwait, Oman, Qatar, Saudi Arabia, and the United Arab Emirates; the holdings for individual oil exporting countries are not available. (US GAO)

- China (26 percent)
- Japan (22 percent)
- United Kingdom (8.8 percent)
- Oil-exporting countries: Saudi Arabia, Venezuela, Libya, Iran, Iraq, the United Arab Emirates, Bahrain, Kuwait, Oman, Qatar, Ecuador, Indonesia, Algeria, Gabon, and Nigeria (4.9 percent)
- Brazil (4.2 percent)
- Caribbean (3.7 percent)
- Taiwan (3.2 percent)
- Switzerland (3.2 percent)
- Hong Kong SAR (2.4 percent)

- Canada (2 percent)
- Russia (1.9 percent)
- Luxemburg (1.7 percent)
- Singapore (1.3 percent)
- Germany (1.3 percent)
- Thailand, Ireland, and France (1 percent each)
- Belgium, South Korea, India, Turkey, Mexico, Chile, Poland, Italy, Philippines, Norway, Sweden, Netherlands, Israel, Malaysia, and Spain (each with lower than 1 percent shares) (US Department of Treasury).

Any debt, be it private or that held by a country, could potentially be used as a noose by a lender and, in cases where governments are concerned, as potential political leverage. With regard to the debt owed to other countries, this could create additional exposure for the United States or other borrowing countries in the eventual case one or more lending nations decide to dump the securities held.

As best explained by the GOA, government securities are attractive to investors because they are backed by the full faith and credit of the US government, are offered in a wide range of maturities, and are exempt from interest rates.

Only debt held by the public is considered as a liability, while debt held by government accounts is considered an asset to those accounts but a liability to the Treasury, offsetting each other in the consolidated financial statements of the US government.

How Do Countries Borrow?

In the United States, the president and the Congress can make laws to limit the total amount of debt that can be outstanding by the federal government, thereby creating a legal ceiling. This limit, however, cannot restrict Congress's prerogative and ability to ratify spending and revenue legislation that can affect the level of debt or otherwise restrain fiscal policy. The debt limit confines the Department of the Treasury's authority to borrow in order to finance the decisions enacted by the Congress and the president.

Since 1995, the statutory debt limit has been increased twelve times to its current level. The Department of the Treasury recently notified Congress that the current debt limit could be reached soon. The Congressional Budget Office (CBO) projects that under current law debt subject to the limit will exceed $25 trillion in 2021.

According to the Congressional Budget Office, in the United States, the federal government can borrow by issuing securities to the public that for the most part are marketable (sellable), meaning that they can be resold by whoever owns them while a small portion of securities are nonmarketable, meaning they are registered to the owner and cannot be sold in the financial market. US savings bonds are an example.

These securities consist of bills, notes, bonds, and TIPS. These are offered in a wide range of maturities to appeal to the broadest range of investors, as best represented by the below diagram.

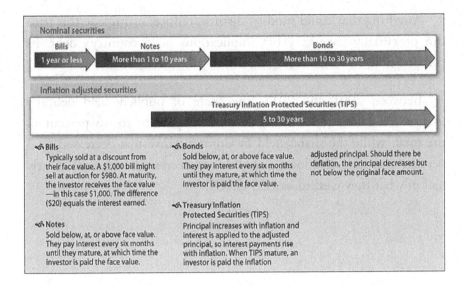

Source: (US Department of the Treasury)

The following are key reasons that investors purchase Treasury securities:

- They can easily be traded;
- There is good demand. Many people are interested in buying and selling at any given time;
- Treasury securities accounted for about half or more of the trading volume in US bond markets between 2001 and 2011;
- Treasury securities were viewed as a "safe haven" investment;
- The United States offers a stable political system and possible favorable returns;
- The US dollar is still considered to be the world's dominant reserve;
- The dollar was involved in more than 80 percent of activity in global foreign exchange markets in April 2010. The euro was second;
- Fundamentally there is trust in the system!

Anything that could modify, disturb, reduce, or impede this trust can potentially have very big implications on a country's debt, its composition, its value, etc.

Between 2001 and 2011, the share of publicly held debt by international investors increased from 37 percent to 46 percent of the total, while the shares held by domestic investors decreased by 3 percent and state and local governments decreased 6 percent, nearly half of what they used to be (US GAO).

What If a Country Cannot Pay Its Debt?

Is a country's debt a one-way street, where debt is accumulated continuously? While this might be the true track record of some countries, it cannot be considered a general rule for all. In the last decade the United States has had periods when debt was kept to a minimum and others when it went beyond its GDP, as best depicted in the chart below.

US Government Debt Trend

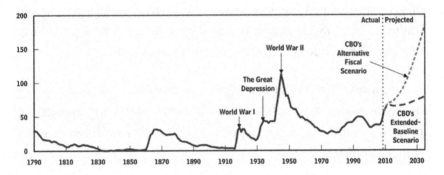

Source: Congressional Budget Office and Office of Management and Budget
Data from 1797 through 1969 available through CBO, Long-Term Budget Outlook June 2009 (see Additional Data). Data from 1970 through 2011 from OMB, Budget of the United States Government for Fiscal Year 2013—Historical Tables. For 1797-1969, year refers to calendar year. For 1970-2011, year refers to fiscal year. For the years prior to 1929, CBO notes they estimated GDP from several sources. (US Congressional Budget Office)

A country's debt is not enforceable, as one might be led to perceive. Should a country simply decide not to honor its debts, it can do so, as was the case of Germany with the rise of Adolf Hitler to power.

Though many safeguards were put in place after World War II to avoid such eventualities or limit their damage, state/country defaults have occurred in the recent past. There are international agencies, such as the International Monetary Fund and World Bank (which are funded by participating countries) that can exert some pressure on or help provide solutions for countries in difficulty.

Theoretically there are no internationally enforceable debt ceilings on sovereign countries, as these are set by their relative governments that, on a yearly basis, pass budgets on expenses they deem of public utility and propose ways to finance these through their legislative bodies and eventually concert these through official channels with these extra governmental bodies.

If the ceilings should be exceeded, governments have the power to authorize their treasuries to take extraordinary measures to cope with such emergencies, as was the case in 2009 and 2011, when the US debt ceilings were breached and government intervened to avoid a government shutdown. The US governments new ceiling has be revised in January 2012 to c. $16 trillion (US Department of Treasury website).

The intent here is not to suggest nor promote a state of anarchy but to show that the inability to fully honor debts by countries is not only possible but it has happened (repeatedly) to different states throughout history.

The sovereign status of a state puts it in a unique position and can, in extreme cases, decide not to honor its debts. In most cases, however, debts are restructured so that they can be repaid, such as the London agreement on German external debts, signed in 1953, or the most recent debt restructuring that was signed with poor African states or the Argentine debt crisis in early 2000 and now the Greek debt crisis.

Defaults were faced by Spain repeatedly during the 1500s, France after the French Revolution, the United States after its confederation, the newly formed USSR after the communist revolution, the Italian states in different historical periods, and Germany during the Weimar Republic. The list is long, and it is not limited to poor or less developed countries.

The following is a mere list of countries that have faced defaults, were near insolvency or restructured debt for synthesis some countries were not included on the list (Reinhart & Rogoff, 2009):

- Algeria (1991)
- Angola (1976, 1985, 1992-2002)
- Antigua, Barbuda, Bolivia (1875, 1927, 1931, 1980, 1986, 1989)
- Argentina (1827, 1890, 1951, 1956, 1982, 1989, 1991, 2002-2005)
- Austria (1938, 1940, 1945)
- Brazil (1898, 1902, 1914, 1931, 1937, 1961, 1964, 1983, 1986-1987, 1990)
- Cameroon (2004)
- Canada (1935)
- Central African Republic (1981, 1983)
- Chile (1826, 1880, 1931, 1961, 1963, 1966, 1972, 1974, 1983)
- China (1921, 1932, 1939)
- Congo (1979)
- Cote d'Ivoire (1983, 2000)
- Colombia (1826, 1850, 1873, 1880, 1900, 1932, 1935)
- Costa Rica (1828, 1874, 1895, 1901, 1932, 1962, 1981, 1983, 1984)
- Denmark (1813)
- Dominica (2003-2005)
- Dominican Republic (1872, 1892, 1897, 1899, 1931, 1975-2001, 2005)
- Ecuador (1826, 1868, 1894, 1906, 1909, 1914, 1929, 1982, 1984, 2000, 2008)
- Egypt (1876, 1984)
- El Salvador (1828, 1876, 1894, 1899, 1921, 1932, 1938, 1981-1996)

- France (1812)
- Gabon (1999-2005)
- Germany (1932, 1939, 1948)
- Hesse (1814), Prussia (1807, 1813), Westphalia (1812)
- Greece (1826, 1843, 1860, 1893, 1932, 2012)
- Ghana (1979, 1982)
- Grenada (2004-2005)
- Guatemala (1933, 1986, 1989)
- Guyana (1982)
- Hungary (1932, 1941)
- India (1958, 1969, 1972)
- Iran (1992)
- Indonesia (1996, 1998, 2000, 2002)
- Honduras (1828, 1873, 1981)
- Jamaica (1978)
- Japan (1942, 1946-1952)
- Kenya (1994, 2000)
- Kuwait (1990-1991)
- Liberia (1989-2006)
- Madagascar (2002)
- Mexico (1827, 1833, 1844, 1850, 1866, 1898, 1914, 1928-1930s, 1982)
- Mongolia (1997-2000)
- Morocco (1983, 1994, 2000)
- Mozambique (1980)
- Nicaragua (1828, 1894, 1911, 1915, 1932, 1979)
- Nigeria (1982, 1986, 1992, 2001, 2004)
- Panama (1932, 1983, 1983, 1987, 1988-1989)
- Paraguay (1874, 1892, 1920, 1932, 1986, 2003)
- Peru (1826, 1850, 1876, 1931, 1969, 1976, 1978, 1980, 1984)
- Russia (1839, 1885, 1918, 1947, 1957, 1991, 1998)
- Rwanda (1995)

- Sierra Leone (1997-1998)
- Spain (1809, 1820, 1831, 1834, 1851, 1867, 1872, 1882, 1936-1939)
- Sudan (1991)
- Surinam (2001-2002)
- Sweden (1812)
- Trinidad and Tobago (1989)
- Tunisia (1867)
- Turkey (1876, 1915, 1931, 1940, 1978, 1982)
- South Africa (1985, 1989, 1993)
- United Kingdom (1822, 1834, 1888-89, 1932)
- United States (1779, 1790, 1798,1862, 1933, 1971(Nixon Shock))
  - 9 states (1841-1842)
  - 10 states and many local governments (1873-83 or 1884)
- Venezuela (1826, 1848, 1860, 1865, 1892, 1982, 1990, 1995-1998, 2004)
- Zambia (1983)
- Zimbabwe (1965, 2000, 2006).

This data is also available in different formats in UN web sites and under the Creative Commons Attribution in open information web sites.

Nonetheless, governments can face pressure from lenders and be isolated from the international community for long periods. Even though many argue that global world isolation is becoming a deterrent, that is proving to be less effective as an instrument.

They suggest that it cannot last long and usually ends up with a restructuring of the debts owed, even in worst-case scenarios, such as in war reparations, meaning when a country loses a war and is subjected to paying the damages to the winner(s).

Extraordinary items such as reparations for war damages can go on for decades and constitute a very sizable portion of their total debts. In the case of World War II, reparations go back seven decades and still weigh heavily on the shoulders of generations of people who had nothing to do with those wars. This is also true for the few remaining survivors, too old and economically less capable to be held to account (should they even be accountable, it is likely that in many cases they had nothing to do with these wars either).

Another heavy encumbrance on public debt is the huge sum that accumulates as a result of interest. Sometimes this becomes such a big piece of the total debt owed that the country finds itself only paying the interest portion. The exponential cumulative effect of interest builds up over time, preventing states from ever really being able to address their full debt, forcing some of these countries into insolvency that, in many cases, might also be burdened by market, industrial downturns, social unrest, regime changes, and, in some cases, wars, revolts, revolutions, etc.

De facto in recent history only a few countries were able to settle all war reparation debts. It is a process that can take decades, and its success is not guaranteed. Governments change. As time progresses different variables, such as trade issues, can weigh heavily on the need to change the agreements. Consequentially to assure adequate indemnifications are received, countries that win wars, in recent history, find new ways to increase their chances of reparation by relying on sources different from money.

For example in the first Gulf War was a program called "food for oil," or obliging a country to give its future business in order of priority to specific countries. After World War II this translated into agreements, such as the Potsdam Conference that foresaw the transfer of machinery and manufacturing plants to winner countries, along with the transfer of patents and technological and scientific know-how. In the case of Japan, the generations that had nothing to do with the war found themselves with a staggering 1.3 trillion yen in war reparation bills.

Other strategies seem to have been more successful and produced beneficial effects instead of emphasizing punishment or stripping know-how. One such strategy was the adoption of the Marshall Plan by the United States. The plan focused on the reactivation and development of western European states, and according to many sources it seems to have worked.

Considerations on Public Debt

The amounts of public debt faced by many countries today are astounding. The United States is not the only one to be in such a situation. According to the 2010 CIA World Fact Book (accessed July 2012) the following is a list of industrialized countries that well exceeded their GDP in 2009 (these numbers will most probably differ after the book is published—the site is constantly updated and the reader is invited to access the website to have the most recent update):

Gross Debt over GDP (%)

- Japan: 204-208 percent   with total debt of $8 trillion
- Greece: 130-165 percent   with total debt of $0.5 trillion
- Italy: 119 percent   with total debt of $2.1 trillion
- United States: Over 100 percent with total of $15 trillion
- Portugal: 97 percent   N/A
- UK: 94 percent   with total debt of $1.7 trillion
- Ireland: 93 percent   with total debt of   N/A
- France: 87 percent   with total debt of $1.7 trillion
- Germany: 85 percent   with total debt of $2.4 trillion
- Austria: 82 percent   N/A
- Netherlands: 82 percent   with total debt of $0.4 trillion
- Spain: 74 percent   with total debt of $0.8 trillion

Emerging nations, such as China, India, Brazil, and Russia, are running significantly lower ratios and total debt amounts in absolute terms. Could the coincidence suggest that development could play a critical role in a country's national debts, should external or internal factors slow economic development, or should development in a country reach its relative critical mass and saturation level, as it seems to have in developed nations? May this translate into an appreciable modification of the national debt of emerging countries?

National debt by country is more vividly depicted on The Economist web site (http://www.economist.com/content/global_debt_clock). As dates in the future are chosen the number of countries reaching alarming levels of debt and hence portrayed in red or shades of it increase—practically covering most all of the worlds primary, secondary and tertiary economies including countries such China and India, US, Canada, all of western Europe, Australia (accessed March 22, 2013 - this data is subject to constant change).

According to the US Government Accountability Office, with this rate of increase in debt, sometime between the next coming years and 2040, "mandatory spending will exceed government revenues" toward a "fiscally unsustainable" path. Might this hold true also for many other developed countries?

States in this condition seem to be exposed instrumentally to large market forces and investors to conform and adopt certain measures, such as those being imposed on many countries in the Western world.

Should the total debt figure ($45 trillion) for the world be true (as reported by the previously cited The Economist web site) or close to it, US debt represents 33 percent. Whatever the real total number for the planet, it is of overwhelming proportions. What will the real additional impact of the following factors be on government debt?

- Growing population age;
- Growing pension and health-care costs;
- Persistent high unemployment. According to the CBO, the past three years were "the longest stretch of high unemployment in this country since the Great Depression;"
- Moreover, the CBO projects that the unemployment rate will remain above 8 percent until 2014. *The official unemployment rate excludes those individuals who would like to work but have*

not searched for a job in the past four weeks, as well as those who are working part-time but would prefer full-time work; if those people were counted among the unemployed, the unemployment rate in January 2012 would have been about 15 percent. Compounding the problem of high unemployment, *the share of unemployed looking for work for more than six months "topped 40% in December 2009 for the first time since 1948* when such data began to be collected; it has remained above that level ever since" (US Congressional Budget Office Understanding and Responding to Persistently High Unemployment, 2012);

- Trade deficit (i.e., United States importing more than it exports even with a weaker dollar);
- Investment focus shifting away from real economy to financial markets. As the US Congressional Budget Office put it, with business ventures becoming less attractive investments vis-à-vis investing in government securities, theoretically less and less funds could be available to produce real products and services, further impacting the economy;
- Structural impacts reducing growth capability (e.g., mismatched skill needs and locations, erosion of management capability as a result of mass layoffs);
- Erosion of adequate or competitive technology due to limited investments in recessive period;
- Effects of the credit crunch on business closures and resulting job losses that also add to reduced tax intakes.

The White House blog referred to the president's speech on the US national debt: "$12.7 Trillion were added to the Debt over the last Decade . . . to make matters worse, the recession meant that there was less money coming in, and it required us to spend even more—on tax cuts for middle-class families to spur the economy, on unemployment insurance; on aid to states so we could prevent more teacher and firefighters and police officers from being laid off" (The White House, Macon Philips).

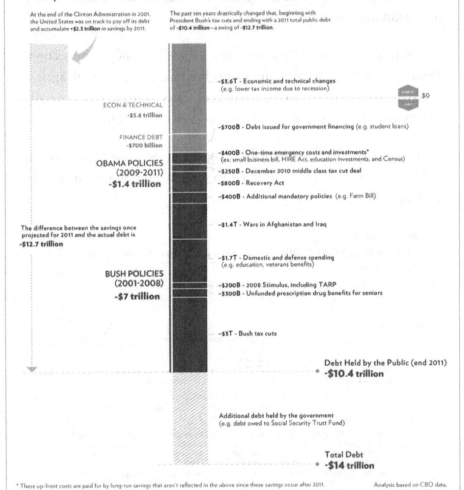

U.S. National Debt

$12.7 Trillion Added to the Debt Over the Last Decade

At the end of the Clinton Administration in 2001, the United States was on track to pay off its debt and accumulate +$2.3 trillion in savings by 2011.

The past ten years drastically changed that, beginning with President Bush's tax cuts and ending with a 2011 total public debt of -$10.4 trillion—a swing of -$12.7 trillion.

ECON & TECHNICAL
-$3.6 trillion

FINANCE DEBT
-$700 billion

OBAMA POLICIES
(2009-2011)
-$1.4 trillion

The difference between the savings once projected for 2011 and the actual debt is
-$12.7 trillion

BUSH POLICIES
(2001-2008)
-$7 trillion

-$3.6T - Economic and technical changes
(e.g. lower tax income due to recession) $0

-$700B - Debt issued for government financing (e.g. student loans)

-$400B - One-time emergency costs and investments*
(ex: small business bill, HIRE Act, education investments, and Census)
-$250B - December 2010 middle class tax cut deal
-$800B - Recovery Act
-$400B - Additional mandatory policies (e.g. Farm Bill)

-$1.4T - Wars in Afghanistan and Iraq

-$1.7T - Domestic and defense spending
(e.g. education, veterans benefits)

-$200B - 2008 Stimulus, including TARP
-$500B - Unfunded prescription drug benefits for seniors

-$3T - Bush tax cuts

Debt Held by the Public (end 2011)
-$10.4 trillion

Additional debt held by the government
(e.g. debt owed to Social Security Trust Fund)

Total Debt
-$14 trillion

* These up-front costs are paid for by long-run savings that aren't reflected in the above since these savings occur after 2011.   Analysis based on CBO data.

(The White House)

Though according to the CBO there are signs of slight economic recovery and the deficit seems to be shrinking, it remains very large by historical standards. The effects, implications, and fallout are not just those that refer to the here and now but the long-term effects. The measures that are being studied require incredible amounts of energy on behalf of many. The problem is that many of these impact the national debt to varying degrees. It is a catch-22 scenario of very large proportions.

Each January the CBO prepares a baseline budget projection. These are not forecasts of future events but rather a benchmark against which policy changes can be measured. These projections generally incorporate the assumption that current laws are implemented.

In January 2012 the CBO's budget and economic outlook for fiscal years 2012 to 2022 projected the following trend for debt held by the public:

Summary Figure 1.   **Return to Reference**

Federal Debt Held by the Public Under CBO's Long-Term Budget Scenarios

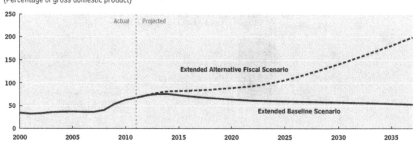

Source: Congressional Budget Office.

Notes: The extended baseline scenario generally adheres closely to current law, following CBO's 10-year baseline budget projections through 2022 and then extending the baseline concept for the rest of the long-term projection period. The extended alternative fiscal scenario incorporates the assumptions that certain policies that have been in place for a number of years will be continued and that some provisions of law that might be difficult to sustain for a long period will be modified.

Debt does not reflect economic effects of the policies underlying the two scenarios. (For analysis of those effects and their impact on debt, see Chapter 2.)

Source: (US CBO)

Under current law, substantial tax cuts and spending policies are scheduled to take effect within the year. The CBO has also projected an "alternative fiscal scenario" in which some current policies (i.e., Bush tax cuts) are assumed to continue.

Under the extended baseline scenario the projected relative fall in the deficit will be mostly due to the expiration of recent or scheduled tax provisions, such as those that lower income tax rates; limit the reach of the Alternative Minimum Tax (pushing more taxpayers into higher tax brackets and making more taxpayers subject to AMT); and impose new taxes, fees, and penalties.

The effects of budget cuts, statutory caps, and other instruments used to control government spending are projected by the CBO to be offset by the effects of increased spending requirements due to a growing percentage of the aging population (i.e., social security, Medicare, Medicaid). Moreover, according to the same projections, the accumulation of debt, along with rising interest rates, forces the cost of financing that debt to rise from 1.4 percent of GDP to 2.5 percent in 2022.

According to the same document, "the agency expects that the US economy's output will remain below its potential until 2018 and that unemployment rate will remain above 7% until 2015." What might this mean on competitive edge lost? The document goes on to say that, in developing the alternative fiscal scenario, the following assumptions were made:

- Extension of expiring tax provisions (other than payroll tax reduction);
- The AMT is indexed for inflation after 2001 (for Italian citizens, this is a similar concept to the *Scala Mobile*, which means escalator—that was used instead to increase salaries to match inflation);
- Medicare payment rates for doctors' services are held constant rather than dropping by 27 percent and more thereafter;

- Leaving in place the discretionary caps established by the Budget Control Act.

The CBO states that under this alternative fiscal scenario, the projected deficits till 2022 will be significantly higher. Only the portion of debt held by the public will climb to 94 percent of GDP in 2022, the highest since World War II. The distinction is that the world needed much economic development after the war, which is by no means intended to convey that war is good. Quite the contrary, as the four recent wars in Kosovo, Gulf I and II, and Afghanistan would suggest. *We need an alternative plan to make sustainable long-term development possible!*

The CBO's baseline and its alternative fiscal scenario do not include the aging of the population, rising costs for health care, and rising costs of social security. These will push such spending considerably. Coupled with the effects of revenues that are held close to the average historical share of GDP over the last forty years, "the resulting deficits will increase federal debt to unsupportable levels."

The CBO suggests limiting growth of spending, increasing revenues, or a mix of both. But might this be reminiscent of more of the same? On the other hand, these are the tools allowed by our current model.

The hard choices lawmakers will need to make will have significant impact on public debt in the years to come (US Congressional Budget Office: The Budget and Economic Outlook Fiscal Years 2012 to 2022, 2012).

Alarmingly, it is not clear if these projections consider the impact of any other external elements, such as Eurozone effects, financial market-driven effects, growth or slowdown of emerging markets, the aggravation of an international crisis (Middle East), the psychological effect on the credibility of the systems, and the impact of changes in the environment and natural resources.

Even more distressing is that so far most of the emphasis has been on the United States (because of access to data and transparency), but what are the combined effects of all these aspects on a global scale? If the debt situations elsewhere in relative terms are as bad, if not worse how could these impact each other? what amount of cumulative destructive/destabilizing energy could they potentially hold back and what is the breaking point?

Slower economic or GDP growth has many effects on budget and debt levels, activating self-consuming cycles, for example, that sooner or later, as the virus spreads across borders, provokes undesired effects, such as reducing income, lowering consequent revenue for governments from taxable income, lowering possibility and propensity to spend, increasing the need to borrow more, and impacting interest to be paid back. All of these, in turn, affect the economy not only nationally but internationally.

Might the current modality of generating and accounting for debt still be right? Wrong? Superseded? Can it be done differently? Some time back, given the reference model, someone decided it made sense doing it this way and did so with the fullest set of good intentions and goodwill. So long as everything worked, they were the best methods we could use.

But is there a limit beyond which the importance of nations, individuals, families, communities, and businesses supersedes the best of intentions, the best capabilities of existing models, to come up with policies that resolve real issues for investors, businesses, and people? Today's policies affect the lives of billions on a planetary scale for decades to come.

With the benefit of doubt, and respect for equidistance and objectivity, though many are surely working with fullest dedication and earnest interest to address these very important issues, in the midst of the many fervent political and academic debates, there is a legitimate concern building up.

Is there a dichotomy forming even in our national debt models? Are we sure the current public debt models are adequate for today's reality and, more importantly, those of the immediate future?

Are we trapped inside a logic bubble? Can we evolve to something that can address issues that can no longer be postponed? There are a few differing perspectives that are being evaluated currently, this book provides an additional one.

There is potential for a new chapter in economic development. Do we wish to start a new phase of structural reforms?

MONETARY POLICY: WHAT'S IT TO ME? WHY SHOULD I BOTHER?

The intent here is not academic—there is plenty of literature on this subject—but to explain the general concept and see how monetary policy contributes to the overall picture, and to focus on the so-called "so whats" of this economic variable.

A brief premise of what is meant by monetary policy is obligatory before going further. Monetary policy, and its implementation, is another variable of the existing economic models. More precisely it is one of the tools used by central banks or generically a country's monetary authority with the hope of steering the economy.

Monetary policy refers to policies and strategies that are applied to control the availability or supply of money in an economy through a set of tools, such as interest rates and reserve requirements, hopefully with the intent of promoting economic stability and/or growth.

In the United States, for example, the Federal Reserve "sets the nation's monetary policy to promote the objectives of maximum employment, stable prices, and moderate long-term interest rates. The challenge for policy makers is that tensions among the goals can arise in the short run and that information about the economy becomes available only with a lag and may be imperfect" (The Federal Reseve System).

Though the final intent of a monetary policy is to bring about a stable economic platform that promotes growth, it is so important a variable that if elements of it are applied or executed wrongly they can produce inflation or hyperinflation, recession, liquidity traps, unemployment, high interest rates, and even economic depression.

Some actions taken by the Federal Reserve, together with other agencies, to curb the devastative effects of the 2008 financial crisis, avoiding a possible meltdown, to stabilize the banking system, anchor inflation, and hopefully produce the conditions for a recovery were to

- use lender-of-last-resort policy to help stabilize the system;
- lower interest rates to affect longer-term rates to help stimulate the economy, encouraging the purchase of houses, capital goods, etc.;
- enact large-scale asset purchases (LSAPs), thus reducing thirty-year mortgages and anchoring inflation that so far has remained low; and
- lead the stress test on the largest US banks, arresting possible runs on financial institutions.

Given the unprecedented scale of the crisis, the objectives achieved are short of a human miracle. Equally objective in confirming that no one has the magic wand—notwithstanding the desired outcomes—the economy's response to the hard work, dedication, goodwill, and willingness of the many that went into the creation and implementation of the monetary policy has been "sluggish."

The chairman of the board of governors of the Federal Reserve, Dr. Ben Bernanke, noted,

> "But the pace of recovery has been extremely sluggish compared with post World War II cyclical recoveries, as a result job prospects have improved only gradually and the employment rate remains painfully high . . . A resurgent housing market normally helps economic

recoveries, but not this time . . . Very tight lending standards on mortgages have blunted some of the effects of low mortgage rates. Declining house prices discourage new construction . . . and make consumers feel poorer, and thus less willing to spend . . . For small businesses, credit conditions remain tight but appear to have begun to improve. Concerns about the European fiscal and banking conditions have also stressed financial markets and led to more conservative lending and diminished confidence . . . Many people who have been unemployed for a long time see their skills erode. And longer term problems like rising federal deficits, have not gone away (The Federal Reserve System)."

Independent of the intellectual effort that goes into this, getting monetary policy right is not an easy task. In Zimbabwe, for example, hyperinflation in July 2008 reached annual rates beyond 20,000 percent, equivalent to a doubling of prices every month and a half. This phenomenon has not touched only Zimbabwe but many others also see World Bank historic inflation figures.

Some Background Information on Monetary Policy

Monetary policies in most of the industrialized countries are developed by independent monetary authorities (i.e., central banks, Federal Reserve System). In small or less developed countries these policies are managed directly by the ruling governments or so-called currency boards because of a lack of means given the relative size of their economies, historical foundations, or simply the types of governments they have.

Central banks apply different monetary strategies according to the perceived needs of their country's economy to hopefully achieve the economic goals (e.g., slowdown of inflation or stimulus to economic activity) that foster growth. In doing so they adopt different policies. Some target inflation (e.g., Australia, Brazil, Canada, Chile). Others place the focus of their policies on indexes, such as consumer price indexes, while others focus on exchange rates (China), aggregates, gold, or a mix of factors (e.g., unemployment, consumer price indexes), such as in the United States. They can work independently of each other or in concert with a limited number of other central banks, intending to achieve particular economic goals.

Fundamentally, to control the availability of money in an economy, central banks can utilize any mix of the following actions (McKenzie. R; Tullok Gordon), (US Federal Reserve; European Central Bank; US Treasury):

Increase money supply in an economy by

- reducing reserve requirements;
- increasing loans to commercial banks; and
- buying its government bonds and securities.

Decrease money circulating in an economy by

- increasing reserve requirements;
- decreasing loans to commercial banks; and
- selling government securities.

Many economists agree that the concept of independence of central banks from the executive branch is relatively recent (starting in the 1980s), while other sources say it stems from the 1970s Nixon Shock. Still others state that its origins are rooted in the Bretton Woods agreement. To provide an example, the current Bank of England (founded in 1694) became independent of its government by an act in 1998.

The Bretton Woods agreement owes its name to the location in New Hampshire, where representatives from forty-four allied nations got together in July 1944 while World War II was still raging, with the intent of agreeing to a new economic system. This gave rise to what later became known as the three super governmental agencies—namely, the International Monetary Fund, the World Bank, and the International Bank of Reconstruction and Development. The Bretton Woods agreement also laid the foundations for a system of rules and procedures to govern the monetary interaction among the member states. One of the cornerstones of this new system was a commitment of each member state to adhere to these rules, one of which was to fix their exchange rates to the dollar.

Some economists suggest that the Bretton Woods agreement in spirit was a revisited version of a previous monetary policy used in the Western world prior to World War II, which tied the monetary supply and its value to a country's gold reserves. The agreement remained in place until 1971, when then—US President Nixon terminated the Bretton Woods arrangement unilaterally, declaring the US dollar free-floating and no longer tied to gold (hence, the Nixon Shock).

The value of the US dollar from then on was merely backed by a virtual promise of the US government and the trust people had in the currency. According to a very well-organized synopsis of US Department of Treasury history, the concept of the currency's virtual backing is not new; in fact, it was adopted for the first time in the United States on June 2, 1779, when the Continental Congress "authorized the Board of the Treasury to sign continental bills of credit. Bills of credit were backed by nothing more than a promise by the United States to be paid back at some point in time" (Treasury). Well ahead of its time, it failed to achieve its goals in a very short time frame.

One of the reasons for this new change in the paradigm in 1971 was that the economy was growing much faster than the gold supply availability; remaining attached to such a direct link could have provoked more damage to the economy than benefits. The adoption of the new paradigm liberated the currency and its value to a physical requirement, allowing economic growth to find new dimensions and possibilities of growth internationally. It was a step-level evolution toward a new economic plateau.

There are many schools of thought regarding monetary policy (e.g., Keynesian, Austrian, neoclassical), and each bases its considerations on a set of assumptions and statistical, macroeconomic, or historical data, theories, possible outcomes, and behaviors of consumers. For example, if interest rates are lowered, it is hoped that these should promote increased availability of the money supply in the market, easing credit toward businesses and families and, therefore, reviving the economy. The expected results of a monetary policy on any economy, however, are at best physiological stimuli and do not necessarily produce the desired outcomes, especially in difficult times. Variables are numerous, and their interactions are hardly predictable, such as the current case of the European Central Bank, which provided banks across Europe with large amounts of cash at very low interest levels through different "facilities"—this has not (to date Q2 2013) produced any of the desired results.

These problems are even more amplified in developing or poor countries for a plethora of reasons—the simple lack of historical capability, lack or complexity in obtaining economic data, level of freedom of market mechanics, degree of dependence from government, or eventual pegging of their currencies to other currencies.

Monetary Policy and Considerations

Monetary policy uses a set of tools in trying to address challenges posed by a country's economy. These challenges grow each day as new variables are introduced, such as paradigm-changing technological innovations that give way to new business models, which influence employment needs and utilization. Newer challenges come from globalization and interconnectivity of systems over international borders; evolving market, banking, and financial dynamics; new financial products; emerging markets; sustainability; aging population needs; environmental and energetic considerations; etc.

This excludes challenges posed by new dimensions, such as complexity, the amounts involved, the additional and different layers of concurrence needed, and the social repercussions that transcend national boundaries.

An example of these added dimensions might be the G-2, G-3, G-7, G-8, and G-20, the Eurozone scenario where a group of countries are desperately trying to find a balance between naturally contrasting national priorities and those imposed by multilateral agreements that might have been ratified by member countries not too long ago.

This Eurozone scenario is aggravated by the fact that though there is a "legal" union and possibly a beginning of a social union between individuals who appreciate the possibilities provided by free movement, shared values, unified money, etc., but that de facto have not yet truly translated in real factual unification in terms of:

- political unity (i.e., though there is a European Parliament that tries its best to represent Europe as a single entity, citizens of the European Union do not directly elect their leader or a government that represents the majority of their common interests);

- fiscal policy;
- true unity of strategic priorities; and
- those things necessary to take the next step in becoming truly one entity.

Each country is naturally inclined to put national priorities over those of any virtual or legal union, because the mandate each government leader receives is from their national parliaments and citizens. The benefits of a nation within a union (even in unprecedented crisis) sometimes could be in sharp contrast to what might benefit the group as a whole. The German interest vis-à-vis that of other member countries is an example in this current state of affairs. Additionally there are many independence seeking movements in Europe that are more or less active that add additional layers of complexity to the issue (e.g.: Basque and Cataluña regions in Spain, areas of high sensitivity in the Balkans, Padania region in northern Italy, etc.)

If it is already difficult for monetary policy to address current concerns, if its effects on the economic recovery are demonstrably of little stimulus, how much longer can it sustain growing feats without evolving to a new plateau? These problems are compounded by the titanic sums involved: transactions, movements, and speculations of billions or trillion of yens, dollars, or euros, where fractions of a percentage point differential in interest rates or exchanges can translate into millions (in losses or profits) that could potentially strain entire economies with a domino effect on many other markets, nations, and economic systems.

Failure to acknowledge, appreciate, and accept possibly reaching a level of complexity beyond effective resolution fundamentally will not allow us to see beyond the boxes and will trap us in a logic bubble.

STRATEGIC MARKET SECTORS

Historically some economic sectors have been deemed strategic to the prolonged success of nations. Private and state-funded research and development initiatives and organizations are deemed to be strategic for almost all nations in varying degrees. This includes sectors such as the energy, oil, and gas; utilities; information systems and telecommunications; aerospace and defense; transportation and logistics; agriculture and fishing; airports; ports and waterways; and natural resources.

These sectors provide quintessential elements to a region's sustainability, long-term development, security, and, if leveraged and managed correctly, growth. Deficiency in any of these key sectors translates to dependence on others to properly address these needs. In the real world, however, this is not always practical or achievable for many reasons, including the limited availability of resources, economies of scale, economic viability, etc.

Though of strategic importance, this does not mean using a blindfold extremist approach in keeping such sectors running at whatever cost. The approach should be dictated by realism, pragmatism, and cost benefit mix in the best interest of a nation. Proper leverage of an evolutionary process is essential for these to continue their healthy growth and contribution. Not all countries have the luxury of having these sectors, and in these cases the best strategy is to leverage what they can realistically achieve.

Naturally any lack of indigenous capability may be filled by international trade, hopefully reaching a balance between what is being given and taken in exchange. Imagine the amount of exposure a country faces if it has to depend on electric power, access to seaports and shipping lanes, and international economic unions. Imagine the vulnerability a country could face if it decided to depend upon others for defense equipment.

It might come as a surprise that these realities do not happen just to landlocked and/or poor states. As far-fetched as this might seem, these things happen on a daily basis in well-off countries. A growing number of countries are following this trend. Not many persons, for example, know that England has opted for a similar policy for its defense industry.

Since the end of the Cold War and the fall of the Berlin Wall, Westland, Marconi, and a plethora of other large and mid-sized aerospace and defense sector companies, which once formed the pride and glory of Great Britain, have been left to slowly spin off or be left for acquisition on behalf of foreign counterparts. BAE, Rolls-Royce, and a small group of other niche players are still active, yet most of their business is done outside national turf.

There is nothing wrong with the policy undertaken by the UK and the many other states that have undertaken this path. If put in the framework of the socio-economic-political and historical moment in which these decisions materialized and if there is a strong political union, the reasoning is simple and logical and if the benefits outweigh the costs then that is perfectly fine.

Europe is a larger entity, and with the fall of communism it is not under known imminent symmetric threat of attack (at least for now). The logic is industries present in Europe in this arena should be stimulated to become more competitive in an open market. This lowers the tax burden on the country's budget and translates into public policy not to invest in the sector. But counter to this logical reasoning are brutal facts—who's jobs will be cut; who's national economy will be effected to achieve a unified strategy? In the case of the Eurozone might the only beneficiary be Germany for example as many analysts and journalists seem to indicate?

The same reasoning has been applied to just about all the other key strategic sectors in the UK, from transportation, to energy and utilities, to IT and telecommunications.

Most of these companies have some similarities. They are mostly capital- and manpower-intensive industries, for example. Their cost structure inhibits them from being competitive. Due to their strategic importance in terms of job-creation potential, many of their programs are subsidized and, in many cases, have been incentivized.

With the worst economic crisis to hit the world, if left aside, these private industries have no profit incentive to maintain their presence locally. It is a simple pragmatic case of profit and loss. Private concerns cannot run anything at a loss. FIAT, for example, has moved de facto the core of the business to the United States. The largest Finnish shipbuilding concern is considering selling off to a Chinese conglomerate.

Some of the alternatives companies operating in these sectors are considering are:

- finding other markets (i.e., delocalizing, expanding or growing international markets);
- developing new value-added killer technologies (with lower R&D budgets);
- selling off nonperforming businesses;
- restructuring, rightsizing, and outsourcing;
- finding lower equilibrium points and selling goods and services at lower prices;

- innovating; and
- closing the business or dying a slow death.

On the other hand, if unemployment continues its current negative trend, there will be diminishing demand for goods and services. For example, before spending on a new car, a family suffering unemployment will probably give priority to goods and services needed for survival. New economies of scale will need to be addressed as larger numbers of businesses close or reduce their size furthermore.

In previous chapters we also saw how it is critical to a nation's survival and continued success to maintain local capability and expertise.

In the specific case of strategic sectors key to a nation's or region's prolonged security, there is a point beyond which it will become arduous to turn back. So what is the eventual policy to adopt here? Will it be wait and see? In some countries that enacted privatizations decades ago, large critical national infrastructures have become dated, obsolete, and potentially hazardous to public safety and competitiveness. Such is the case of the US electrical power grid, for example, (as it is the case with many other nations) which is in dire need for modernization in many parts of the country.

Continued modernization of critical national infrastructure is key to a nation's capability in keeping itself, its citizens, and its industry in the inner circle of countries that count.

In absence of long-term policies, these industries can be taken over by investors for pure economic motives to increase international market share and/or other motivations. No matter which way you turn, these will become political bargaining chips somewhere down the line!

So where is balance struck? When do the benefits from giving away strategic sectors outweigh the consequences? Delocalization of production of much less strategic industries toward two giants made the fortunes of today's China and India. Sometimes strategic intent in selling could include: draining the competitor of resources selling-off bad assets to start fresh with new funds—while that of a foreign buyer to drain remaining expertise, market share and know-how while slowly suffocating any remaining life of a company or economic concern.

Possibly the logical strategy is to strike a winning balance. What elements might be most important for a nation or a union of nations? The following are some of the more important aspects that need to be considered in terms of developing capability: scientific and engineering excellence, know-how development, innovation capability, research and development, key production processes, evolutionary capability (ability to continuously evolve to new plateaus), strategic interconnectivity with education sectors, international cooperation with strategic partners and nations, and strategic vision.

What is being suggested here is also collaboration (not isolation), continued healthy economic development, adequate strategic localization, and sustainable growth. But is this being done? Can these objectives be still achieved via current models?

EMERGING NATIONS OVERTAKING IN INTELLECTUAL CAPABILITY?

Two decades ago or so, some companies started giving away all production that was deemed unwanted or costly, at growing rates, to less developed countries. At the time there was limited indigenous know-how and capability. Most of the concern was about reverse engineering and in some cases the illicit copying and replication of products and processes on behalf of local businesses.

A decade or so on, many things have evolved. One of these is the number of native engineers that are being produced and absorbed by these economies. There is much discussion about everything from the number of graduates to the quality of their education, their qualifications, etc., in newly developing countries.

According to an article written by Geoff Colvin, the number of engineering Ph.D. students graduating from top universities in China exceeds the total of US graduates, the majority of which are non-US citizens (Colvin, Geoff, CNN Money). According to another source, Duke University's professor, Vivek Wadhwa, and his testimony before the House Committee about a study conducted on competitiveness of US engineering colleges, the number of engineering students in 2004 in each country follows (Ed Brunette ZDnet.com, Extracted April 27 2012):

United States: 137,437
India: 112,000

China: 351,537

Citing the same source, David Epstein produced substantially different numbers (David Epstein; Vivek Wadhwa: Duke University):

United States: 222,335
Indian: 215,000
Chinese   644,106

The point in case is not about the precision of the numbers, as both articles correctly state that Dr. Wadhwa's findings and testimony to the House Committee clearly pointed out the flaws of such numbers, which did not factor in important variables, such as the difference in classifications of graduates in the different academic systems and the quality of education.

While this data is very important and valuable, the fundamental point is not about when emerging nations might catch up with the developed ones form a purely technological point of view, nor is it about forecasting the specific demarcation point in time when this event could take place. It is about being cognizant that the reality of these nations is moving rapidly from reproducing technology to developing new technology!

Similar debates took place in England from the late 1800s to the 1930s. The United States—then still a young country with hardly anything comparable to the might, resources, know-how, technological and research base, investment capabilities, etc., of the British Empire during the period of its maximum splendor and power—advanced at such a pace that it surpassed the incumbent giant by leaps and bounds without England ever being able to recuperate.

Provided new technological enablers and the hunger for knowledge and prosperity, it would be highly unrealistic to think that developing countries might wish to stop or slow down. In response there are many options from which to choose: wait and see, watch and learn, flank, if you can't beat them join them, conflict, or being cognizant of an evolutionary process and a need for a step-level transformation to develop and implement a new wining paradigm.

Moreover, a country's competitive advantage is intrinsically derived from the sum of many additional variables (e.g., infrastructure, capabilities, social advancement, civil liberties, education system, legislative and judiciary environment, health, property rights and the general organization of society). The most important aspects though seem to be the ability to keep at the forefront of development of the preceding and the opportunity to realize dreams—things that have grown hand in hand with the advancement in developed countries, not things that can be replicated easily.

In a state of affairs where things are relatively stable and the economy is running at a decent rate, governing the sale of strategic assets is relatively easy. Under the current state of affairs, the implications of easy handedness in policy affecting beyond the horizon periods (medium to long term) concerning matters that affect strategic sectors is increasingly important. Their domino effect, or exposure to risks and overdependence, should not be underestimated.

Again we are not talking about the liberty in making open-market investments in these sectors as shareholders, investors, and employees, but safeguarding capability in sectors strategic to the long-term well-being, success, and independence of nations whilst maintaining free market.

Furthermore, the number of engineers, doctors, and laureates only has sense when you factor in crucial elements such as a country's/market's capability in absorbing this intellectual capability. It is not only degrading for those millions of engineers who work precariously in fast-food retailers as cashiers or as call center operators selling services over an extended period of time, but it is a shameful waste of extremely valuable resources. A systemic failure! A key to long-term development and prosperity depends on these capabilities but also a healthy economy.

POPULATION GROWTH

With a total world population of 7 billion allegedly reached on October 31, 2011, according to data from the United Nations Population Division, the world population has grown by 1 billion since the start of this century, while another billion were added between 1987 and 1999.

According to the same official sources and an article by Eric McLamb, today our planet's population is "twice what it used to be in 1968" (McLamb).

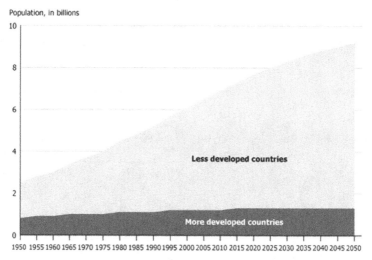

Sources: United Nations Population Division; Population Reference Bureau (extracted from prb.org/educators/teachersGuide/humanPopulation/populationgrowth/.aspx. April 27, 2012).

The projections for the near future are even more telling. The World Bank estimated that the world population grew by 30% in just a decade (1990-2010) and that the largest growth in number of individuals occurred in India with 351 million (greater than the US population) and 196 million in China in just ten years.

During the same decade, growth in terms of percentages narrate a totally different story the highest increase in population in percentage terms occurred in the United Arab Emirates 315 percent and Qatar 271 percent to be followed by Nigeria 62.4 percent, India 40.2 percent, and Bangladesh 41.3 percent. The surprises are China that has grown by 17.1 percent while the US by 22.5 percent (UN Department of Economic and Social Affairs Population Division).

According to the same source our planet's population should stabilize around the 9 to 10 billion mark by the end of this century.

But this information alone does not convey whether or not a ten billion population can be sustainable or when the tipping point might be reached.

There is a wealth of information for the reader on the web and other media on this subject matter but for the purposes of this book we to ask if this variable been factored into the current solutions for the economic crisis we are facing? To what extent? What do these foresee? Can our current models cope with this added challenge?

Some of the alternative scenarios we might face include the following:

1. Population pressure cannot be managed and can lead to increasing risk from exposure to unwanted events unfathomable today in terms of potential effects (e.g., increase in poverty, pressure on environment, sustainability and resources, outbreak and spread of diseases, food shortage, famine, war, and new factors such as an increase in deposition of oxidized nitrogen and other toxic gases (Galloway et al.);

2. Population growth strategies are developed and implemented to some degree, and commitment on behalf of governments is achieved by reducing or stabilizing the growth rate on a future date.

Unless things change, or currently unknown external factors influence population growth trends, these growth rates coupled with current global socioeconomic scenarios only exacerbate and increase the challenges of finding viable solutions through current economic models.

So are we condemned? Or better yet, if we cannot find alternatives, will we be faced with increasing challenges?

FISCAL POLICY—TAXATION: WHEN IS IT ENOUGH?

Fiscal policy is the set of fiscal measures, laws, treaties, etc., that determine the amount of revenues that it will collect in the form of taxes and levies from its citizens, legal entities, and residents and any foreign source subject to taxes in that country. It provides valuable data to form government budgets and cash management and expenditure decisions.

The Investopedia website (Investopedia; Reem Heakal; et al) further defines fiscal policy as one "used in various combinations in an effort to direct a country's economic goals."

According to historical records, taxation has been with humankind at least since the beginning of the first societies. In its primordial form it probably served as a means of sustaining the livelihood of the group of persons (e.g., priests, shamans, chieftains, and hunters who probably also served as soldiers in times of need) that were not involved directly in productive activities, such as farming, herding, producing iron, nurturing, and the like if they were to produce the benefits they were elected to produce. Each person within the community chipped in, probably even voluntarily at the onset, for the benefit of the group.

Members of the community had a concrete benefit from this, and the cause-and-effect connection between the levy and its benefits might have been as evident as it has probably ever been since.

As societies grew, they became more sophisticated. Agglomerations of huts became villages that later became city-states that depended ever more on trade. Walls had to be erected; roads had to be created; and armies had to be trained, armed, and fed. Hierarchies started growing and formally consolidating; new types of "differently productive" figures emerged within society and this demanded defending the acquired status. At this point taxation started becoming ever more similar to what we know today.

Taxation has also been one of the motives for revolutions and wars throughout history. The American colonial war against the British was one of the most emblematic example in recent history. Though there were many other underlying motives, "taxation without representation" fueled discontent and disenchantment among the people living in the new world. Taxation has also been considered unconstitutional in particular moments of history. This happened, for example, in the early days of the United States as states assembled under one nation (US Department of Treasury).

It is easy to link taxation only to our immediate source of revenue (e.g., our paycheck or our profit-and-loss statements), yet taxation goes much beyond this. It is everywhere and in everything traded, sold, purchased, leased, rented, negotiated, advertised, published, licensed, patented, stamped, imported, exported, produced, wasted, dismantled, wrecked, claimed, possessed, transferred, owned, owed, entrusted, donated, shipped, ferried, towed, posted, parceled, airlifted, flown, consumed, used, elaborated, transmitted, transferred, projected, filmed, written, played, displayed, expensed, explored, imagined, invented, formulated, worn, applied, enforced, paid, received, accrued, depreciated, appreciated, devolved, donated, confiscated, serviced, tooled, accessed, entered, entertained, weighted, measured, destructed, constructed, built, engineered, examined, sent, delivered, received, recuperated, found, housed, deposited, inventoried, judged, bailed, decommissioned, employed, unemployed, fired, waged, salaried, optioned, exercised, implemented, supplemented, merged, spun off, split, constituted, contracted, traveled, leisured, visited, formed, associated, incorporated, partnered, parented, schooled, educated, fixed, adjusted, protected, vouched, guaranteed, insured, declared, claimed, invested, profited, lost, accumulated, margined, grossed, fished, milked, raised, cooked, served, fueled, gassed, powered, generated, metered, bit-rated, baud-rated, voltaged, watted, acred, hectared, galloned, litered, dosed, damaged, parked, planted, smoked, sown, raised, cropped, marketed, retailed, shopped, frozen, liquefied, purified, sterilized, boxed, packed, canned, translated, notified, notarized, actuarized, and even double- or triple-taxed.

Theoretically just about every single thing and/or activity is potentially taxable. Yet what should be the most remunerative tax-exempt business in the world does not seem to cover our society's costs. So what is wrong? Why is it that, notwithstanding the growing amounts each citizen is burdened with, we seem to only be accumulating more and more deficit? Should we not be thinking of a better, more equitable modality of chipping in a fair share for the common good?

Here are some examples of questions being posed by a growing number of economists, analysts, journalists, business leaders, policy makers, and citizens of many different countries: Should the returns or benefits from taxation be more tangible or closer to local communities? Where is the line drawn between what is fair taxation and no longer sustainable or acceptable imposition? Is it right to pay more tax than the value of a product or service (e.g., low-cost airline tickets)? Or for something that is already yours? What is the legitimacy of taxing the same item multiple times under different voices? Or the logic behind taxing something without this tax producing any real tangible benefit for the society.

Some economists explain that the reason governments don't turn to simply printing money is justified by fear of entering a hyperinflationary economic vortex. History is full of such examples that date as far back as the Chinese dynasties and as recently as the Weimar Republic.

Fiscal policy can influence an economy in several ways. It can influence the way income is distributed among different echelons in society and, hence, their propensity to spend, the aggregate demand, and the way revenues and funds are allocated to different budgets. As with monetary policy, there are long-standing discussions as to the efficacy of different types of fiscal policy among politicians, economists, and interest groups.

The levers used here are basically two:

1. How much government lowers or raise taxes;
2. How much government spends.

Granted, it seems like a pretty straightforward axiom based on seemingly only two variables, but there is no agreement amongst economists and policy makers as to the validity of one strategy versus another nor as to what the right mix might be for any given moment in time.

For example, some Keynesian economists state that in times of economic downturn governments should spend more and decrease taxes, as was the case during the depression of the twenties and thirties in the United States, with the enactment of the New Deal—de facto creating deficits to promote, economies to stimulate, and jobs to create in the process. The reasoning is that once economies pick up again, governments can increase taxes and reduce government spending to substantially reduce public debt in those years.

Other schools of thought disagree with this theory and state that high spending creates only bubbles in the economy that burst cyclically, aggravated also by the high deficits produced by high spending. This puts further pressure on the economy (e.g., the subprime crack). The promoters of such theories favor instead governments cutting both their expenditure and taxes on its citizens, deeming that only investments in the real economy (i.e., the private sector) truly bring a rebound in the economy. Others instead still believe instead that increasing taxes and implementing austerity measures is the way to re-activate an economy—reasoning that bringing numbers to match a theoretical set of objectives (a certain debt level) will create traction in the economy and that business and people will start spending in view of a future economic start-up, while they are being heavily taxed and suffocated—but the question is: if you don't have any money or reduced sources of income is that what a business or a citizen realistically be thinking of in their daily quest for survival in these extreme conditions?

After decades worth of debates and disagreement among Keynesian, classical, neoclassical, and Austrian thinkers about the effectiveness of different types of fiscal policies, we have reached a stage where the real question becomes: Does it really make a difference who is right at this stage? Are any of these producing any concrete results in resolving possibly the worst economic crisis mankind has ever faced?

Additionally, what justifies the complexity surrounding taxation? Do things need to be complex to collect more taxes, promote job creation, revive the economy, or provide competitive tools to businesses? To paraphrase a brilliant phrase coined by the Austrian Schools of Economic Thought (though not in this context), do we need entire groups of persons who dig holes with shovels while another group refills the same holes soon after in order to create jobs (in and around taxation issues)? What do ruthless facts of everyday life tell us instead?

While there are many efforts on behalf of policy makers around the world to address these exact questions, will they provide any premise for resolving the even-greater challenges that we all will be facing in the near future?

Additional examples of questions being raised include: Does complexity in tax laws produce value-adds to the society it should serve? What is the difference between providing complicated possibilities of tax elusion instead of giving a simple reduction for the total value derived from tax elusion? What is the true value-add of tax complexity, and what is its cost to society? Is the trade-off between cost and benefits of complexity still viable, equitable, sustainable, and practical? Does it make sense any longer? Is it truly necessary?

In many countries direct income tax brackets have exceeded the 50 percent mark. Should one add all the other taxes mentioned, the total tax burden on citizens, investors, companies, and enterprises grows substantially.

Is it equitable to work more than half of the year for the government with decreasing returns? Is it fair to accept cuts to essential needs and services and their quality levels, such as police, hospitals, firefighting, care for disabled persons, veterans, national security, defense, and highways—everything that until not long ago made the difference between a civilized society and an less civilized one?

Is there a reason modern societies and current generations should opt for less services or quality while being asked to contribute more? This is not about a choice between a capitalistic or socialistic model any longer, is it?

Have we not crossed invisible lines of sustainability and economies of scale that inhibit any further increases in tax burdens from being truly productive or in making real-life contributions to the long-term prosperity of citizens within the framework of current economic models and boxes?

Are we sure taxation will still satisfy its raison d'etre? Will the same set of paradigms hold true for the future? Can we evolve from this and move toward evaluating possible new perspectives? Can we afford *not* to evolve toward a model that allows us to address the many challenges we face (e.g., unemployment, business closures, Web inclusivity)?

Again, the questions posed are not in any way meant to promote fiscal anarchy. Exactly the contrary. This would add only another problem to the already-enormous challenges we are facing. The purpose here is to ask ourselves if there are possible alternative perspectives that can help us in identifying the appropriate tools to address the new challenges of an evolving economic model.

Fortunately there might be. It depends on us. Additionally any possible practical solution is a process of migration, and its success depends on the possibility of adding the effects and desired outcomes of new variables. We are not talking about this being better than that or doing away with what you have but how to improve upon it and evolve it in line with everything else.

WHAT GOVERNMENTS ARE DOING TO REVIVE THE ECONOMY

To assure a balanced view and and objectivity this chapter sheds light on some of the most important measures governments and policy makers are trying to implement around the world to address the global crisis. Being of public domain, a few of these measures have been added here verbatim, in order to not distort the real intentions or meanings of these policies.

The roots of the current crisis go back at least a couple of decades. In an effort to find solutions to the prolonged economic crisis, many governments and international organizations developed and adopted several different strategies/policies. A few of these are mentioned below. For brevity, some of the more emblematic have been selected.

The Washington Consensus

Though this strategy has been cast aside amidst very animated debate by a growing number of economists, it is one that, leading up to the 2008 crisis, was initially envisaged and implemented around the world with varying degrees of accomplishment by G-20 countries.

"First embraced by many G-7 and G-20 nations (in full or in part) and then abandoned to varying degrees, the so-called Washington Consensus entailed embracing the following "ten broad sets of relatively specific policy recommendations" (John Williamson; Peterson Institute for International Economics):

1. Public debt reduction and fiscal policy discipline;
2. Redirection of public spending from especially indiscriminate subsidies toward services like primary education, primary health care, and infrastructure investment;
3. Tax reform, broadening the tax base, and adopting moderate marginal tax rates;
4. Interest rates being market determined and positive (but moderate), so as to promote investments and reduce government debt;
5. Competitive exchange rates;
6. Trade policy: import liberalization, with particular emphasis on elimination of quantitative restrictions (licensing, etc.); any trade protection to be provided by low and relatively uniform tariffs;
7. Liberalization in favor of foreign direct investments;
8. Privatizations of state enterprises;
9. Deregulation: abolition of regulations that impede market entry or restrict competition, except for those justified on safety, environmental, and consumer protection grounds, and prudential oversight of financial institutions;
10. Legal security for property rights.

The following are a small sample of polices being currently undertaken in the United States and internationally among the G-20. This data has been gathered from US Department of Treasury, White House, Federal Reserve, and international organization (such as the World Bank and IMF) websites.

Wall Street Reform

The Dodd-Frank Wall Street Reform and Consumer Protection Act address key deficits and flaws in the system to reduce the probability of future financial shocks and their consequences. This is essential to investor confidence and the safety, stability, and integrity of the financial system, allowing for capital to finance businesses, innovation that hopefully produces jobs. The Dodd-Frank Acts are believed fundamental to restoring a pro-growth, pro-investment financial system. It helps achieve those objectives in the following ways:

- by promoting a safer, more stable financial system focused on sustainable growth and job creation;
- by putting in place a dedicated watchdog for consumers;
- by bringing the derivatives market out of the darkness and into the light of day;
- by providing new tools for winding down failing firms without putting the economy in jeopardy.

Housing Finance Reform

The plan provides reforms to address important flaws in the mortgage market through stronger/improved consumer protection, transparency, underwriting standards, and other critical measures . . . providing targeted and transparent support to creditworthy but underserved families that want to own their own home and affordable rental options.

Recovery Act

This was an effort to jump-start the economy, create or save jobs, and put a down payment on addressing long-neglected challenges. The act is an extraordinary response. It includes measures to modernize US infrastructure, enhance energy independence, expand educational opportunities, preserve and improve affordable health care, provide tax relief, and protect those in greatest need.

G-20: Sustainable External Imbalances and Orderly Global Adjustment

President Obama made the following proposals to G-20 countries (US Department of Treasury; The White House):

- "Bolster cooperation to achieve sustainable current account balances; reduce external imbalances across the global economy, treating surplus and deficit economies symmetrically;
- Assess persistently large imbalances against indicative guidelines to evaluate the root causes of impediments to global adjustment;
- Move toward more market-determined exchange rate systems, and enhance exchange rate flexibility and refrain from competitive devaluations of currencies;
- Pursue structural reforms to boost and sustain global demand and deliver on commitment to medium-term fiscal responsibility;
- Undertake additional regulatory reforms to safeguard and strengthen financial systems and economies;

- Keep global markets open, and resist trade and financial protectionism given the serious risk that proliferation of protectionist measures could derail the recovery.

The global recovery will be stronger—and the U.S. recovery more vigorous—if the shift in U.S. growth away from consumption to investment and exports is complemented by a shift away from export dependence by those countries that traditionally have run large and current account surpluses. The commitments agreed-to will lead to a more balanced pattern of global demand—and therefore a more robust, job-rich recovery in the United States. The combination of commitments to pursue balanced demand growth, flexible exchange rates, financial and structural reforms, and sustainable public finances will lead to a stronger and more sustainable growth path globally and in the United States, and to the good jobs that our citizens need."

Financial Reform in G-20 Agenda

Subsequent to the Dodd-Frank Wall Street Reform and Consumer Protection, the United States promotes a race to the top so that all international financial firms face the same tough standards everywhere on a level playing field. The main points declared in the G-20 agenda are:

1. End to "too big to fail";
2. More capital and better quality capital: . . . discourage excessive leverage. Institutions should have an appropriately long transition period to implement these new requirements to reduce banks' incentive to take excessive risks, lower the

likelihood and severity of future crises, and enable banks to withstand—without extraordinary government support—stresses of a magnitude associated with the recent financial crisis;

3. Safer, more transparent derivatives market to help Main Street businesses: "Standardized over the counter derivative contracts should be traded on exchanges . . . and cleared through central counterparties" . . . all OTC derivative contracts should be reported to trade repositories. *The Dodd-Frank Act will benefit those businesses that use derivatives to manage their commercial risks. That is good for every farmer and every manufacturer that uses derivatives the way they were meant to be used.* Derivatives reform will also help prevent a future AIG;

4. Close loophole in regulation of major financial firms: particularly careful oversight given their systemic importance of large financial institutions to address the moral hazard caused by these . . . create accountable regulation for all firms that pose the most risk to the financial system. Purpose is to end the ability of financial firms to avoid tough standards by manipulating their legal structure;

5. Bring transparency to hedge funds: "Hedge funds or their managers will be registered with SEC and will be required to disclose appropriate information on an ongoing basis to supervisors or regulators;"

6. Constrain the size and risks of the largest firms: Risk posed by systemically important financial institutions should be subject to more intensive supervision and additional capital, liquidity, and other prudential requirements. The largest and most interconnected firms should be subject to mandatory international recovery and resolution planning. In the United States, the Dodd-Frank Act prevented financial firms from growing by acquisition to more than 10 percent of the liabilities in the financial system;

7. Reform pay practices at financial firms: "Excessive compensation in the financial sector has both reflected and encouraged excessive risk taking" and endorsed the financial stability board's implementation standards aimed at aligning compensation with long-term value creation, not with excessive risk taking;

8. Separate banking and speculative trading: Reform must have "clear incentives to mitigate excessive risk-taking practices." The "Volcker" Rule in the Dodd-Frank Act protects taxpayers and depositors by separating risky, speculative "proprietary trading" from the business of banking. These reforms *will* make clear that banking entities must focus on their customers, and not on proprietary trading or hedge fund or private equity investments. It will also limit the derivatives activities of banks to derivatives regarding traditional banking products;

9. Strong consumer protection: Develop options to advance consumer protection internationally through disclosure, education, and protection from fraud and abuse through establishment of the Consumer Financial Protection Bureau to protect consumers across the financial sector from unfair, deceptive, and abusive practices. There will be one agency instead of seven, dedicated to establishing and enforcing clear rules for banks, mortgage companies, payday lenders, and credit card lenders;

10. Crack down on the abuses in mortgage markets to protect consumers, depositors, and investors against abusive market practices. Require, for example, that mortgage brokers and banks consider a family's ability to repay when making a loan. The act also requires lenders and Wall Street securitizers to keep skin in the game when selling off loans to investors and make full disclosure so investors know what is in those packages. Reforms of credit rating agencies will help make

sure that investors do not rely unwisely on their ratings on these packages;

11. Support long-term job growth by helping prevent future crises: G-20 leaders recognized that we "must take care not to spur a return of the practices that led to the crisis. The steps we are taking here, when fully implemented, will result in a fundamentally stronger financial system that existed prior to the crisis." Further, leaders noted that we "want growth without cycles of boom and bust and markets that foster responsibility not recklessness." The Dodd-Frank Act will ensure that businesses have a more stable and predictable source of credit throughout the business cycle and will reduce the risk of a sharp and sudden cut-off because of financial panic. By making the financial system safer and stronger, the Dodd-Frank Act will reduce the chances that a financial crisis deprives businesses of the credit they need to grow and to create jobs.

IMF and Other International Organizations

International Monetary Fund (IMF) and other international organizations (e.g., UN, FAO) are involved in realizing many different initiatives to address issues around the world. Please visit their websites for more detailed information.

Conclusions

This is all a testament that things are being done, and efforts and energies are being spent. If implemented properly they might help to address some of the many questions posed thus far, especially those stemming from the banking and financial system.

A question remains: Are the above measures that have painstakingly been put in place to create said benefits translating into a systemic recovery for economies, investors, businesses, and citizens of these countries? It is not a question of lack of will here.

These efforts are very important and many might become part of the long term solution. Incredibly they might be even more effective within the framework of an equally up-to-date model. Some of these have produced some benefits and others might hopefully start to yield some positive results and signs of recovery. Yet, provided the number of new variables incapable of being elaborated by our models (e.g., virtualization of activities, processes, Web inclusivity, etc., numerous systemic blocks, and important dichotomies) that go beyond some vertical sectors, such as the banking sector for how long can current models be overwhelmed, overstretched, and overexerted before something gives?

Should there be the slightest doubt that the measures might not be able to address these structural and systemic challenges, might it be worthwhile to start considering the possibility of looking at these important issues from a different perspective or even an evolved modality?

The chapter that follows presents the official reports, expert assessment of authoritative government agencies and international organizations. They provide the official authoritative picture of where we stand today and what the foreseeable future might be.

They consider the effects of all the measures being taken.

OFFICIAL ASSESSMENT OF THE CRISIS, EFFECTIVENESS OF MEASURES UNDERTAKEN, AND FUTURE OUTLOOKS

The press, specialized media, institutional reports, articles studies and papers from different authoritative sources provide ample evidence of the economic scenario that the global economy will be facing in the immediate future. The reader is invited to visit these institutional, continuously updated sources and websites to augment their understanding of the depth, breadth, extension and growing ramifications of the global economic crisis—this in relation to the many efforts being undertaken by policy making bodies around the world.

The following is a mere non-exhaustive collection of assessments of the current global crisis, as seen by just a few of the many different authoritative government institutions and international organizations. In order to avoid the risk of the very important information being taken out of context or used instrumentally, some excerpts from these publicly available official reports will be presented here.

US Department of Treasury

Reforming Wall Street, Protecting Main Street (US Department of the Treasury, 2012):

- "The financial crisis shows that the cost of inadequate oversight can be devastating;"

- $19 trillion lost in household wealth (Q2 2007-Q1 2009);
  - 8.7 million lost jobs (December 2007-February 2010);
  - millions more Americans in poverty (2007-2009).

- US financial systems are safer and stronger. Consumers are more protected, regulators have more tools to monitor and mitigate threats to the financial systems, and business conditions are gradually improving although we need faster economic growth;
- While the size of financial markets has grown dramatically over the last decade, the number of regulators to police them has not;
- Opponents of Wall Street Reform have repeatedly tried to roll back, delay, and weaken the rules. Since the legislation passed in July 2010, opponents have:

  - Mounted legal challenges that have blocked investor protections, would prevent derivatives rules from taking effect, and would dismantle other important aspects of the legislation;
  - Proposed more than 50 bills and countless amendments to gut or slowdown Wall Street Reform—including full repeal of the legislation;"
  - Budget cuts could further undermine implementation and enforcement of Wall Street Reform.

Federal Reserve System

Monetary Policy Report to Congress
(The Federal Reserve System, 2012)

"Economic recovery appears to have slowed during the first half of this year, with real GDP having risen only modestly. The rate of job gains has diminished recently, and, following a period of improvement, the unemployment has been at an elevated level since January.

A number of factors will likely restrain economic growth in the period ahead, including weak economic growth abroad and a fiscal environment that looks set to become less accommodative.

Uncertainty may also restrain household and business spending. In addition, credit conditions are likely to improve only gradually, as are still-elevated inventories of vacant and foreclosed homes.

Moreover, the possibility of a further material deterioration of conditions in Europe, or of a particularly severe change in US fiscal conditions, poses significant downside risks to the outlook.

Eurozone

The Eurozone fiscal and banking crisis has remained a major source of strain on global financial markets. Tensions increased again in the spring as political uncertainties rekindled fears of a disorderly Greek exit from the Euro area.

Mounting losses at Spanish banks renewed questions about the sustainability of Spain's sovereign debt and the resiliency of the Euro-area banking system.

Yields on the government debt of vulnerable European countries rose toward new highs. Euro-area responded with additional measures in late June 2012, including increasing the flexibility of financial backstops and recapitalization of Europe's banks.

The Greek government concluded a restructuring of its privately held bonds, which reduced the face value of that debt by slightly more than half, and negotiated a second program with the EU and the International Monetary Fund (IMF) worth about €170 billion.

EU authorities lifted the ceiling on the combined lending of the region's *rescue facilities*, the *European Financial Stability Facility* and its successor, the *European Stability Mechanism* (ESM), from €500 billion to €700 billion, and they accelerated the schedule for capitalizing the ESM.

In addition, G-20 countries and other IMF shareholders *pledged* about $450 billion in new financing to the IMF, which should enable the IMF to substantially increase its lending capacity.

Notwithstanding these initiatives, events in Greece and Spain heightened financial stresses throughout the region as concerns about Spain's public finances and the cost of stabilizing the banking system mounted.

With economic activity declining, unemployment on the rise, and the budgets of regional governments under considerable strains, the Spanish government missed its 2011 budget deficit target by a wide margin and raised the country's deficit target for 2012.

There were renewed calls for Euro-area countries to move toward greater fiscal and financial union.

EU leaders pledged to further integrate the supervision of European banks to allow the Euro-area *financial backstop facilities to directly recapitalize banks* (as opposed to requiring sovereigns to borrow to support their banks) and to provide greater lending in support of growth and employment.

All told, European economies still face significant challenges. Euro policy makers must restore confidence in the region's banks and in the sustainability of sovereign finances. But risks to the stability of domestic financial systems remain.

The region must also find ways to stimulate economic growth and improve competitiveness in the most vulnerable countries even with major fiscal consolidations.

Over the longer term, EU policy makers need to establish an effective institutional framework to foster economic, financial, and fiscal integration and, ultimately, to increase the resilience of the monetary union.

Financial Markets

Financial markets were somewhat volatile over the first half of 2012, mostly due to fluctuating views of Euro area and the likely pace of economic growth at home and abroad.

As investors' concerns rose with data releases, broad equity price indexes rose, and risk spreads in several markets narrowed.

. . . However, market participants pulled back from riskier assets amid renewed concerns about the Euro area and evidence of slowing global economic growth.

On balance since the beginning of the year, broad equity prices rose as corporate earnings remained fairly resilient through the first quarter.

. . . Meanwhile . . . budgets for state and local governments remain strained and federal fiscal policy is likely to become more restrictive in 2013.

Household Sector

US Housing activity remains low and continues to be held down by tight mortgage credit conditions for all but highly rated borrowers . . . this tightness reflects the uncertain economic outlook and the high unemployment rate.

Total mortgage debt decreased further, as the pace of mortgage applications to purchase a new home was sluggish.

Refinancing instead increased over the course of the second quarter but remained below levels reached in previous refinancing booms despite historically low mortgage interest rates.

Indicators . . . continued to reflect strains on homeowners confronting depressed home values and high unemployment.

The fraction of current prime mortgages becoming delinquent remained at a high level but inched lower, over the first five months . . . likely reflecting, in part, stricter underwriting of more recent originations.

Additionally . . . mortgage delinquency . . . inventory of properties in foreclosure, continued to linger near the peak in the first quarter of 2012.

Real Business, Corporate Profits, and Business Finance

Slowdown in equipment and software (E&S) investment growth in the first quarter was fairly widespread . . . surveys of business sentiment and capital spending plans, may signal renewed caution on the part of businesses.

Businesses more cautious about increasing investment or materially expanding their payrolls have led households to remain quite pessimistic about their income and employment prospects.

Private spending continues to be weighed down by factors including uncertainty about developments in Europe and the path for U.S. fiscal policy, *concerns about the strength and sustainability of the recovery, the still-anemic state of the housing market, and the difficulties that many would-be borrowers continue to have in obtaining credit.*

Aggregate operating earnings per share for S&P 500 firms rose about 7 percent at a seasonally adjusted quarterly rate in the first quarter of 2012. *Financial firms accounted for most of the gain*, while profits for firms in the nonfinancial sector were unchanged from the high level seen in the fourth quarter of last year.

Long-Term Unemployment

The following chart represents a long-term unemployment trend from 2006 to 2012. Any other additional comments might be superfluous.

34. Long-term unemployed, 2006–12

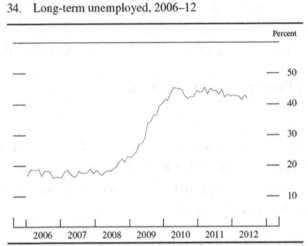

Note: The data are monthly and extend through June 2012. The series shown is the percentage of total unemployed persons who have been unemployed for 27 weeks or more.
Source: Department of Labor, Bureau of Labor Statistics.

Exports and Imports

Real exports of goods and services rose at an annual rate of 4.25 percent, supported by relatively strong foreign economic growth. Exports of services, automobiles, computers, and aircraft expanded rapidly, while those of consumer goods declined. The rise in exports was particularly strong to Canada and Mexico.

Real imports of goods and services rose a relatively modest 2.75 percent in the first quarter, reflecting slower growth in U.S. economic activity. Imports of services, automobiles, and computers rose significantly, while those of petroleum, aircraft, and consumer goods fell.

The rise in imports was broadly . . . from Japan and Mexico showing particularly strong growth.

Commodity and Trade Prices

Easing of geopolitical tensions and increased crude oil supply—production by Saudi Arabia has been running at near-record high levels—have also likely contributed to the decline in oil prices.

Price of Brent plunged $25 a barrel in March to $100 per barrel in mid-July.

Prices of many other commodities followed a path similar to that shown by oil prices. As with oil prices, broader commodity prices fell in the second quarter, reflecting growing pessimism regarding prospects for the global economy.

The Current and Financial Accounts

The nominal trade deficit widened slightly in the first quarter of 2012. The current account deficit deteriorated from an annual average of $470 billion in 2011 to $550 billion in the first quarter, or 3.5 percent of GDP.

The financial flows that provide the financing of the current account deficit reflected the general trends in financial market sentiment and in reserve accumulation by emerging market economies (EMEs).

International Financial Markets

International financial markets were affected as political and banking stresses in vulnerable European countries resurfaced.

Increased uncertainty and greater volatility have pushed up the foreign exchange value of the dollar about 4.25 percent against a broad set of currencies.

The dollar has appreciated against most currencies but depreciated against the Japanese yen. The Swiss franc has moved very closely with the euro.

Flight-to-safety flows and the deteriorating global economic outlook helped push government bond yields for Canada, Germany, and the United Kingdom to record lows.

Likewise, Japanese yields on ten-year bonds fell well below 1 percent.

Equity prices abroad declined significantly in the second quarter, more so than in the United States. Indexes tumbled in the nations at the center of the Euro-area fiscal and banking crisis.

News that Spain had partly nationalized the troubled lender Bankia and would need to inject an additional €19 billion into the bank and its holding company added to unease about the region, eventually leading to plans for an official aid package of up to €100 billion to recapitalize Spanish banks.

Apprehension about bank health was widespread . . . European bank stock prices have tumbled since mid-March.

At the same time . . . the CDS premiums on the debt of many large banks in Europe have risen substantially while issuance of unsecured bank debt, which had previously recovered, has fallen.

Advanced Foreign Economies

Eurozone real GDP was flat in the first quarter of 2012. Output fell sharply in more vulnerable countries, including Italy and Spain.

Growing financial tensions and fiscal austerity measures appear to have further restrained the Eurozone economy in the second quarter, as evidenced by declining business confidence and a further downdraft of purchasing managers' indexes.

In the UK, real GDP continued to fall early in the year, with indicators pointing to further weakness fueled by tight fiscal policy and negative Eurozone spillover effects.

In Japan, output rose but recent data suggests that activity decelerated in the second quarter.

The Canadian economy continued to expand moderately in the first three months of the year, supported by solid domestic demand and a resilient labor market.

In most AFEs, headline inflation rates continued to decline in the first half of the year as the effects of the large run-up in commodity prices in early 2011 waned.

Several central banks eased further their monetary policy stances. The BOJ increased the size of its *asset purchases* from ¥30 trillion to ¥40 trillion in April, and then to ¥45 trillion in July.

The ECB, after having conducted the second of its three-year longer-term *refinancing* operations in late February, cut its policy interest rates to record lows in early July.

In July, the Bank of England increased the size of its *asset purchase* program from £325 billion to £375 billion, and, together with the UK Treasury, introduced a *new Funding* for Lending Scheme designed to boost lending to households and firms.

Emerging Market Economies

Economic growth continued to *slow* in China and India. Moreover, recent indicators suggest that the pace of economic activity decelerated in most EMEs going into the second quarter.

In China, real GDP registered 7 percent in the first semester, down from an 8.5 percent pace in the second half of last year reflecting weaker demand for Chinese exports, as well as domestic factors, including moderating consumer spending and the restraining effects on investment of government measures to cool activity in the property sector.

Concerns about growth mounted. The People's Bank of China lowered banks' reserve requirements by fifty basis points in both February and May and then reduced the benchmark one-year lending rate by twenty-five basis points in June and thirty-one basis points in July.

In India, economic growth has also moderated as slow progress on fiscal and structural reforms and previous monetary tightening stalled investment.

Some credit rating agencies warned that India's sovereign debt risks losing its investment-grade status.

In Mexico, growth moderated somewhat in the second quarter.

In Brazil, real GDP—restrained by flagging investment and weather-related problems in the agricultural sector—making it the fourth consecutive quarter of below-trend growth.

Industrial production, which has been on a downward trend since early 2011, continued to fall through May, suggesting that economic activity in Brazil remained weak in the second quarter.

Headline inflation generally moderated in the EMEs, reflecting lower food price pressures and weaker economic growth."

IMF International Monetary Fund
(IMF—World Economic Outlook Update, 2012)

New Setbacks, Further Policy Action Needed

"Global recovery, which was not strong to start with, has shown signs of further weakness. Growth in a number of major emerging market economies has been lower than forecast.

Forecasts, however, are predicated on two important assumptions: that there will be sufficient policy action to allow financial conditions in the Euro-area periphery to ease gradually and that recent policy easing in emerging market economies will gain traction. Clearly, *downside* risks continue to loom large, importantly reflecting risks of delayed or insufficient policy action.

In Europe, the renewed deterioration of sovereign debt markets highlights the priority of timely implementation of these measures, together with further progress on banking and fiscal union.

In the United States, avoiding the fiscal cliff, promptly raising the debt ceiling, and developing a medium-term fiscal plan are of the essence.

In emerging market economies, policy makers should be ready to cope with trade declines and the high volatility of capital flows.

Developments during the second quarter, however, have been worse. Relatedly, job creation has been hampered, with unemployment remaining high in many advanced economies.

The Euro-area periphery has been at the epicenter of a further escalation in financial market stress, triggered by increased political and financial uncertainty in Greece, banking sector problems in Spain, and doubts about governments' ability to deliver on fiscal adjustment and reform, as well as about the extent of partner countries' willingness to help. Escalating stress in periphery economies has manifested itself along lines.

Data for the United States also suggests less robust growth underlying the loss of momentum.

Negative spillovers from the Euro area, limited so far, have been partially offset by falling long-term yields due to safe haven flows.

Growth momentum has also *slowed* in various emerging market economies, notably Brazil, China, and India. Domestic demand has also decelerated sharply in response to capacity constraints and policy tightening over the past year.

Many emerging market economies have also been hit by increases in investor risk aversion and perceived growth uncertainty, which have led to equity price declines and to capital outflows and currency depreciation.

In global financial markets, yields on safe haven bonds (Germany, Japan, Switzerland, and the United States) retreated to multi-decade lows.

Commodity prices have also fallen. Among these are prices of crude oil, given the combined effects of weaker global demand prospects, easing concerns about Iran-related geopolitical oil supply risks, and continued above-quota production by the OPEC members.

Global growth weakened through 2012 in both advanced and key emerging market economies, reflecting the setbacks to the global recovery discussed above.

Growth in advanced economies is projected to expand by only 1.4 percent in 2012 and 1.9 percent in 2013, a downward revision of 0.2 percentage point for 2013 to reflect Euro-area issues.

Growth in emerging and developing economies will moderate to 5.6 percent in 2012 before picking up to 5.9 percent in 2013, a downward revision of 0.1 and 0.2 percentage points in 2012 and 2013, respectively, relative to the April 2012 WEO.

The global recovery remains at risk. Downside risks to this weaker global outlook continue to loom large. The most immediate risk is still that delayed or insufficient policy action will further escalate the Euro-area crisis.

Other downside risks relate to fiscal policy in other advanced economies. In the short term, the main risk relates to the possibility of excessive fiscal tightening in the United States, given recent political gridlock.

In the extreme, if policy makers fail to reach consensus on extending some temporary tax cuts and reversing deep automatic spending cuts, the US structural fiscal deficit could decline by more than 4 percentage points of GDP in 2013.

US growth would then stall next year, with significant spillovers to the rest of the world. Moreover, delays in raising the federal debt ceiling could increase risks of financial market disruptions and a loss in consumer and business confidence.

Another risk arises from insufficient progress in developing credible plans for medium-term fiscal consolidation in the United States and Japan—the flight to safety in global bond markets currently mitigates this risk. In the absence of policy action, medium-term public debt ratios would continue to move along unsustainable trajectories.

A lack of progress could trigger sharply higher sovereign borrowing costs in the United States and Japan, as well as turbulence in the global bond and currency markets.

Concerns remain that potential growth in emerging market economies might be lower than expected. Growth in these economies has been above historical trends over the past decade or so, supported in part by financial deepening and rapid credit growth, which may well have generated overly optimistic expectations about potential growth.

As a result, growth in emerging market economies could be lower than expected over the medium term, with a correspondingly smaller contribution to global growth. Also of concern are risks to financial stability after years of rapid credit growth in the current environment of weaker global growth, elevated risk aversion, and some signs of domestic strain.

Commodity exporters are vulnerable to further erosion of commodity prices.

In the medium term, there are tail risks of a hard landing in China, where investment spending could slow more sharply given overcapacity in a number of sectors.

Once the agreed-upon single supervisory mechanism for Euro-area banks is established, the European *Stability* Mechanism (ESM) would be able to *recapitalize* banks directly.

In addition, the leaders reaffirmed a willingness to consider secondary purchases of sovereign bonds by the European Financial Stability Facility (EFSF) and the ESM.

These tasks require credible commitment toward a robust and complete monetary union, a unified supervisory framework, a banking union, a pan-European deposit insurance guarantee scheme, and a bank resolution mechanism with common backstops.

The EU monetary union must also be supported by wide-ranging structural reforms to increase growth and resolve intra-area current account imbalances.

Additionally the ECB should continue to provide *ample liquidity* support to banks under sufficiently lenient conditions. This might require nonstandard measures, such as reactivation of the Securities Market Program, additional LTROs with lower collateral requirements, or the introduction of QE-style asset purchases.

Furthermore, fiscal consolidation plans in the Euro area must be implemented.

In other major advanced economies, monetary policy also needs to respond effectively, including with further *unconventional* measures.

It will be critical to reach bipartisan agreements to avoid a fiscal cliff in the near term and to raise the federal debt ceiling well ahead of the deadline (which will most likely be early in 2013).

At the same time, both the United States and Japan need more credible plans to put medium-term government debt on a downward track.

In Japan, a full Diet approval of a gradual increase in the consumption tax rate is essential to maintain confidence in the authorities' resolve to put public debt on a sustainable trajectory.

In emerging and developing economies, potential growth could be lower than expected. Policy makers should stand ready to adjust policies, given spillovers from weaker advanced economy prospects and slowing export growth and volatile capital flows. In economies where inflation and credit pressures have not eased, targeted measures could be considered should bank liquidity or funding pressures arise.

Finally, with growth slowing and after many years of rapid credit growth, enhanced risk-based prudential regulation and supervision and macro prudential measures that address financial risks should take top priority.

IMF Global Financial Stability Report:

Restoring Confidence and Progressing on Reforms
(International Monetary Fund)

This is a brilliant document produced by a group of experts. It is available on IMF's website, and I invite all to read directly. It confirms to a certain extent what has already been covered, but its outlook seems slightly more pessimistic than the preceding information, especially with regard to perceived risks in many domains (e.g., lower growth, public debt, Eurozone issues and spillage risks, austerity measures, tax issues, business recovery, unemployment).

highly recommend additional reading:

- IMF Pilot External Report;
- "Taking Stock: A Progress Report on Fiscal Adjustment." October 2012. http://www.imf.org/external/pubs/ft/fm/2012/02/fmindex.htm.

The information provided by all these authoritative sources is constantly being updated, it is important to rely on the the most updated versions as time progresses.

CONSIDERATIONS ON THE AUTHORITATIVE FORMAL ASSESSMENTS

In evaluating the formal assessments—one of the obvious question that emerges is; if all the meticulous efforts by many in providing more liquidity (through different financial "facilities," "financial asset purchases" . . .) to the system delivering profound results? Is this money injected producing enduring real growth, jobs, and businesses? Are reforms yielding systemic improvements? Is there something else at the very heart of the system that does not allow a true-to-form *lasting and structural* recovery this time around? Will these be able to effectively address the many new variables that are already influencing our economic/business models creating known (and currently unknown) endemic dichotomies and blocks?

Provided the efficacy measures and official assessments, should we not allow ourselves to start making an allowance for other possible perspectives? Bearing in mind the nature of the profound changes and challenges that we are experiencing, will it be able to factor in all the game- and paradigm-changing variables we saw in preceding chapters? What effect might these have on the efficacy of the aforementioned measures? There is no doubt that there will be short cycles of mini recoveries as business and jobs are shed and new lower levels of economic plateaus are reached augmented maybe by facilitations such as lower interest rates for example. Will these though provide structural remedies?

Would we wish it to recover structurally and possibly open a new era of development and prosperity? Or should we instead decide to linger on, wait and see, continue as is, and focus all our energies within the framework of the same walls and boxes? What world will we have in the next three to five years?

Could we contemplate a parallel strategy? A winning strategy rather than a patch and fix one or be satisfied with bursts of short duration cycles of mini recoveries without truly addressing the underlying problems.

Provided the inefficacy of our search for appropriate solutions with existing models, some are starting to reason that they might be content passing on leadership, reaching an illusionary second place in the global economic scenarios with respect to other economies that might seem to <u>temporarily</u> benefit from an ephemeral positive growth rate.

This reasoning would suggest the following (non-exhaustive list):

- the acceptance that little or nothing can be done (loss of resilience);
- relinquishing to a theoretically dominant position;
- the cognizance of not having answers;
- conscientious acknowledgment of lack of independence and acceptance of dependence;
- the acceptance of a new mono-polar world rather than a multipolar one.

Others contend that there might be nothing more wrong than this seeimgly logical conclusion, stating that: If the scales tip toward an economic leadership on behalf of others, one thing that might need to be considered is that succumbing societies will need to adhere to the rules, living standards, ways of thinking, social structures, political and individual liberties, and levels of freedom dictated by these others.

Additionally we must remind ourselves they might be on similar boats in a not so distant future. What sense would it make to arrive second and be subjected to someone who is in the same dire position, if not worst?

Civil liberties, freedoms, and advancements in all fields, matured through centuries of evolution and wars, will be lost in shorter time frames than one could ever imagine. Recent revolutions set a perfect precedence. Furthermore, what sense would it have to move towards archaic models if the citizens of many developing countries are increasingly seeking democracy, be it with different shades of it, to the point of risking their lives and those of their loved ones.

It is easy to jump to the first logical conclusion and think that this is between East and West or North and South. In reality, this can regard any geographical context vis-à-vis any other. It could regard regions such as Southeast Asia, the Caucasus, or the Austral-Asian scenario. Small, maybe insignificant, samples of these seem to be emerging in the news (e.g., litigation over islands among Japan, Philippines, and China).

Although there is room for debate, there are two certainties. Historically, moments of extreme frailty lead to voids, and voids are filled at faster rates than our logical thought processes might wish to accept. Once filled, tips in balances change, especially those of leadership. Once independence is relinquished, if ever regained it is only at an excessive cost.

This is already happening all around us, yet as individuals we fail to see beyond our own daily challenges. With uncertain stock markets, enormous sums that are still searching for speculative higher-yield or flight for safety investments. This has generated unjustified pressures on governments to implement arguably quasi-authoritarian-style austerity measures on their citizens (e.g., Greece, Italy, Spain, Netherlands, Ireland), fueling social unrest, dangerous rebirth of historical sentiments, and discriminatory thought processes of preoccupying proportions for the first time after World War II.

European countries are surprisingly being affected one by one in a curious domino effect because of their national debts, never requiring such extreme steps.

The point in case is not a pro or contra EU stance but that of contemplating on these facts.

The US and EU economies are not by any stretch of the imagination where they could or should be; better yet, no economy in the developed world is where its citizens might like it to be.

Unfortunately, in the absence of new ideas that become *formally* accepted and bring real growth and sustained recovery, austerity and an increase in taxes are proving to only suffocate business and economic development in the processes.

Are investment, business, market, and employment opportunities being created structurally? Should the answers be unsure, it is time to change survival strategy.

It is hard not to agree that humanity is at a very big turning point in history.

Our actions today will determine the world we choose to live in tomorrow (literally)! Those that begin earlier are bound to take on a leadership role.

Do we wish to give up leadership and independence while we reach the next evolutionary step in mankind's history, probably the biggest epochal leap yet? Are we instead willing to take the challenge to evolve our systems and models into even better ones, or do we wish others to do it for us?

The well-being of a society affects everything, including its organization and freedoms. Freedom is a concept that has seen its birth and rebirth in several countries across the globe, yet it is a concept that was enriched by evolution throughout the contributions of many across the world. It is the result of innumerous that fought and died against slavery, racism, and totalitarian rule of the many different ideologies and countries that adopted them, against those that committed genocides, those that suffocated freedom of thought, of creed, of assembly, against those that prohibited free trade, movement of persons and ideas, against all those that oppressed and segregated, and against those that used hate and fear to dominate others.

It owes its existence to the cumulative sacrifice of all persons across the planet—from Greece to England, the United States to Iraq and Afghanistan, from North Africa to South Africa, from China to India, from the middle east to southeast Asia, from South Korea to Israel, and from Canada, the Scandinavian countries, and all the countries making up the former Soviet Union—in anyplace the quintessential nature of man desires its reaffirmation.

Freedom does not belong to a country or physical place rather it is implemented and exercised by those who desire it. It does not need to be exported or imported. It is an idea that lives a feeble existence and walks on a thin line between two daunting and damning extremes. It is what has provided mankind with its biggest leaps in advancement and explosion of ideas individually, as a society, and spiritually.

The democratic process today is not perfect, but it's the best system mankind has been able to produce. It is up to us to face the challenge of improving it and evolving it towards new levels of civilization. The new model proposed herein promotes and provides some of the most significant building blocks for such progress.

Hence, a more salutary strategy might be wishing to maintain a healthy and balanced innovative leadership in evolving the economic model to the next level of sustainability and long-term prosperity, paving the way for a new area of opportunity, well-being, and progression of civilization.

IS THE CURRENT MODEL
GEARED TO FAIL?

As seen in earlier parts increasing numbers of new model-changing variables are being introduced at growing rates and will continue to be introduced probably at even greater rates. They include:

- systemic dichotomies
- Web inclusivity and TIAI
- Mobint
- nanotechnologies, robotics
- innovations and advancements
- investment evaporation, business closures
- preoccupying levels of increasing unemployment and remuneration availability
- growing numbers of new poor
- immigration, emigration, alarming levels of taxation and public debt
- population growth
- delocalization, technological transfer
- growing dependence, loss of independence, geopolitical and financial power shift
- growlingly structural trade imbalances
- growing numbers of social revolts and social unrest and exposure to potential ideologically fueled extremist actions
- increasing organized and unorganized criminal activity.

A growing number of endemic systemic blocks are destabilizing the economic model that no longer responds and is overwhelmed by new variables with which it was not meant to deal, consequently touching most aspects of the lives of billions of individuals.

Examples of the effects can be seen everywhere.

The formal photograph or where we stand not only today but an outlook of where we might stand in the foreseeable future, notwithstanding all the titanic efforts put in place by many, existing models might not be fully equipped to provide concrete answers to the challenges posed by the multitude of new paradigms and variables.

Each of the primary elements composing the foundation of the existing economic models are possibly already overstretched in addressing existing complexity and the crisis. This is evidence of multidimensional dichotomies of the new variables and paradigms that only add more complexity and exacerbate the response capability even further.

There are incremental probabilities for potentially virulent systemic events, as new paradigm-changing elements and remedies are introduced into the existing economic models that are not able to elaborate and or process these adequately.

A picturesque analogy could be similar to an older-type PC, connected in an elementary network with other old PCs, running on prior-generation operating systems, extremely limited CPU capacities, and dated circuitry and logic. They use earlier programming languages with no-longer-valid interfaces, and they are not geared to work with today's programs, interfaces, connections, data volumes, and transfer rates. What has happened is that we have connected this rudimentary network to the Internet via a high-speed connection with applications running in a cloud environment. For now we are managing to maintain frail connection and minimal processing capability with many patches.

The more the existing models are solicited with new variables and paradigms, the greater the number of multidimensional dichotomies created, generating additional challenges and substantially escalating the possibilities for systemic failures and unwanted effects. The interaction between the primary pillars of the existing economic models is becoming growingly nonresponsive. Current policies are struggling in yielding concrete results in the recovery process, let alone lasting solutions. Nonetheless the worst might yet to come in terms of the necessity in addressing paradigm-changing variables.

Considering the last couple of market bubble bursts, the effects of the self-consuming systemic vortex might be depicted as something similar to the following and its implosive/explosive cycle (similar to the cycle of a dying star).

Effects of the Self-Consuming Systemic Vortex/Paradox and
Its Implosive/Explosive Cycle in the Last Two Market Bubble
Bursts and Financial Systems Near Meltdown

From Implosive **Toward Explosive**

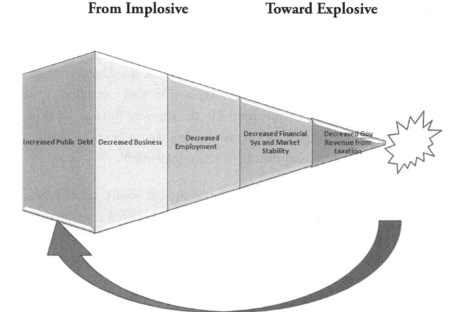

Provided the complexity of the current scenario, all the above
considerations might only be of purely intellectual relevance and may
be a subject matter of curiosity for future historians.

DEER-HEADLIGHT FIXATION: A SYNDROME TO FRET

The risk of remaining fixated on man-made norms and not being prepared to adopt an alternative winning strategy, even when it is apparent the old norms might bring about defeat at exorbitant costs, is real. History books are full of these catastrophic consequences when some remained stuck to old methods. A few examples follow:

- As paradigm-changing machine guns made their way in the battlefield, entire armies would still use old-style maneuvers, assembling entire battalions of soldiers in perfect company or platoon-sized units that would literally walk in militaristic fashion toward the enemy in suicidal death;
- Cavalry units were used as recent as World War II against new tank battalions;
- The famous Maginot Line, built after World War I by the French to defend their northern border from Germany at exorbitant costs to its citizenry, was completely vain, as a new German Blitzkrieg strategy completely flanked the entire French defensive line, attacking France through the Belgian border;
- The introduction of pc's in a world dominated by large mainframes or still manual processes produced a revolution—those business models that failed to adapt quickly were exposed to considerable consequences.

Consider the geometric impact of the invention and concept of a needle, a simple fishing hook or that of a nail has had on the creation of a plethora of industries from its prehistoric origins till today—from fishing, to its use many uses in medicine, in leather-made products and textiles, to armaments (a firing pin), from recording industry (before it created the necessary step towards digitalization) to its use in skin care and orthodontics, from its use in furniture manufacturing to its use in the automotive industry . . . or that of a nail in construction.

What to say about the invention of glass and its geometric resonance and impact on vision; building and construction; medical; scientific; automotive; aerospace and defense; shipping; appliances; kitchen-ware; etc.

These examples (deliberately of relatively small significance) demonstrate how seemingly meaningless single variables, innovations etc. can determine the most impressive and/or gravest consequences with geometric effects.

If this is true for a small paradigm-changing innovation, let us imagine what the combined impact of many advancements already here might have on entire economies, nationally and on a global scale.

Are we sure our current models provide the tools to address these challenges appropriately?

CONFLICT: ECONOMIC PARADIGM OF LAST RESORT?

History confirms a relation between conflict as an economic revival strategy of last resort (and sometimes even earlier). It is one of the major shortcomings of the existing economic model and its predecessors.

These are unquestionably very hard times, and we cannot allow ourselves the luxury of not considering alternatives to conflict, especially if adopted solutions do not produce results.

To start with, there is no guarantee who might win a war—even in a proxy war (engaging in conflict on someone else's territory).

Until World War II, for millennia the model could presumably rely on a simple axiom: that full-scale destruction brings with it a period of production during a war and a period of reconstruction and economic revitalization after it.

The wars in the last fifty years instead, on a growing scale, do not necessarily result in the same expected outcomes—widespread lasting economic reactivation.

Additionally, paradoxically in today's interconnected world, defensive might in military power does not necessarily equate to invulnerability. In reality, historically, it probably never has been. There are substantial examples of scenarios where the sizably smaller adversaries were able to bring or pose considerable threat, damage, and in some cases defeat to previously "undefeatable" realities.

Today's exorbitant public debts render an impracticable new arms race, but then again weren't also Germany and Russia fully indebted before the rise of Nazism or during the birth of the Soviet Union? Military doctrine is split among the need to maintain high-impact visible power projection capability and asymmetric strategy. The reality is that you might need both, but more importantly the ability to win a conflict before it ever begins through a solid economy and valid and dynamically updated deterrents.

Asymmetry is not a new concept; it dates back several thousand years and may have always been used as far back as the first conflicts between two contenders with considerably different forces and resources. In essence, it is the use of weakness as a strength that sometimes determines, at the very least, psychological defeat.

Today the use of technological asymmetric strategy is also inherent to cyberspace and nanotechnology. The news is full of examples of "real" virtual wars taking place in cyberspace today, inflicting real damage to the military, intelligence, critical infrastructure, business, economy, and individuals.

Increasing budgets are being dedicated to what could be called the fifth dimension of warfare after land, sea, air, and unmanned dimensions. It is fundamentally different from other dimensions in at least two primary areas:

- It does not need proximity to inflict damage (physical distance to the battle-space and/or enemies assets);
- It has "one-to-many" damage-inflicting capabilities exponentially higher than any other weapon ever made by man. Theoretically with an algorithm that could penetrate all the other dimensions, it could debilitate these through the same single asset.

Fifth-dimension asymmetric strategy can potentially be used as a debilitating first move and might require, at least initially, the involvement of only a handful of individuals, probably unaware of one another, who are simply sitting in many different parts of the world, operating from a laptop to start their assignments. And they do not necessarily need to be military personnel. Each might acts in his official capacity as journalists, system administrators, investors, etc., to initiate the engagement. For all practical purposes they might not even necessarily be aware of the repercussions of their actions, or theoretically they might even not be the enemy but simply an unwary individual with the only fault of having purchased a PC belonging to a very particular batch.

Cyber deterrence or offensive capability is achieved through substantial investments in very strong cyber strategies, resources, applications, etc., both of offensive and defensive natures that in many countries might not even show up in publicly declared budgets. These domains could include:

- Offensive cyber warfare (examples)

    o Access inhibition/denial, application destruction, data loss, etc.
    o Economic cyber warfare through deliberate coordinated economic transactions
    o Intelligence (i.e., sniffing, phishing, intelligence gathering, decryption, info distortion, manipulation)

- Defensive cyber warfare (examples)

    o Cyber protection, firewalls, system/data protection, etc.
    o Counterintelligence.

An even more subtle strategy might reside in what could be called *"end-user product pre-fitted destructive, manipulative, and inhibitive logic* (or PDMI-Log)" onto ordinary electronic circuitry.

In other words, it refers to the incubation or infestation of simple logic that could potentially include implanting hard-to-detect, deeply embedded logic or applications in firmware of innocuous-looking circuitries or chipsets of any nature (at different points of their manufacturing processes) that either self-destruct, inhibit or manipulate a system, its data or way of operating.

As an example, imagine a chipset or miniature circuitry embedded in seemingly innocuous day-to-day appliances, such as a washing machine, that could be deactivated or activated to operate differently at a distance by an innocuous electric pulse, a particular yet simple radio wave, or other means.

Now imagine a theoretical, purposely exaggerated scenario of a washing machine being prompted from a distance to open its door as it is running, dumping the water it contains on the floor of one's home. Now multiply this effect on a neighborhood, town, city . . . .

Theoretically this sort of embedded logic might go in not only a washing machine but also a food or medicine-dosing subunit that controls the accuracy of dosage of various ingredients in common medicines; a smartphone; truck-breaking or fuel systems (70 percent of US goods are moved on trucks); hospital emergency systems; ventilation systems on ships or submarines; fuses in military machinery, aircraft, and platforms; an elevator command module; an emergency center control room's sprinkler system; hazardous material-handling rooms in research centers; the temperature control indicator of a reactor; a metro's signaling system; a civil aircraft's fuel engine valve controller, rudder control, or landing system; a city sewage pump's valve control unit; a motorcycle engine's spark ignition system; a dam's electrical generation unit's circuit breaker subsystems; the keyboard circuitry on PCs and servers; Wi-Fi and cell phone relay station replacement sub-circuitry or displays; HVAC system shut-off circuit in server farms around the world on which clouds and terabytes of websites' information and data reside, including that of financial institutions; a factory's conveyer belt speed control unit; a car manufacturer's inventory control logic and bar code laser printer; computer or printer file management logic that sends this data every time connection to the Web is activated; e-mail server's deleted files bin logic; the handsets of emergency responders (e.g., police, ambulances, firefighters); downloaded music; etc.

The potential use of similar strategies is not only within the capabilities of developed nations and emerging economies but even those with the least amount of technological capability.

Seen from this additional perspective, questions that might be posed by geopolitical strategists include: will dependence, "cost only"—focused economic logic, delocalization, or relinquishment of know-how and strategic sector sell-off still be as fancy and strategically or economically viable as they've sounded thus far?

Independently of what has been discussed in this chapter, we must remember that different from other historical moments, in the unwanted event of a future conflict of substantial proportions, after a brief reconstruction period, the survivors will be confronted by the same dilemmas and challenges we face today-the numerous game-changing paradigms and systemic paradoxes that inhibit the proper functioning and prolonged success of the current economic model—unless of course Albert Einstein's prediction is correct that whomever survives the next war will revert back to a technologically more primitive society.

While it might not be hard to predict what balance of forces a conflict might be commenced with among two contenders, there are two things that are not foreseeable: the outcome and the price at which this comes (both during and after the conflict).

Theoretically, for the first time in human history, changing the economic paradigm might help add a possible protective layer, or cushion between the economic motivation for war (deriving from conflict-based economic axiom/paradigm) and the need for conflict itself. The need to maintain strategically strong deterrence in different domains is a totally different story.

PART 2:

A Possible Solution

INTRODUCTION

In a world where all productive human activity is being virtualized, how is it possible to think of continuing to resolve issues with unfit/dated/ unresponsive models—our existing models? Provided the potentially unknown number of new variables and paradigms we face and will continue to face, we will need equally evolved models to address these.

Today's evolving needs, challenges and technology are altering and influencing our models at increasing speeds—existing models working within defined boundaries have difficulty keeping pace with the added complexity, and are no longer able to provide solutions to mounting obstacles on the one hand while impeding us to exploit opportunities that reside just on the other side of the same coin.

Seeking a possible solution can no longer be achieved from within the boxes constituting the current economic model that is losing traction, as solutions and change are external to these.

To succeed at this feat one needs to step outside the existing framework and distance himself at such a range as to see the true extent of the wider picture.

It is impossible to think that evolution will happen overnight.

Transition toward a new plateau must be planned, and migration will need to contemplate soft switchovers to new models and modalities, facilitating the step-level evolution toward a new plateau of long-term development, prosperity and civilization.

In the following chapters we will step back and visualize the wider picture, appreciate where we stand, and evaluate how we are impacted and the options at hand. Next, a possible solution will be introduced.

New concepts, models, and protocols will be defined and explained, providing a sample high-level road map together with possible migration and transition tools. Finally, a diversified set of concrete examples will be provided as evidence for the real-life applicability of the model and concepts to a set of different economic sectors and economic dimensions, such as public debt and employment. The reforms henceforth discussed are structural and systemic in nature and aimed at achieving short-term economic recovery with long-term impact on national economies and prosperity.

This book does not provide the solution to all dilemmas or a magic-wand approach. Rather, it provides a possible alternative perspective from which the solution can be developed.

The proposed solution introduced here is presented as an open, baseline framework, one that is modular and scalable, leaving ample room for the contribution, improvement, and completion of many experts from different fields.

This book is intended to reach as many persons as possible, because the evolutionary trek we are undertaking regards everyone. Hence, in order to reach such an objective, the following chapters will make substantial use of analogies, similitudes, and references to everyday notions to explain new concepts, models, and protocols—hopefully to render the matter more understandable and enjoyable to read.

A purely academic version of this book will be published shortly.

MOUNTING CHALLENGES

Summarizing what has been discussed thus far, based upon the formal assessments of authoritative and official sources (see earlier chapters) and the factual evidence we see all around us, the economy (local, national, international) faces mounting, growingly irresolvable challenges that contribute to complexity and the generation of additional potentially virulent systemic blocks and dichotomies—the following is a non-exhaustive list:

- Loss of "economic traction": Traction is created and led by such basic things as demand, availability of income, propensity to spend, etc. The more an economy fails in this, the greater the increased loss of "economic traction" and the challenges of restoring it. An analogy here could be the mechanism similar to that of a bicycle's eroded dented disk that fails to properly hook the chain, allowing the energy applied to the pedals to be transferred to the rear wheel for traction. Continued erosion and mis-engagement of the chain initially creates short, dangerous slippages of the chain that, in turn, erode the dents even further. Ultimately and beyond a certain point, any energy applied to the pedals will yield lesser advancement, and any additional energy applied simply adds cost;

- Debt, tax, and structural dichotomies: Excessive public debt, its implications (e.g., fiscal cliffs—we need to remember that under the existing models these problems do not disappear but can only be diluted), increased tax collection, and growing austerity measures only exasperate the general economic environment, activating a negative self-consuming vortex and additional systemic blocks;

- Liquidity quicksand: Continued massive injections of liquidity through differently denominated "facilities" in the banking and financial sectors, while having been useful in partially stopping hemorrhage or simply postponing risks, have not produced their additional objectives: liquidity distribution to, or permeation into, the wider economy, as intended to help recovery;

- Systemic failure of industrial life support: Distribution of different types of "incentives" to industry have had short-lived effects—in most cases these have failed to produce long-term *systemic* traction and the virtuous capability of regenerating lasting development, business growth, increased stakeholder value, and long-term employment;

- Increased exposure to risk: Financial institutions' increased shift of focus of their core business toward investments in innovative financial instruments irrespective of numerous and theoretically valid policy measures is de facto increasing the potential exposure derived from putting all eggs in one basket;

- Increased endemic volatility of markets deriving from:

    a) structural and systemic uncertainties (e.g., Eurozone, debt);
    b) objective success of reforms;
    c) increasing levels of risk associated with growing numbers of highly speculative financial instruments;
    d) excessive over- or under-valuation of a growing number of equity (share) prices; and
    e) prolonged adverse economic conditions of a growing number of listed companies.

- Reduction and/or disappearance of sources of revenue and income affecting a growing number of corporations, businesses, entrepreneurs, individuals, and families pertaining to all echelons;

- Propagation of excessive real inflation in a growing number of countries: independent of formal inflation figures, real inflation is reaching alarming levels in many countries (both in growing economies and those hit by the crisis);

- Income/spending dichotomy paradox: This is produced when sources of income are reduced or disappear while real inflation, austerity measures, and tax pressure increase at the same time, producing a systemic exacerbation (be it on companies, investors, families, or simply individuals);

- Critically increasing unbalanced polarization of economic activity toward geographical regions that leverage hardly replicable economies of scale and disproportionate cost structure advantages achieved only through exploitation of very cheap labor from a practically endless supply basin, given the numbers of persons that can be instantly jettisoned and replaced, as their unit cost rises;

- Increased endemic and systemic loss of competitiveness: The preceding point references only the cost disadvantage element, whereas in reality competitiveness is lost as a result of many other factors, such as loss of:

  a) capability and know-how (e.g., as key resources relocate, others find better-paying jobs in healthier ecnomies, are laid off, etc., and/or key technologies, licenses, patents, etc., are sold);
  b) resilience (e.g., as companies become inwardly focused, fixated on "cost-only" paradigms);

c) positive economic environment (e.g., influence on a company's general operational environment and relations with customers, suppliers, bankers, financiers, shareholders, and innovation sources who, in turn, are affected by negative economic environments);

d) motivation (e.g., as a consequence of continuous restructuring, change in leadership, prolonged periods of uncertainty, organizational confusion, lack of visibility, change-management overdose, devaluation of work, professionalism and results, growing precariousness and resulting sense of uselessness of efforts);

e) independence (e.g., relocation and delocalization of processes, business segments, and/or units; increasing dependence on external factors; loss of vital entrepreneurial independence and decision-making capacity);

f) value-generation capability (e.g., emptying the business of value through the sell-off of a growing number of its pieces); and

g) strategy (e.g., reduced strategy development capability as companies lose important assets).

- Disproportionately different standards and applications of sustainability, health and safety, and eco-environmental protection models used by some nations: These exert incalculable negative effects on both societies that are directly impacted by them and those that become indirect recipients of these effects, be it through natural propagation or through the purchase of the goods they produce and export. The world is a closed-loop system, and effects in one area will impact other areas—disregard of environmental issues in one area is of direct concern to other regions;

- Increasingly unreasonable fiscal/taxation pressures on individuals, businesses, and investments only increase burden on economic recovery and are more and more being perceived as enforced impositions rather than contributions to general well-being;

- Liquidity distribution imbalance and induced credit crunch on growing number of concerns across all economic sectors:

  - homeowners
  - construction
  - businesses and corporations
  - enterprises and investors
  - research and development.

- Deterioration and aging of critical national infrastructure increase the level of exposure to associated risks;

- Risks from and repercussions of extreme speculation (not investments);

- Saturation of credibility (economic, political, etc.), perceived leadership, and the shift of real geopolitical and economic power balances;

- Reduced funding for and deterioration of fundamental services:

  - education
  - law enforcement
  - environment management, natural disaster recovery, and mitigation
  - public transportation
  - emergency services

- road and highway maintenance
- national defense
- public health and quality of services
- national resilience mega projects.

- A general environment of growing social unrest (potentially concerning millions of individuals) and potential breeding ground for ideologically fueled extremism.

- Short duration mini recovery cycles induced by downward vortexes of further business closures, job cuts and or artificial means only shift the effects and accumulate the potentially destructive energy.

The cost-focused paradigm will only naturally force delocalization of greater economic activity to geographic locations with cost bases impossible to match, creating "terra bruciata" (burned terrain) in the economies they abandon.

Note that in all the above we have not even considered the impact of new technology, paradigm- and game-changing variables, Mobint, Web inclusivity, etc., that, as we saw in earlier chapters, are and will continue to be the inremental challenges, ones that cannot be addressed through the current models.

The matter here is grave. It no longer can be affronted with patchwork solutions, postponement, or dilution strategies. The world economy is approaching unknown levels of exposure to risks with potentially devastating effects. Any and all actions/reforms thus far undertaken should have produced tangible results. Pragmatism and realism call for evaluating or at least considering viable alternatives.

Unfortunately we need to seek answers soon. Signs both formal and informal are preoccupying. In some countries, for example, the economic crisis is leading to riots that are growingly involving the silent majority, and the middle class is becoming more common.

Desperate strike actions are becoming more resolute. Unsolvable dichotomies are deepening, adoption of democratically dubious policies such as citizen tax spying (spying on one's neighbors life style, spending habits, and reporting anything that can lead to a verification and investigation) and citizen spending investigation are becoming ever more common and demanding. In some cases recent headlines suggest that we might have stepped over a demarcation line of reasonableness both in terms of what is being asked and modalities chosen.

The matter is so serious that a growing number of newspaper articles have even suggested that some of these measures are reminiscent of very dark periods in recent history. True or not and to what degree is a matter of debate. The real question is how far down this line do we wish to go before something gives?

If the economy is not running structurally (not through artificially induced mini-recoveries), and money is not flowing, how can the public debts be expected to be covered with rising taxes? Worse, what sort of context do we wish to find ourselves in if things continue down this path? Historically, there are many studies confirming a direct cause-effect link between prolonged economic downturns and increase in social unrest, petty crime, organized criminal activity, revolts, etc.

COST FOCUS:
SELF-CONSUMING PARADOX

As we mentioned earlier, one of the fundamental elements or building blocks of the existing models is cost. Should one step back and look at our current economic models from a distance, a new perspective is formed. What will be noticeable is, though declared to be market-based/driven, the existing models are predominately also based on the notion of "cost"—so much so that it has even influenced language and human behavior. Cost is the fundamental building block /base of the current economic models and has been so since the beginning of recorded human economic activity.

How much any item "costs" versus its perceived benefit is what makes or breaks any decision:

- We cannot compete because of an un-replicable cost structure;
- We cannot be profitable because of a certain cost issue;
- We cannot afford determined things (investments, research, projects, programs, etc.) because of the cost concerns;
- We cannot invest because of how much this costs, etc.

Cost centricity, cost focus, cost vortex, and the self-consuming cost paradigm discussed in earlier chapters are what renders, for example;

- maintenance or refurbishment of critical infrastructure, noneconomic or economically unattractive (e.g., maintenance of roads, railroads, dams, highways, electrical grids, but also aircraft fleets, shipping fleets, trucking fleets, plants, equipment and machinery, networks, offices, hotels, housing, and assets of public utility such as schools and parks);

- projects and programs critical to a nation, a business, an investment, etc.; continued economic development; success; prosperity; competitiveness; attractiveness; etc. uneconomical, not viable; and

- research, development, and advancement in many fields, including those vital to our own health and survivability —financially unattractive due to cost;

- Environmental clean-up—economically unattractive, etc.

To find a way out, we must find a new alternative or a new perspective from which to look at the problem. If one were to look closely, it appears that cost, is in reality made up different states/ elements: a) the first is one of immediate value generation capability, b) the second; different levels of latent/intrinsic value generation capability and the third c) currently non definable value generation capability.

The immediate value generation capability states/elements are represented by those aspects which are instantaneously identifiable as being able to produce benefits. For example, in the case of the maintenance cost of an aircraft engine (or of any given item); the benefits derived from a properly maintained jet engine are among other things: passenger and crew safety, increased operation of the aircraft, positive impact on sustainability, increased revenue generation possibility, efficiency, savings in fuel consumption, reduced risk of failure and maybe savings on insurance etc.

The latent/intrinsic states/elements in this specific example are represented by those aspects that have been seen as mere cost till today but that could, as these concepts evolve over time and we mature a better understanding and appreciation of new dimensions, be considered as those having the potential to generate value i.e.: the cost in terms of time, materials and resources utilized, the hazardous waste generated etc.. In the case of hazardous materials for example; the opportunity to reduce, neutralize, re-cycle, etc. represent latent capability in generating research, investment, processes, business and job opportunities.

Currently non-definable value generating elements such the cost associated with wages, taxes, . . . while considered mere expenses today—need more time to be investigated. Over time we may find new intrinsic value generating capabilities as the model evolves and new frontiers are rendered visible, as we will see in later chapters.

Extrapolating this notion to all those elements that today are solely seen as costs by an individual, a business concern or a government, new dimensions become perceptible. How many opportunities these may hide then become the real questions and the true enterprising quest.

In the next chapters we will address these aspects more exhaustively.

For now we could say that: just adding this small perspective on the make-up of cost we open a new set of dimensions.

Segregating and leveraging the positive elements of costs will provide new, innovative modalities also in many additional areas. Just to mention a few; we go from accounting for cost, to attributing value for the positive aspects to incentivizing virtuous behavior, new opportunities and business models.

WHAT MIGHT A POSSIBLE SOLUTION NEED TO ADDRESS?

Any solution geared to resolving the challenges that were discussed thus far in essence need *at least* be able to (the following represent just a subset):

- address new paradigm-, game-changing variables such as innovations, Web inclusivity, etc., in a continuous manner as they emerge;
- create lasting virtuous economic traction, regeneration, development, and prosperity;
- create an environment for continued natural incentive to grow business ventures and provide new opportunities and investments;
- be implementable independently of geography (not needing to be dependent on exploitation of cheapest resources or cost-focused paradigms) and using the capability of building economies locally; realigning competitiveness;
- find an appropriate replacement for self-consuming paradigms (e.g., cost) that also impede proper leveraging of new variables, advancements, and vital elements such as sustainability; and
- unblock current systemic blocks and dichotomies discussed earlier and unleash hidden potential. And be realizable in reasonable time frames.

A model that is anchored on deeply rooted, systemic reforms made to address new paradigms creates possibilities for new virtuous and lasting economic renewals that are based on new evolved concepts, such as "value creation," and what can be called "value balance" (as elaborated later).

THE BIRTH OF A NEW ECONOMIC MODEL AND A NEW PERSPECTIVE

The existing pillars of the current economic models may not be able to sustain the economy for long, especially in light of new challenges. Everything around it has changed and will continue to transform our lives.

Should we wish to look carefully, we might be able to perceive the actual formation of a new economic model. The reason for the objective difficulty in seeing it is that the evolved economic model is forming on a totally new set of definitions, connotations, forms, requirements, technologies, modalities, interactions, networks, relations, mediums, logic, cause-and-effect relationships, and a whole new set of underlying truths and premises—on a new and totally different, higher plane (plateau) explained in the next chapter. Paradoxically it is of our making.

The sooner we are able to grasp this reality, the faster we might be able to leverage this opportunity and evolve, increasing our chances of achieving economic recovery in the short run. But even more importantly, maybe we will begin a new phase in human evolution by using an evolved model to exploit new potential for long-term sustained development and prosperity.

This requires sage decision making and action to be successful in achieving a step-level transition toward an economy made by man for man—sustainable and one that can develop continuously to new levels, keeping pace with advancement (technological, economic, and otherwise).

The following chapters will introduce the following concepts:

- A new plateau of long-term development and prosperity;
- The newly forming Value-Based Baseline Evolutionary Economic (Prosperity) Model (BEM[HESD]);
- The Alpha-e Protocol;
  a) Definition
  b) Set of conversion, transition, and migration tools (samples)
     i. Evolutionary Conversion Process
     ii. eVolve Migration Process
     iii. Organization
     iv. Implementation and transition strategy
- The evolved "value creation" and "value balance" concepts;
- An evolved governance and equilibrium framework.

In order to go from where we are to where we need to reach, we must step back from the existing models, look at the bigger picture, assess where we are, decide where we wish to go, and only then establish what we need to do to get there. Let's see how this works.

NEW ECONOMIC PLATEAU

*Should we wish to look at matters from a more relevant perspective,
we might notice that we are in the presence of a step-level evolutionary
event and a newly forming economic model that works on a totally
different plateau with very evolved characteristics, requiring evolved tools,
frameworks, and reference models.*

To explain the concept of a different plateau, we must make reference
to the preceding and existing ones. The following image better
conveys this concept.

Step-Level Changes in Economic Plateaus

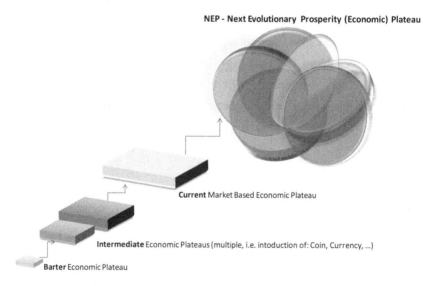

NEP - Next Evolutionary Prosperity (Economic) Plateau

Current Market Based Economic Plateau

Intermediate Economic Plateaus (multiple, i.e. intoduction of: Coin, Currency, ...)

Barter Economic Plateau

In essence, the number of economic plateaus that have evolved
with humanity's innovation capabilities has been high (not just
limited to the above stages).

The barter economic plateau was miniscule and limited compared to its successors until reaching the current economic plateau, which has been depicted as fourth for simplification of the diagram, also to denote that the current economic plateau is bound by its current borders and limitations.

A new evolved plateau is forming, and it is doing so as a result of our activities. In fact, it is this evolved plateau that could be called NEP (newly forming or next evolutionary economic/prosperity plateau) that will allow us not only to find new possibilities to address the innumerous paradigm- and game-changing variables, dichotomies, and blocks we are faced with today, but also allow us to finally see and exploit currently unperceivable opportunities as we migrate to and use this different, higher plane (plateau), one that can contain the evolved reference model that has the capability of dynamically identifying new variables and the ability to address each, finding equally evolved solutions to paradigm-changing innovations, needs, requirements, advancement, etc., that the future might have in store.

Though a shape has been given to the next evolutionary economic plateau (NEP) to make the point in a simple way, in reality the next economic plateau is shapeless (amorphous), dynamically evolving and multidimensional.

Where We Are

Basic Legacy Model

The existing basic legacy model (below) which lies on the current economic plateau, is based on the following basic concepts and generic cycle:

Basic Legacy Model

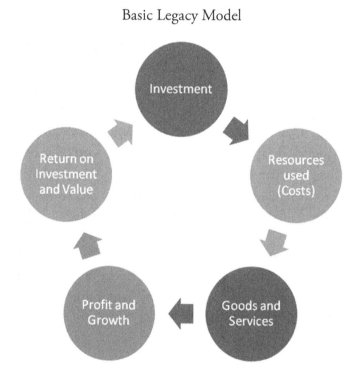

The idea here is to present the concept in generic terms, because what matters is not the fiscal accuracy or level of detail of the model but how it flows overall.

To describe the flow of the current model, we could say:

a. Capital is pooled and invested in business enterprises (e.g., production, services, retail);

b. These enterprises bring together, organize, and utilize resources (human, machinery, natural, etc.) according to plans and objectives; to produce goods and services

c. Goods and services are sold to markets with the intent of growing a company's market, increasing profits, and producing a return on investment and stakeholder value;

d. The remuneration from these activities forms the basic incentive to provide additional investment from different sources, such as shareholders, banks, and individuals, reactivating the loop again.

In essence, there is a sequence in the cycle where each element follows the preceding one. This model has worked more or less in the same way since the inception of a money-based economy. The second element in the loop (human and nonhuman resources) has till today constituted and been treated as a cost to an enterprise.

Intermediate or Hybrid Legacy Model

The intermediate or hybrid reference model is where we stand today. It is a small but significant evolutionary step away from the previous basic legacy model, but in a position too risky to maintain/sustain for long, as it represents the current global market scenario. It is too dangerous to remain in the turbulent waters we find ourselves in today.

This model can be witnessed if one looks at the very big picture forming. The differences from the original basic legacy model might seem subtle. In reality they are substantial and game changing in their impact. They create short circuits in the basic legacy models that have fueled the economy for centuries, affecting the survivability of the rest of the elements within the model.

What we are witnessing more and more today is that the hybrid model and the search for immediate, higher reward and or and less risky returns or simply flight to safety, leave out some of the fundamental elements of the legacy model, leaving ever fewer resources to these and substantially modifying the paradigm.

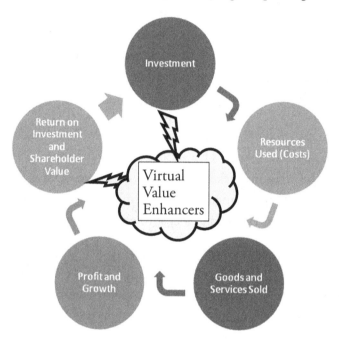

The following paragraphs describe the general flow of the hybrid model.

1. With the introduction of new paradigms and elements, such as innovation, technology, and Web inclusivity, the economic returns from historic activities based on the current models' cost focus are becoming less remunerative, attractive, and, in some cases, riskier than they used to be with respect to more virtual forms;

2. Remuneration possibilities offered by more virtual means, which we can call "Virtual Value Enhancers" (e.g., innovative

financial instruments, speculation, Web inclusivity, intangibles), form the basic incentive to lure increasing amounts of investment from increasing numbers of actors and sources (e.g., investors, markets, shareholders, banks, individuals) toward these, short-circuiting and reactivating the loop without necessarily fueling the rest of the elements/ domains within it—de facto bypassing them and depriving them of necessary resources, lymph, and/or oxygen (e.g., investments, liquidity);

3. To compete for investments, legacy model-based enterprises (e.g., industry, manufacturing, retail, services, paradoxically including banks, financial institutions) are growingly forced to find new ways to survive in both form and substance.

The following diagram provides another depiction of the consequences and the systemic imbalance that is generated when more and more financial resources are diverted toward Virtual Enhancer and away from real business in today's models.

Diversion of Investments toward Virtual Value
Enhancers rather than Real Business

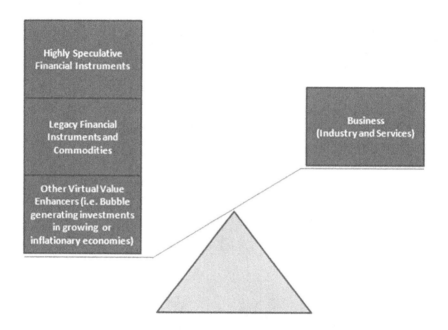

As more financial resources and potential investments are diverted toward Virtual Value Enhancers for remuneration rather than being invested in business ventures, the hybrid scenario we live in today will most likely leave a growing number of businesses, enterprises, professionals, and persons from all walks of life out of the economic model, one that will continue to drain any remaining possibility and energy.

It is important to understand that these very important transformations are in addition to the cracks and systemic dichotomies forming in the fundamental pillars (e.g., public debt, unemployment, monetary policy) of the current models. These additional transformations only exacerbate the current models' sustainability capabilities.

Money will continue going where it finds growth possibility, preferring the shortest and easiest route and the one of least resistance and complexity.

Evolution came about when the limits posed by a model were no longer sustainable. They acted as impediments to growth, giving way to a new mechanism that was globally recognized and, in turn, gave way to the existing legacy or hybrid model.

But this is not all. Today's economy unequivocally relies on trust in the system, together with its fundamental "governance frameworks" (e.g., policies, laws, norms, rules), more so than it has probably ever needed to.

Imagine the legacy economy as any object delimited by a set of dimensions—a square, rectangle, octagon, etc.—anything with a length, width, and height, set within a definable shape (as with the square below).

Legacy Economy

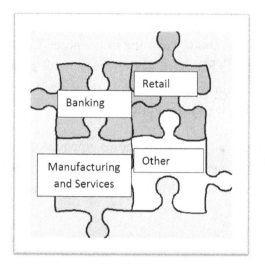

Then imagine that the rules governing this area have been tailored to a similar length, width, etc., covering the underlying legacy economy. Each time a new area formed in the economy, a patch was added to it (see below diagram).

Legacy Economy with Overlay of Legacy Governance Framework

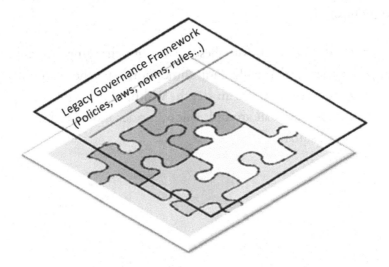

As time progressed, adjustments were made to the rules (governance framework) to fit the growing size and complexity of the underlying legacy economy (the square). The two dimensions grew mostly hand in hand.

Now imagine the increasing number of changes (paradigm-changing variables) that the world has experienced just in the recent two decades, adding new dimensions to this model and its needed governance framework.

The invention of computers, wireless communications, digital communications, and network-centric communities, the production of services shifting away from industrialized nations to growing economies, streamlining of processes, revision of human organizations, the growth in concerns over sustainability, exponential growth in population and immigration, not to mention the effects of the Web on the traditional brick-and-mortar business, the inclusive nature of the Web and technology, the invention of more recent technology such as the fusion of the Internet with mobility, nanotechnology, and all the other recent technological advancements are already substantially modifying the way we live, communicate, work, interact, and do business.

Now imagine each of these paradigm-changing variables as non-geometrically definable multidimensional patches not only on the horizontal axis but also in depth, width, and height, occupying new amorphous areas all around, below, inside, above, and in tangent to the original square.

Intermediate Hybrid Economic Model with the Effect of Overlay of New Paradigms, Variables, etc.

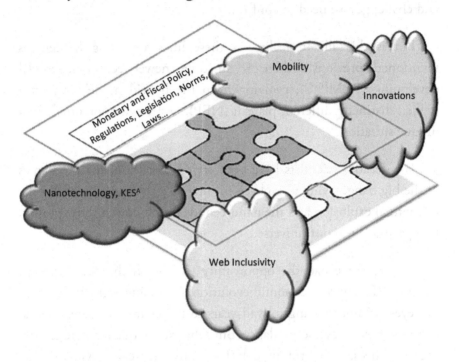

We have de facto created a new reference model for the economy, one substantially different from our legacy model, the one we have habituated for centuries.

To be fair it is easy not to see it. Some fail to recognize it because they are fixated on the legacy model, while others might perceive its existence but, given the myriad of new variables and paradigms, either tend to force the new variables within known boxes or might simply shy away from visualizing the general picture.

Independent of the reasons why it is not easily visible this scenario provides a new perspective from which to develop a starting point.

Taking a step back, we start noticing how the systemic dichotomies being created will only increase the level of complexity and challenges we need to confront.

But is this all? In reality, as these lines are being written, as mentioned previously there is an even newer economic model developing (BEM^{HESD}), evolving from the hybrid model, but on a higher, distinctly different plateau (NEP), and we are potentially in a unique situation.

For decades scientists have been trying to fathom the mechanics of the big bang, trying to go back in time to reach the moment of the primordial explosion and the nanoseconds that followed the explosion that gave birth to our universe.

It is as if we had the opportunity to witness the occurrence of this big bang in an economic evolution, occurring right in front of our eyes, without having to wait years to understand its fundamental components in reverse modality. But what we witnessed here is only the intermediate hybrid model. It is not the real newly forming economic model.

We might, in fact, be in the presence of the nascence of "Evolutionary Development and Prosperity Genomics," as a new economic science for the new evolutionary economic model that is being generated (BEM^{HESD}).

Virtus—The Newly Forming Value-Based Baseline Evolutionary Economic Model: BEM^{HESD}

The name chosen for this model is the Value-Based Baseline Evolutionary Economic (Prosperity) model (BEM^{HESD}) or for simplicity Virtus as will be explained later.

- It is newly forming because it is at the beginning of its development, evolving away from the hybrid model on a higher, distinctly different plateau.

- It is "value-based" because it moves away from a cost-focused paradigm of existing models. The primary objective of the evolved model is to create value continuously, be it in the form of investments, business, employment, sustainability, etc.

  - "Value" forms the DNA, quintessential traits of the evolved model (BEM), and it is expressed within the superscript letters ^{HESD} (introduced below—please note that the superscript letters are not to be taken as a mathematical formula or expression but merely to denote the DNA makeup of the new model).

- It is baseline because it provides the underlying framework for future models. This framework is open, modular, and scalable.

- It is evolutionary because it is not meant to be static. It will be a model that continually evolves dynamically. Any model henceforth must be able to leverage new opportunities and to face, address, and master new variables, paradigms, and challenges.

- I have used only one letter, "E," in the BEM acronym to represent both words that begin with the same letter ("Evolutionary" and "Economic"). I have opted to use the same technique for successive acronyms to avoid excessively long acronyms. Later on we will notice that we might wish to change the name of "Economic Model" to fit a more appropriate definition, one that could be connotative of long-term development, well-being, and prosperity, a new level of civilization (i.e. Prosperity).

- The superscript letters "HESD" enclose the models' fundamental characteristics or DNA properties/traits. The acronym is made up of the letters representing the initial DNA, fundamental characteristics, traits, and properties of the BEM. All elements inserted into the new model must be able to contain the same DNA (i.e., creating "Value" to guarantee long-term development and prosperity).

In other words, in order to find answers to new variables and challenges, be able to come out of the recession, create long-term economic traction, and be able to step up to a new plateau of development, the model must create value (e.g., investment, business, or employment opportunities). This means that each globule, element, component, and subcomponent of BEM will need to produce/yield one or more of the following (HESD):

- **H**uman centricity (putting mankind at the center), **H**olistic (not focused on just single aspects or dimensions), etc.;

- **E**volutionary (being able to continuously evolve in a positive way), **E**nterprising (promoting and creating a premise for generation of advancement, ideas, definitions, processes, modalities, means, levers, etc.), **E**conomy generation (fostering initiatives that keep it producing positive results, value, equilibrium, etc.), Education (long-term knowledge enhancement, etc.);

■ Sustainability (finding viable solutions to the limitations set by our planet), Security, Stability, Survivability of ecosystems, Strategic inclusive Survivability (i.e., eye toward the future, natural disaster protection, space exploration and exploitation) Strategy, etc.;

■ Dynamicity and a focus on Development of opportunities, long-term prosperity, and well-being (such as virtuous cycles of innovation, investment and business opportunities, paradigm-changing strategic mega projects), etc.

Now that we have established a starting point, we will introduce the fundamental building blocks from which one could elaborate the concept further (note that each letter forming the ^HESD acronym is not limited to the few descriptions or traits thus far outlined, as these provide only examples).

As it will be clear later, these in reality include other traits that have not been mentioned, for reasons of brevity, and those traits that need to be added by experts from different fields (i.e., those that might form the evolutionary "Transition Task Force" or any other organization that might be elected to perform an eventual transition. This concept will be elaborated in the next chapters).

WHAT DOES THE BEM^HESD LOOK LIKE?

Virtus or BEM^HESD—the newly forming Value-Based Baseline Evolutionary (Prosperity) Economic Model—forms the first version of a continuously evolving model. As it evolves into newer versions (EPM^HESDX: Evolutionary Prosperity Model, as it is no longer baseline), it will be more and more amorphous, multidimensional, and dynamic. It will continuously mutate into new forms as it is faced with new challenges.

The following is not fully representative of how BEM^HESD might look today or in the future. It is impossible to portray all the globules, components, and dimensions of the evolved model on a two-dimensional page. The following drawing has been provided only to simplify its initial understanding.

Virtus (BEM^HESD)

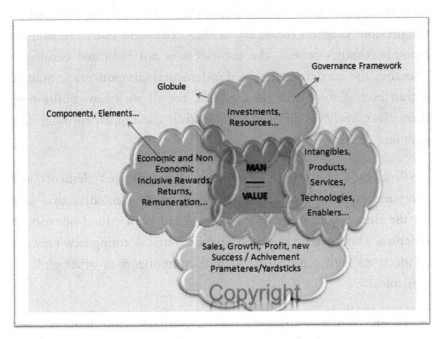

Key characteristic of the newly forming BEM^HESD:

Given the challenges, an evolved model must be dynamic if it is to remain successful. Provided this particular feature, a depiction of it would also be impossible, because, as in a movie, the emphasis is not on a single frame.

What is important here is the fact that nothing in the evolved model is static. Each variable entering the evolved model must have the same DNA.

Nothing impedes the addition of others globules or their intersection, interaction, convergence, separation, deletion, reductions, additions, and transformations. These will occur, be included, or be shaped, as deemed necessary.

Provided its dynamic nature, one should not become fixated on the titles or localization of components and elements depicted in the previous diagram (these are neither exhaustive nor complete, for example, though central, the ecosystem is not indicated because it underlies the model, etc.). The fundamental components contained within each globule will change, and, for all we know, positioning themselves freely in different areas within the model, forming new globules, deleting others, etc.

A globule refers to a temporary aggregation of elements and components (temporary aggregation of single elements) that join for the time required and can be connected via a virtual network of synapses. These can be activated or deactivated, forming new network connections with other elements and components in other globules dynamically.

Being multidimensional, the relations, interactions, and positioning of each element contained within each globule will also be prone to constant evolution, transformation, and change, moving progressively away from the sequential nature of the current models.

The globules forming the model could be imagined as permeable. Their elements can easily mix with others and create new components and networks and synapses pertaining to other globules as things evolve, creating the base for an incalculable number of new perspective, possibilities, and opportunities in all sectors and professional spheres. If applied correctly, the domino effect on the economy could be geometric.

For example, a globule could bring all elements used in providing measuring tools and performance yardsticks for the BEM[HESD] or its future versions, EPM[HESDX], under the same umbrella. These components could include components, such as return on investment net income, return on sales, and other key performance indicators.

Each of these, in turn, could create synapses with other globules, components, elements, etc., outside of its own, as required. In the previous example (the globule of measurement yardsticks) could create inter-connections with other globules such as that of Jobs, creating new currently unimaginable remuneration criteria.

Any element can also be contemporaneously part of different virtual globules. A globule's length of existence depends on its utility and value creation capability.

All in all, the only constants of the newly forming evolutionary economic model BEM^{HESD} are value creation, versatility, transformability, and evolutionary capability. In essence they are all focused on the centrality of man, sustainability and the preservation of ecosystems and habitats.

This means that each element making up the BEM^{HESD} in the future must provide the above characteristics, which are vital to the continued success of the economy, our lasting well-being, prosperity, and survivability of evolving civilizations/societies/ ecosystems with a time horizon to cover surely the short term, ideally at least the living generations and possibly the immediately successive one each time it is revised.

The evolutionary step between our legacy or hybrid model and the BEM^{HESD} is so marked that it is highly probable that we might need new terminology to replace the word "economy" with something that is more linked to "long-term prosperity, well-being, and advancing our civilization to a new level."

The word "economy," in fact, in many languages still denotes an ancestral legacy to the concept of scarcity. This is in no way meant to imply that we should lose sight of sustainability or depletion of resources. Quite the contrary, it is how to best manage sustainability going forward in producing greater prosperity.

The models in use today (legacy or hybrid) cannot match the dynamically changing shape or nature of the global BEM^{HESD}, especially as it continues to evolve in unpredictable ways. Current remedies or stimuli that work along dated or totally different assumptions, configured around a completely different set of paradigms, cannot be effective in providing lasting solutions.

OPTIONS

What options does this leave us with? How will we be able to address the new form the global economy has taken and will continue to evolve into? In this scenario we are possibly left with the following set of primary alternatives:

1. Ignore the existence of a newly forming reference model. Continue as is;

2. Acknowledge the existence of a newly forming baseline evolutionary economic model, BEM^{HESD}, but continue addressing issues with current (i.e., legacy/hybrid) policies, tools, and remedies (e.g., austerity, indebtedness, increased taxes);

3. Take drastic action. Force the BEM^{HESD}, new paradigms, and variables to conform to the previous framework, intervening with a set of radical approaches to shape the multidimensional amorphous evolutionary model back into its primordial legacy form (i.e., the square), potentially increasing exposure to drastic, extreme, or unwanted outcomes. In many ways is this not what we are currently doing through some of our current remedies?;

4. Alternatively, tackle the issue from a totally different perspective, allowing us to master the BEM^{HESD}, leveraging potential new windows of possibilities with which these new frontiers could provide us.

Should the first three options not bring desired results, choosing the last alternative (i.e., taking the issue from a different perspective) implies first having answered the set of very important questions:

- Can we do away with the current advancements (in all fields)?
- Can we afford to, or do we wish to, go back?
- Are current remedies providing solutions?
- Can legacy and hybrid reference models provide answers for the future?
- Does it make sense to force existing models to achieve what they can no longer reasonably accomplish?

The winning alternative might reside in choosing a different strategy, one with a greater potential for success in the long run. Viewing the challenges we face from an evolved perspective allows us to drive the BEM^{HESD}, harnessing the potential for new perspectives that are invisible to us today because they currently reside on the higher plateau.

This is the real shift in the paradigm, potentially one similar to the one witnessed by mankind when transitioning from the barter system to the currency-based system.

However, this approach is not sufficient, because if we fail to provide this strategy with an inbuilt equally dynamic and evolving governance framework—as human needs and the economy evolve, we quickly will lose control over the outcomes—we will be in a similar position as we are today.

If left alone (as we are doing today), the BEM^{HESD} will be driven by unknown forces rather than be governed (this word has nothing to do with the free-market concept or its inverse).

In other words, if we fail to govern the new ship—steer it, hoist or lower the sails, and man the rudder—we will lose all control over our destination! Moreover, *if we don't do it, someone else will by filling that void!*

Evolution is the real challenge. This is what we are truly up against. An evolved model is what is required to master if we want to find solutions!

Just as we had a framework of policies, laws, rules, regulations, and norms that govern the current (legacy or hybrid) models, we need an analogous framework for the newly forming evolutionary model, one that has the same DNA of the evolved model. An evolutionary governance framework that can address the BEM^{HESD} is one that addresses the constantly changing variables.

If handled correctly overall, this situation could possibly turn out to be a chance for this and future generations to undertake the next evolutionary step—permitting ourselves to focus on those aspects of our lives that really matter and providing new unfathomable possibilities in terms of business, investments, and personal and professional achievements.

A step-level evolutionary change similar to the one man faced when he decided the winning strategy was no longer a nomadic one but that of the creation of communities led to a totally new economic and sustainability model that has lasted over the last centuries.

In some form, this new scenario could provide mankind with new means to liberate it from impediments (technological or otherwise) that have hindered man from being able to go beyond current limits in pursuing material aspirations in business or professional realms and allowing enrichment in nonmaterial spheres (i.e., relational, intellectual, or even spiritual), realizing personal life projects, opening new possibilities unforeseeable till today.

Performance/achievement metrics that made sense till today, such as growth or profitability, might no longer be the sole measure of success or failure of human initiatives. They might be augmented by a myriad of other more valuable dynamically changing metrics.

More properties might be added in the future as needs and requirements evolve. As future evolutionary models evolve, these will give way to different versions, namely evolutionary prosperity models that might also require transformations in terms of their DNA (EPM^{HESDX}, where the P stands for prosperity and X for other value-generating properties that might be added in the future).

To assure effectiveness, each new variable that becomes part of the BEM^{HESD} and its successive versions (EPM^{HESDX}) must be "tested" for its DNA traits. Those traits that match can easily contribute to the enhancement of the model. Traits that do not provide immediate value to the model can be considered for transformation, temporarily frozen until they become of value, or become a new DNA trait. The subject matter will be elaborated further on.

Imagine the new variables being introduced (through a new technological advancement), which should be tested to verify their contribution to the following areas:

Business and investment opportunities: if we are to find long-term opportunities, the answer lies in adopting those that (for example):

- put mankind at its core and address issues holistically (H);
- allow room for evolution to promote an environment that increases opportunities for investments (E);
- are sustainable; contribute stability, security, and growth of markets (not just financial); and have a positive effect on inclusive survivability of ecosystems that become a source of business possibilities that till

today were not economically attractive in a virtuous cycle (S); and

- allow dynamics and focus on long-term development of new opportunities, prosperity, and well-being, fostering innovation (D).

Employment: if we are to find long-term solutions to this issue, the answer lies in adopting those options that (for example):

- put mankind at its core (H);
- allow room for evolution to be able to provide new forms of evolving opportunities and remunerated continuous knowledge enhancement (E);
- are sustainable and contribute stability and security (S); and
- allow dynamics and focus on long-term development of new opportunities, prosperity, and well-being (D).

And so on for public debt, etc. If done properly it is not hard to see the multiplier effect this will have in the long-term development, prosperity, and well-being model (economy). We will elaborate on these concepts further on.

HOW ARE WE IMPACTED?

So what does this mean to anyone? How will this affect our lives? In reality, the questions should be posed the other way around, as the model is already here and evolving. The real question becomes: how can we best leverage the naturally forming evolutionary model to improve our lives, businesses, employment, investments, remuneration, opportunities, and possibilities sustainably?

Now that we have a notion of the newly forming BEM^{HESD}, we can probably better perceive its existence all around us. Continuing on the path of avoiding its existence is possible, but this might mean having to endorse the continuous onslaught of thousands of businesses shutting down every day while others delocalize in the hope of survival. In the process, we'll sacrifice any leftover economic, political, and technological leadership, know-how, employment, research, development, and possibly independence.

MIGRATING UP TO A NEW LONG-TERM DEVELOPMENT PLATEAU THROUGH BEM^{HESD}

The best way to explain this concept is by learning from the past. Mankind made a step-level evolutionary improvement when he evolved from the hunter/gatherer model to the food maker model as a new set of needs emerged.

In taking this step, they found themselves on a new socioeconomic plateau of opportunities and civilization that were previously unfathomable. As they did, additional new ideas took form because of this step-level evolutionary transition.

New needs gave way to the adoption of a new model. New needs arose that led to even newer requirements, which in turn fed continuous cycles of new opportunities and necessities. The step-level evolutionary migration to a food maker model gave way to new requirements to organize a first nucleus of early society, with completely new roles and specializations: farmer, herdsmen, food and material processing experts, etc.

Soon new food storage requirements, and those stemming from urban growth in the early villages, gave way to new housing needs (e.g., brick dwellings rather than tent dwellings) and, with it, new building and storage techniques that provided sturdiness and adequate protection that led to the first baked mud brick production, which led to new specialized professions (e.g., brick makers, construction workers).

New step-level evolutionary plateaus would be reached as these first human agglomerations evolved into the first city-states (e.g., Sumer, Ur, Jericho, Thebes), *opening the way for a totally new set of specializations, processes, organizations, opportunities, and socioeconomic realities that would have remained hidden had there not been a need that led to a new evolutionary step.*

The following are a few new elements made available by the newer plateaus:

- The first rudimentary city planning, agricultural, and infrastructure projects

  - More complex irrigation, dikes, dams, canals, waterways, under-earth water transport systems to guard against evaporation, port facilities, and embankments
  - More evolved urbanization concepts, roads, paving, first rudimentary resting stations (caravanserais), etc.

- New farming and herding techniques to increase production
- New tools from managing/casting/molding
- New materials (e.g., steel, copper, silk)
- New transportation requirements/means for trade
- Social organization of city-states and the rise of the first professional services required for:

  - Organizing, direction, regulation, policing, defense, discipline, religious activities, schooling, etc.

- Official social rankings, systems and processes

  - The rise of the first experts/professions (e.g., architects, doctors, scribes, artisans, merchants, soldiers, judges)
  - Taxation that allowed for the above to be financed

- Record keeping (e.g., commercial, judiciary)
- The birth of intellectual, cultural, and artistic specializations (e.g., sciences, music, literature, etc.)
- The birth of schools and formal training facilities
- Remuneration criteria, wages, salaries etc.

- New mercantile/business plateau (in addition to evolving the above)

  - Trade
  - Coinage/legal tender/money
  - Rules, laws, norms, charters
  - Exchange systems
  - Measuring and weighing systems
  - Ownership/legal rights/contracts/terms
  - Lending and financing
  - Payment facilities (rudimentary letters of credit)
  - Enforcement (within and inter/intra city-states)
  - Protection (e.g., goods in transit, contractual, military)
  - Transportation costs and services
  - Central government coordination services.

Imagine how many new, previously unimaginable, requirements, products, processes, services and opportunities this translated into each time a new plateau was reached.

Today we are again in front of a new step-level evolutionary transition and the resulting new plateau of opportunity for business, investments, and employment (that I have termed "life projects"), the likes of which are unprecedented given the incredible leaps technology and innovation have provided us with. Seen now from this new perspective, imagine how many opportunities this might open up.

Different from any other time in the past, the evolved plateau will no longer be two-dimensional but multidimensional, similar to the agglomeration of all the globules it contains—hence, a BEM^{HESD} globule mass, the hidden potential geometric.

Internet exploitation for business purposes was not really achievable till recently. The requirement for the new evolved model for the step-level evolutionary migration toward the new economic plateau could not be appreciated until today.

Today's economy is shackled down by the limits and systemic dichotomies and blocks of the current legacy and hybrid models—underperforming in terms of leverage capability of potential opportunities.

The sooner we are able to lead the evolutionary transition and make the evolutionary passage to the next plateau of economic advancement and civilization, the sooner we will be able to come out of the systemic block and begin a new chapter in human advancement, long-term sustainable prosperity, and well-being, freeing currently blocked potential.

Just as the number of new opportunities brought about by migrating to a new plateau was unimaginable before each new step-level change in history, the same is true here. Yet there is one yardstick we can use to measure a few possible opportunities lying just beyond the horizon.

Though there are many ideas in this direction, they would be a representation of only my ideas. Successful design is the result of the contribution of many, so the following provide only intellectual teasers and hints:

- The fluidity offered by BEM^{HESD} will potentially allow moving toward relationships among elements and globules in the evolved model, impossible in current models

- Networks and synapses can be established dynamically, giving way to possibilities and opportunities thus far not imaginable or achievable through the legacy and hybrid models.

- The number of innovations in each field (e.g., biology, chemistry, nanotechnology, mocynet [mobile, cyber, Internet], medicine, communication, transportation) is incredibly numerous.

Now factor some of these into the algorithm of obtainable opportunities crisscrossed with possible uses and applications. How many new possibilities can one potentially envisage?

Our current impelling needs to find solutions in reviving the economy should foster the awareness and the challenge to evolve to the next step. Accepting this means being able to be equally open-minded in developing, imagining, and generating evolved:

- definitions, descriptions, meanings, parameters, conversion indexes, etc.;
- avenues, means, activities, modalities, requirements, needs, etc.;
- business possibilities, enterprise models, levels of interaction, forms of entrepreneurship, investments, trade possibilities, etc.;
- employability, professionalism, expertise, new roles unimaginable till today, etc.;
- organizations, networks, communications, etc.;
- time management, availability, free time usage, etc.;
- long-term knowledge progression and enrichment, evolved education systems, and organizations fit to cater to new needs, etc.;
- accounting, accountability, measurement, performance yardsticks, etc.;
- attributing value (i.e., assigning value to human contribution, new forms of involvement, etc.);

- remuneration, awarding, recognizing, motivating, prizing, promoting, valuing;
- perceiving, organizing, modeling, conceptualizing, producing, elaborating, providing, servicing; and
- evolved governance frameworks, controls, management, enforcement, audit, etc.

Now factor these into the equation to extrapolate potential new opportunities through new synapses with other globules, components, etc. We might be just looking at the tip of the iceberg.

Many facets of our lives have already changed dramatically, while others will modify and impact new areas. They all contribute to the paradigm-changing event that is seeking to break away from the chains of the current legacy/hybrid models and be free to move in the natural reference model (BEM^{HESD})—today and more so as we progress in time, allowing mankind to achieve even greater feats in the long run, most of which might be beyond our comprehension today.

The following are no longer going to be the same in the immediate future (some already are not, and if they are it is because they are strapped in place and blocked by the current legacy/hybrid models). The following samples are pressing to evolve to a new plateau:

- organizations
- employment, jobs, and work
- business and entrepreneurial models and opportunities
- availability and time management
- education, long-term advancement, and personal enrichment
- retirement and pensions
- banking, financing, investments, and markets
- retail, manufacturing, and services
- taxation

- remuneration, valuation, and recognition
- accounting and accountability.

If one were also to factor into the equation the evolved versions of the above, the interconnection possibilities become more apparent. It's easy to get excited by the potential likelihoods of new opportunities, but we need to be able to recognize and *filter out those that are viable and sustainable and set aside false positives* (until they may become viable provided the right conditions).

We need to be cognizant that identification of all true new opportunities might not be visible at the same time. Some will come before others, some might lead to new variables to provide value, etc.

We need to appreciate that it will be a step-by-step process, and we must comprehend that migration toward the new evolutionary plateau might take effect in different sectors more rapidly than others, due to things such as domino and spillover effects.

We, however, should note that once this process is begun, the effects might be immediate and the general impact on recovery more rapid than we might think. Equally true is that the preparation work is but the first module of an ongoing evolutionary project, and this part can be achieved as fast or as slow as we wish it to happen.

We also must understand these might produce a new cycle of evolved needs, requirements, and challenges to be addressed, which might emerge in parallel.

The most important discourse here is not with how many elements the migration toward the new evolutionary plateau starts out with, but the fact that it has actually begun, independent of our will. How do we wish to address them, leverage them, and start the road to real recovery?

FUNDAMENTAL MILESTONES AND PREMISES

Starting the right way is a key success factor. Hence, prioritizing which elements among those constituting the current legacy/hybrid economic model might need to be transitioned first becomes very important. In other words, deciding which among the elements analyzed in this book (and they represent only a portion), such as public debt, monetary policy, taxation, investments, pensions, and retirement, should be among the first to evolve to their natural reference model (BEM^{HESD}) is a key success factor.

Once this prioritization is achieved, how to go about this migration is another variable that needs to be resolved. In order for each element to transition into the new model and be able to produce sustained development and prosperity and position itself to the new plateau, it should acquire the DNA of the evolved model.

THE ALPHA-E PROTOCOL (BETA VERSION)

Unless we do not wish to lose steering capability in order to facilitate this evolution toward a new plateau, a protocol had to be devised to allow this—namely, the Alpha-e Protocol. Alpha is the first letter in most alphabets and symbolizes the beginning, and "e" symbolizes the evolutionary nature of the protocol. Given the introductory nature of this book, only two sample tools of this protocol have been provided.

Apart from facilitative tools useful in the migration and transition processes, the Alpha-e Protocol deals with aspects such as organization, processes, levers, and in general what is needed to facilitate evolution to the next step.

This is why leadership is so important, as it will set the first set of new parameters and definitions of the evolved components.

Some Tools: Evolutionary Conversion Process (ECP)

In order to allow a smooth transition, it is important to understand how innovations will continue to transform our lives, our investment and business models, employment, processes, etc. What are the implications, and what do the resulting elements and relative frameworks look like whilst they continue evolving? The diagram below provides a simple picture of such a process.

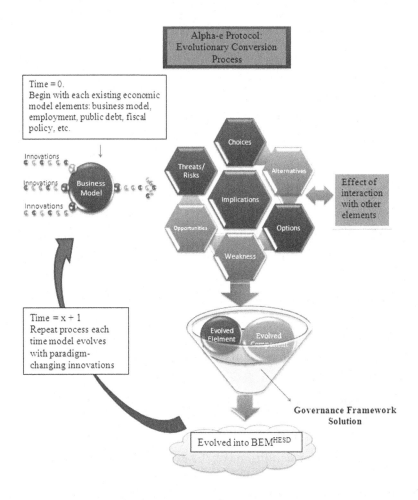

In the preceding example, if a paradigm-changing innovation, one that substantially changes the way things are done at any moment in time, is transforming a particular business model, we must ask ourselves what implication this might have on business opportunity and investment generation, business processes enhancement, intrinsic value, employment, remuneration, new skill sets, public debt and its financing (taxes), social security, pensions, etc.—in general its "value creation capability."

At each turn, we need to ask if the existing model is able to address these issues effectively and appropriately. What are viable alternatives, solutions, etc.? To what degree are these capable of resolving issues? And if these solutions, for example, produce development of new opportunities also in other areas, what evolved governance frameworks might they require?

Once the above answers have been identified, appropriate tools covered in later chapters can be used to migrate elements to leverage their opportunity generation capability.

How Do We Get There?

It has taken us years since the beginning of the near systemic crash and the titanic effort of innumerous many, yet we are objectively still very far away from any structural recovery. The migratory processes that will come about independent of our will can take a shorter or longer time frame than the one we already faced and continue to face for an unquantifiable time frame. It is totally up to us to decide when we wish to start this process (even in parallel with what has already been done) and how fast we wish to achieve lasting economic traction and revival.

Any successful human feat foresees good planning, optimal preparation, and mastery in execution, together with agility, motivation, drive, desire to achieve, focus, and ability to improvise when necessary to overcome unforeseen situations, working in unison toward a common goal. But more importantly, it requires leadership and strategic vision.

Sailing toward distant lands requires advanced planning, plotting and updating your course, sailing your way through nautical miles of different types of weather and sea conditions, mastering the elements, motivating a crew, and maintaining the ship in shipshape form.

This is not about taking on an haphazard, improvised, or extremist set of actions, but embarking on an evolutionary transition/migration, a progression toward continuously improving upon what we have. It is an evolutionary road map, which is a by-product of our own actions from continuous innovations, advancements, and progress in all fields of human endeavor. This step-by-step approach does not mean that we should not set challenging goals and objectives or have reasonably high expectations in seeing substantial benefits in acceptable time frames.

If we seek ultimate success and accomplishment, we need to approach this migration in the correct manner. But this should not necessarily require un-pragmatic time frames, because implementation is a matter of how much we are incentivized to bring about recovery how much priority is given to it, and how many resources are put behind it.

An immediate win benefit could be derived just from the mere news of a new model, spurring an initial revitalization of economic activity, recovery, and renewed trust of markets, investors, shareholders, entrepreneurs, and businesspeople across the globe. The positive economic value of just this could trigger an economic jump start worth millions of dollars across the globe.

Would we rather wait and see how this economic impasse will affect us all on a planetary scale? Or do we wish to start a new chapter in human evolution, one about leveraging the economic model in such a way that it does not hamper our well-being as persons and as a society and that of the sole planet we live on.

As it was for our fathers and forefathers, our future is linked to the liberty and possibility in realizing our dreams and to the invention of new ideas geared toward our well-being. So what are the steps we need to undertake to achieve the shift toward the adoption of the new reference model?

First Step: Recognition of the Problem Transforming the Concept into Action

Recognizing a problem entails acknowledging its existence, impact, effects, potential hazards, options, and ultimately a willingness to evolve if the problem is to be resolved. The effectiveness of this first step and those that follow requires the right mix of statesmanship, leadership, resolve, determination, resilience, strategic vision, and a balancing counterweight to generate equilibrium.

It is not the first time accepted certainties impeded any human organization from looking beyond the unquestionable, coming out of the quagmire. Unquantifiable amounts of effort, time, money, and even lives have been spent trying to answer questions that did not have answers until "sacred monsters" were removed from an equation, simply through a new viewpoint/vision allowing the focus to shift to a different perspective independently of the relative size of impact they might have had(e.g., Lee Iacocca, Jack Welch, Adam Smith, John Maynard Keynes, Galileo).

With the exclusion of natural elements provided to us by our planet, every element making the economy is man-made! And equally man-made are the solutions! Once concurrence is reached in recognizing the problem, it needs to be defined analytically along most of its different major dimensions (fortunately much of this work has already been done by many expert analysts in different fields, and it is a question of putting it all together). This entails:

1. Identification of key causes of each contributing variable to the crisis and domains effected by it;
2. The extent of damage by industries, sectors, business types, and individuals accumulated to date and the potential impact under different economic scenarios;
3. The solutions adopted thus far and results.

The better we define the problem, the better we are able to hone in on the key success factors later on. As the problem is acknowledged and defined, a picture starts to form. This picture will form the underlying framework for the steps that will follow.

Second Step: Action Needs to Be Taken by Key Stakeholders

Given recognition of the problem (the current economic crisis together with the resulting detailed analysis of causes and effects), the next step is concurring that action needs to be taken by key stakeholders.

As banal as it might sound, this is probably one of the most underestimated objectives human organizations fail to achieve.

Notwithstanding it is exactly the same type of effort that goes into international collaboration efforts such as G-20, G-7 Summits, and those efforts that went into the Bretton Woods agreement and the development of the post war system that we have today. Hence it is not about science fiction or utopic reasoning.

Without fully acknowledging that an action must be taken, any successive effort, energy, time, and money used in the initiation of the steps that follow will basically be wasted. Many projects end on dead tracks simply because of a lack of real commitment at the onset on behalf of the key stakeholders. A formal commitment is necessary from primary stakeholders. In this case we are dealing with an economic crisis of unprecedented dimensions that can pour its devastating effects on a planetary scale. A couple of analogies might be D-day or the Apollo program. Had there not been commitment and resoluteness in continuance in the face of seemingly insurmountable challenges, such unparalleled feats would have never been achieved

Consequently, nothing can be effectively done if there is a lack of commitment at the highest levels internationally within government and key international organizations. Pragmatism and realpolitik might be fundamental pre-requisites useful in this phase.

Some of the main phases that might need to be considered for this step are the following: an understanding between a nucleus of a few important countries affected by the crisis that have economic critical mass, and managing the gravitas and momentum that might generate growing membership after the first tangible results of the understanding are registered.

Independent of how many join in forming the first nucleus, the evolutionary steps will achieve a gravitational pull among major businesses, entrepreneurs, and citizens of other nations. At that point, the question might not be who else will join but it might instead focus on keeping a control on the pace. There will probably be a moment when a distinct scenario might develop, drawing a momentary line between those countries, regions, or businesses that lead the opening of the new era and those that stick to the legacy models and methods, inevitably losing many new possibilities in the meantime.

Joining in at the initial stages is not necessarily limited to a set type of economies only. Potentially the more challenges a country is facing, the more benefits it will derive from steps taken toward economic evolution.

Less fortunate economies also might be able to leverage new technological enablers, allowing them to jump over gaps that would have otherwise required substantial investments and years to accomplish.

This is not the first time such a challenge was affronted and resolved. As mentioned The Bretton Woods agreement and G-8's set a precedent.

Third and Fourth Steps

The third step is to agree on the generalities of the fundamental pillars of the new model. This step is the one probably needing the highest level of involvement and facilitation. It is the phase requiring the most strategic vision. This step requires evolving away from a boxed vision toward a new perspective in order to concur on the macro generalities of the fundamental genomes of the new model, because once these find a shared vision, the remaining steps become a consequence.

The fourth and successive repetitive sub-steps are needed to implement the governance framework and allow quick rollout and revitalization of the economy. Once the fundamental variables of the new evolutionary model have been agreed upon, the focus here will be on implementing the governance framework.

The simpler the framework model, the more flexible the solutions. The underlying key success factor will be the governance framework's ability to cover the contours of the continuously changing amorphous economic models' elements in symbiosis with it as it evolves dynamically.

It is, in other words, a matter of developing a framework that can dynamically evolve in unison with the new amorphous forms that current and future economies and needs might evolve into.

The success of these steps is dependent on many factors. Some of the more important ones among these include:

- the quality of professionals that are assigned to the implementation phases;
- the ability to deliver results;
- resources dedicated to the projects;
- sustained commitment form key stakeholders;
- division of the project in quick-win packets; and
- leverage of existing enablers.

This step will be affected by a natural learning curve that, once understood, can be easier to apply, repeat, and leverage to find ever newer opportunities.

If the preceding three steps are done correctly from the onset, the last step will be the one that might require more repetitions as models evolve to confront new challenges. This will also depend on how well we master new technological enablers to aid in this task and level of simplicity and flexibility.

Alpha-e Protocol: Organization

The previous section is a mere example of how the Alpha-e Protocol could be utilized with regard to processes. In this chapter we will introduce how this protocol could be used to organize and identify key players.

The protocol facilitates the definition of organizational aspect needed to address different phases; e.g.: constitution of national and international treaty committee and transition task forces, to arrive at the definition of the initial evolutionary treaty, initial baseline finalization, modular roll-out, and the successive cyclical evolutions of the prosperity model which can be relegated to either a new, nationally independent, modular and networked organization(s), both at national and international levels or, through existing organizations that will need to evolve to best meet and address ever newer and evolved needs and requirements.

To conclude the introduction of the Alpha-e Protocol, it could be suffice to say that it provides different possible alternative baseline frameworks for organizational aspects as well as others, such as, implementation and roll-out strategies. It is clear that these organizations will be constituted and work within the mandates that elected governments, leaders and parliaments (hence forth governing bodies) democratically bestow on them.

On a national level, for example, Alpha-e Protocol's general organization baseline foresees a scalable, networked, and modular structure of three distinct levels, forming an initial national and international Transition Treaty Committee and Task Force, each with distinct roles, professional requirements, responsibilities, and objectives there are several ways this can be achieved.

To facilitate evolution and dynamism of BEM^{HESD}, it could be that a new or evolved internationally networked organization that supports independent national organizations in each country promotes the continual evolution of the Prosperity Model EPM^{HESDX} to address new opportunities at an international level cyclically.

In short the Alpha-e Protocol in its current version is but a baseline framework. It will need the contribution of experts to agree and formally define organization, modalities, processes, milestones, roll-out time-frames, and objectives of each phase.

Ideally the operational Transition Task Force will be staffed by the best (most effective in delivering results) experts, scholars, economists, government officials, entrepreneurs, businesspersons, and high-level expert technicians, each though supported, as necessary, by a lean structure underneath to cover domains being treated in a particular phase, module, or milestone, program governance and steering.

Value is not generated necessarily by vast numbers of participants, but rather by quality, timely, and successful delivery of results.

Though all team members must have strategic vision, an indispensable professional trait of visionary team would surely be to think out of the box while remaining pragmatic. The visionary team refers to another concept pertaining to the Alpha-e protocol i.e.: the concept of a blue and white teams—object of further elaboration for the academic version of this book.

Fundamental Premises

The newly forming evolutionary economic model has underlying fundamental prerequisites built into its genomes, a premise that many times has been taken for granted and encompasses fundamental things, such as a context that provides a society and its individuals fundamental rights and freedoms, including those of free enterprise, movement of persons, ideas, and investments—as these form quintessential traits of the evolutionary concept.

The final "formal" configuration of the BEM^{HESD} of the initial and successive versions cannot but be the result of a collaborative work. In this version, this book cannot but henceforth limit itself to providing an introduction to the baseline framework and principles for the previously mentioned steps necessary to arrive at the full detailed solutions. The realization of any significant feat or project can only be accomplished through the contribution of numerous professionals from many walks of life.

As building a house needs the combined effort of many experts it is only reasonable that the creation of a viable solution to the worst economic crisis the world has faced requires the involvement of a number of well-valued leaders and professionals.

eVolve Migration Process (EMP)

This process is one of the possible tools pertaining to the Alpha-e Protocol.

In order to start leveraging the newly forming model and obtain results in relatively short time frames, activating economic recovery and successive sustainable longer-term development, existing elements should transition toward their evolved versions. In the following paragraphs, a few simplified examples will shed light on how this might be achieved.

The scope here is to take the variables of the existing legacy/hybrid models, starting with the most important, and migrate these toward their evolved versions to liberate them of their dichotomies and systemic blocks, allowing them to produce solutions and expected results. This can be achieved in several ways. One of these is through the use of a migration process, or the "eVolve Migration Process" (part of the Alpha-e Protocol).

To achieve the intended scope, existing legacy elements will need to be stripped of all their accumulated complexity, arriving at the fundamental building blocks of each.

For example, with reference to the fundamental elements making up the legacy/hybrid models, this starts by asking foundation-level questions for each of these elements and components: public debt, monetary policy, banking and financial systems, industry and services (e.g., travel, transportation, hotels, manufacturing, retail, construction, waste management, education), innovation (research and development), pensions and retirement, employment, health care, business enterprise, and strategic national sectors.

The final objective is to evolve the elements to generate "value" (elaborated later).

Specifically this means conducting a detailed analysis of each of the following elements:

Public Debt

- What is the current definition of public debt?
- What was its original purpose?
- How does it serve its primary objective today?
- Can this definition still be applied in the worst financial and economic crisis to date?
- Do the current models of incurring more debt to resolve indebtedness make sense anymore? Can they be used for the future? How well do they fit the newly forming evolutionary economic model?
- Are heavy austerity measures yielding any results? Or are they breaking the back of the remaining businesses, producing unnecessarily massive levels of unemployment?
- Will current models of public debt be able to address additional future challenges that are just around the corner (such as Internet inclusivity)?
- The current model is man-made. It was built based on assumptions that no longer hold true, and it is no longer providing the answers and the benefits it was intended to produce in the first place. Should we seek to build a different model?
- What needs will a new public debt model need to address in order to stimulate current and future development of the economy?
- What flexible and evolutionary model can be used to serve current and evolving needs?

Once each element (in this example, public debt) is analyzed in detail and the lowest common denominators identified, these are then evolved through HESD, providing them with value-generation capability and transforming them into value-creating elements and ultimately "value".

The following diagram describes how the Alpha-e Protocol's eVolve Migration Process or similar one might be used.

eVolve through HESD

LEGACY MODEL   eVolving to BEM^HESD

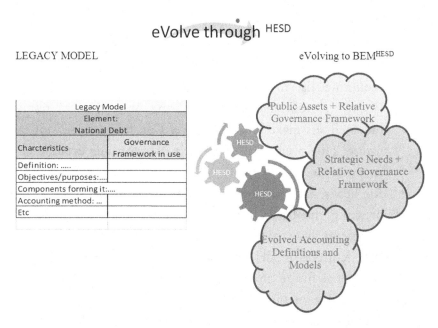

Legacy Model Element: National Debt	
Charcteristics	Governance Framework in use
Definition:	
Objectives/purposes:....	
Components forming it:....	
Accounting method: ...	
Etc	

As each legacy element is analyzed, it is evolved into BEM^HESD. Each acquires evolved definitions, accounting methods, requirements, etc. Evolved perspectives emerge, changing the way things can be organized, managed, and governed, potentially leading to a totally new set of opportunities and levers geared to confront the challenges of a continuously evolving and value-generating economy.

Taxes, Monetary Policy, and Money Creation

The fundamental elements must emerge clearly. Old "sacred monsters" need to be questioned and, if deemed no longer beneficial, evolved or simply scrapped if no longer necessary. We need to arrive at the essence of the issues and provide answers to hard questions that impede or hinder value generation.

We should not be afraid to ask questions that are being asked by a growing number of subject matter experts, policy makers, world leaders, and citizens. What is the true objective of current taxation models? Are they achieving their objectives and at what cost to the citizenry they serve? What tangible benefits do taxes provide its citizenry within the current model? What is the cumulated tax burden from all sources on individuals and business? Is this a reasonable amount?

What is the value of fiscal complexity? Does this complexity provide any benefit to the majority? Does it provide more tax revenues in return? What tangible purpose does it serve? If it is to provide new jobs for highly specialized professions, could there not be evolved models that can provide equally challenging tasks and many more new professional possibilities without necessarily achieving this through complexity?

Alternatively, can a model justify its mere existence on the pure theoretical assumption that complexity was made necessary to catch a limited minority, such as chronic tax evaders, because a small minority will continue evading taxes no matter the system in use? This in no way implicates that tax evaders should not be pursued. Is the current model serving its purpose effectively though? One needs to revert the perspective and evolve toward a system, for example, that allows positive contribution rather than taxation.

Will it be able to address the challenges of the financial and economic crisis? Will it be able to address the dynamic challenges of future economies that lie around the corner in a dynamic and flexible way, one based on simple models that allow fast and effective reaction times rather than complicated ones that impede and stagnate reactivity?

Are there no alternative models that can be created by man in the twenty-first century for today's needs? Is there not an evolved system from the one that is substantially based on the same basic principles and foundations accumulated over two thousand years of history?

This is not about promoting fiscal anarchy but about producing viable results with less complexity, more equity, greater opportunity, and far more benefits to the majority.

Jobs/Employment

Again, here we must strip everything down to its basic elements. We must be able to answer certain questions. What is the definition of a job? What are the fundamental elements of a job? Is it just for the money? For fun? Is it for passion? Motivation? Self-esteem? Fulfillment? Achievement? Sense of contribution or belonging? Professional and personal enrichment? Independence? Stability? Is it a base to create a future family? Is it for involvement and contribution to the community?

Do existing models produce growing employment opportunities? How about the currently evolving model of the economy with the new challenges? Are there solutions that address development of employment opportunities in the current crisis? What new forms are jobs taking and how are they evolving? What elements will most likely change? How will they change? Do we have a model that will address these challenges and turn them into opportunities? What is being done to address these issues? Will the future annihilate currently known jobs, or will it promote new opportunities? How?

The definition regarding jobs and the different dimensions making up a job will most likely evolve in both qualitative and quantitative terms. Tomorrow's jobs, for example, might evolve into other forms on a continuous basis, as evolution is an ongoing process.

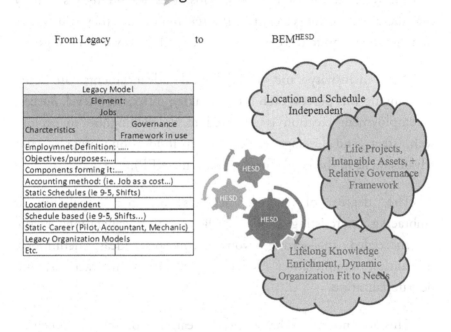

Work, Jobs, and Employment Virtualization: The Next Level

The history of employment is made of several step-level evolutionary changes and mutations, some of which were covered in previous chapters. Today, with all the technological advancements, the world faces yet another step-level evolution in these areas, another step toward further virtualization of work, jobs, and employment.

Data from different sources, such as the World Bank, specialized UN agencies, and national statistical offices of several nations, only confirm this trend, which in its current form is limited to the more service-oriented jobs, especially in developed economies. The data suggests that the more a country develops, the more persons move from agricultural to manufacturing to services. This process can take decades. Today's developed economies register a growing shift toward services that in some cases outweigh manufacturing and agriculture in terms of numbers. This does by no means convey that these will no longer exist in the future nor that they will be less remunerative—quite the contrary—it depends how you do things.

Web inclusivity and technological advancements are only speeding up this process even further, taking us to a new level. Success in employment creation is relegated to the willingness to exploit, seek, steer, and leverage evolutions in innovation, progress, and advancement in the newly forming plateau (NEP).

The degree of success depends on our capability in embracing or resisting similar challenges that generations before us succeeded in—seizing evolved concepts, ideas, definitions, modalities, remuneration models, organizations, interactions, and dematerialization.

This does not mean that we need to earn less or limit the potential to earn more. In more cases than not, if implemented correctly, evolution will be more skewed toward increasing the potential to earn more rather than less, as is the case of the last five years, should we stick to the legacy/hybrid models. Each step-level migration to a higher plateau in history has increased earning and well-being potential. In our current scenario our existing models are instead decreasing this potential.

Evolution will potentially open new windows on more opportunities: from tedious and repetitious to more challenging, from manual to less manual. It will invite more possibilities of breadth of movement into new professions. Employment concepts will evolve into what could be called different "life projects," rather than mere jobs. Evolution will possibly be more linked to one's passions rather than needs, potentially allowing individuals to benefit from additional sources of income otherwise precluded by today's models.

The embracement of new ideas also implies embracing new enablers, such as ideas that can be called personal and professional enrichment and/or knowledge enhancement, to leverage new opportunities as they emerge. This means an evolution of our education systems to provide lifelong support during different phases, adding leverage and new value to our capabilities.

Consequently, evolved remuneration models for these intermediary periods in which an individual develops or enhances capabilities to add "value" have to be devised, according to an evolved "value balance" concept described later, which will allow this. There are no free rides. Additionally, as will be evident later, this has nothing to do with any of the "isms" of actual or historic reality.

The objective is to find viable new solutions to the paradigm-changing factors we will face and for which new answers must be found! The following are just a few of these challenges/opportunities we might need to address:

- a transition away from static schedules (i.e., 9-5, shift-based) toward more time-independent jobs
- a shift towards quality augmentation and value generation rather than a set number of working hours
- a move from full-time involvement toward more dynamic use of time and available free time

- a shift away from location dependency or physical presence but with an equally important shift in maintaining and fostering human relations
- a shift away from physical intervention towards more value added activities, we need to factor in for example the impact of robotics, miniaturization, and automation manufacturing environments, as these will increase the tendency toward remote management, process supervision, on-site intervention from the nearest resource, etc.
- a transformation from static vertical careers (e.g., accountant, mechanic, miner, sales) to new forms of jobs or the possibility of more than one primary type of work experience (hence the evolution from "jobs" to "life projects") or the result of new synapses between new or previously silo careers.

This is why these factors need to be resolved through new models. The only viable answers today are basically more of the same—dated paradigms engraved in stone that have become unquestionable.

In order to find viable solutions, it is necessary to do a few things:

1. Be able to see things from evolved perspectives;
2. Work from an evolved plateau and leverage new opportunities not visible from the current perspective, leveraging new tools, options, frameworks, ideas, etc.;
3. Evaluate different interconnections with other elements.

Opening new avenues means opening the possibilities to many more ways of addressing existing challenges that, in turn, will be geared to produce solutions and the basis for additional opportunities. Hence, the jobs (life projects) of tomorrow depend on how fast we transition over to the next plateau. The job market, the interaction of one's profession with other spheres of one's life, might be based on evolved concepts and new ideas:

- a totally different balance between time dedicated to work and total available personal time from which to leverage
- a more dynamic use of time
- a different concept of long-term personal knowledge enrichment and capability augmentation, allowing one to access new life projects rather that static jobs, increasing possibilities toward leveraging one's innate capabilities and passions rather than "doing it because there is nothing else"
- remuneration modalities and criteria for personal knowledge enrichment and capability augmentation periods that are a prelude to others that create value
- an evolved approach toward virtual work environment no longer necessarily requiring physical proximity or presence but an evolved necessity in keeping, promoting and fostering real (non-virtual) human interaction
- a different approach to retirement, allowing natural turnover and rejuvenation (hence real prospects for young generations), while opening the road to new remunerated options available to those who choose to retire earlier
- an evolved approach toward formal education (from the earliest years through university and beyond which does not necessarily imply moving upwards but also sideways and diagonally) to effectively prepare new and existing generations to leverage the continued evolution of future models.

Being able to reconcile what is currently not reconcilable via current legacy/hybrid models and finally liberate blocked potential from current systemic inhibitors and irreconcilable differences allows us to step up to the evolved plateau of development to exploit new opportunities. But this also implies evolving the current system to a new level—one that offers added motivation and evolved teaching and learning techniques.

Technological enablers, for example, might allow persons to enrich themselves professionally in substantially different ways than today, not necessarily needing to build one's expert knowledge base but rather being able to appreciate a subject matter from a holistic point of view focused, that is, more on delivering value.

For instance, a lawyer today develops his/her skills over years of education that requires an overwhelming amount of human memory capability and an acute appreciation for semantics. As improved logic, or search-based algorithms, allows more accurate and automated responses to search queries, this allows a substantial shift toward more value-added areas of development for the forensic arena, in terms of both augmenting professionalism and opening new spheres of possibilities.

An airline mechanic will most likely be able to place more focus on the global quality and completeness of the maintenance project rather than closing the intervention in the least amount of time, for cost considerations, searching dated, patched tomes of system descriptions that might not have been updated or modified.

Remuneration must evolve to allow similar or equivalent final pay to start growing responsibilities, possibly bringing back the *evolved* notions of careers and seniority (when this is useful, motivated and adds value). If done well, the evolved model will work to improve this.

We might move from structured legacy-based organization models toward evolved dynamic models based more on professionalism and trust rather than hierarchical interactions—from jobs and employees seen and accounted for as costs toward an evolved view and accountability seen and perceived as value contributors and intangible assets.

How much time is spent on work might no longer be the real value associated with a job but the quality and value generated by the activity that will become the focus (which include respect of milestones and delivery time tables).

As each of these dimensions change, they will impact other elements, allowing those to evolve also. If carried out properly, there will be, for example, a progressive mutation in the search process from thousands sending beefed-up résumés to compete for a job to a growing number of persons being sought out for newer fields but who might be busy doing what they are passionate about rather than taking on the first thing that pays or having to endure the professional devaluation that comes with the existing hollow search process in an economy that no longer works or business environments/organizational models that no longer motivate.

Pensions and Retirement

In migrating to the new plateau, we need to answer the following questions for pensions and retirement:

What are the definitions of these words? Are they the demons they are portrayed to be? Has the demonization mantra of the last twenty years resolved anything or provided tangible answers?

What was their purpose? Do these institutions serve the purpose they were intended to serve originally? Are they adequate?

What purpose should they serve in the future? What purpose do we wish them to serve in the future? Our forefathers had the intelligence and the willingness to create these concepts from nothing. Why should we not be able to steer the evolution of these elements to achieve even better results? What benefits do they provide the individual and society?

Are current models fair to younger, aging, and retiring generations? Why should they not have the right to fair treatment? What benefits do they intend to provide? To what degree are they fulfilled? How are they funded? How could they be remunerated instead? Is there anything that would limit our imagination to think up a better model?

Are current retirement models any longer sustainable?

What could reasonable retirement parameters be, from the point of view of both society and the individual? What about pension funds? Do current models provide viable alternatives for the current demographic mix of the growing elderly population?

Do future models need to be one-size-fits-all models? Or can there be better models to serve different purposes and benefits for all stakeholders, retirees, pension funds, markets, and businesses?

What new model can best answer evolving needs, creating new opportunities for retirement while at the same time allowing younger generations to fill a positive natural turnover? Could not added possibilities potentially stimulate the development of new opportunities, ideas, investments, and enterprises? When can we get on with it? More importantly, how are needs and expectations of businesses, individuals, communities, and societies evolving? How can we benefit from these?

Do historically consolidated concepts still hold true? Do we need them necessarily to still hold true? Are we artificially forcing them into place? Does this create more costs than it does benefits? Should we let them go and free progress to take the economy forward? Would these not provide new sets of opportunities that would otherwise remain hidden?

Has an improvement in quality of life over history not created new opportunities? Why should we not take this opportunity to improve possibilities for all stakeholders?

So far we have only skimmed the surface of a few of the many new variables, trying to strip away from the legacy/hybrid models. We have the possibility of evolving these concepts to their next natural level of utilization and value creation.

From our currently limited perspective, we can only start to perceive a few of the potentially many new and evolved areas of opportunity, but today we can only see a blocked retirement/pension model filled with unfeasible contrasts that only contribute to exasperating the economic crisis.

As these fundamental elements are analyzed, transitioned, and evolved through the BEM^{HESD}, each evolved element will start providing many original areas for innovative prospects (e.g., business ventures, evolved pension funds, life projects, sustainability, and quality-of-life improvements).

As each new evolved element is put in relation to other elements, allowing them to interact, network, permeate, merge and influence each other, the number of new ideas that will form is incalculable at this stage. Potentially they could grow geometrically.

Each interaction could potentially produce new requirements, forming new opportunities. Take the example of the interaction of "life projects" (rather than jobs) with the evolved notions of the education system (i.e., knowledge enrichment enabler), pensions, and pension funds.

Just the need for more knowledge acquisition (formal and informal) in ever-growing numbers of personal advancement and development experiences pushes known thresholds (capabilities, business, investments, etc.) continuously further. And unlike the current objectively senseless remedy to push forward retirement age or reduce pensions that produce different types of negative fallouts in the current economic model, the number of potential opportunity synapses under the evolved model are at the very least an additional possibility worth exploiting.

Education, Knowledge, and Capability Enrichment

Consequently, future learning and personal enrichment needs will most probably push toward an evolving type of education, or what we could call knowledge and capability enrichment, most probably much different from the forms we are used to today. Putting the necessary value and importance back in the system. This will require evolution of both mainstream educational systems and the introduction of new concepts, paradigms, educational organizations, new types of expertise, hierarchies and networks creating a plethora of new opportunities at all levels within academia and bsuiensses directly or indirectly linked to their supply or end user chains.

This even from the initial formative years onward i.e., bringing back enriching human needs and experiences with the joy of infancy and childhood, time for natural play with other kids, experience nature, an attention to natural movement to increase central nervous system maturity, increased cognitive learning rather than by memory, allowing for different time frames for individual maturity, respecting a child's or adult's innate/individual attention span and capability, reducing unnecessary performance stress, unhealthy nonpar competition—different from positive motivation and productive competitiveness, identifying and levering individual potential and capabilities making available those assets and progression paths needed to allow maximization of potential.

Personal knowledge enrichment could potentially last over an individual's lifetime, inspiring each to experience other professions and arts (arts as originally intended in Latin to mean all areas of human knowledge). What it should be, is a migration towards an evolved notion; increasingly a willingness to improve one's capabilities rather than today's improvable concepts of study, homework and testing.

Remuneration is also an element that needs to be addressed for knowledge and capability enrichment to allow it to add value.

Closing Thoughts For The Section

The domino effect will occur naturally, since the work done will start at the lowest levels within each element, changing each paradigm from the inside out.

Finding viable answers is achieved by running these through the Alpha-e Protocol and agreeing on what is best for man and the economy and which option provides the most value, if we want to achieve lasting, long-term sustainable development of the economy, unleashing business and economic potential unfathomable till today.

In running future business opportunities, for example, just through HESD's human centricity or opportunity development traits, we will start seeing a number of opportunities that are completely out of our current vision, especially those that will be the result of a network of interactions with new elements. For example, if we run this also through sustainability or quality-of-life elements, more will emerge as it will become more apparent later.

The adoption of this system frees from latches, no longer requiring straightjacket models or forceful agreements or one-size-fits-all approaches (some quick wins may be achieved in some very high-impact areas in relatively short times).

As potential benefits emerge, buy-in will most likely ensue at a natural pace, gathering momentum. At the end of the day, one has to always bear in mind the current alternative. Do we allow ourselves to be affected, for example, by the "inclusivity concept" and the massive business and job losses and retirement system meltdown it entails, or do we master the new phenomena?

What is our true "Problem to Opportunity Transformation Rate Capability" as a society? In other words, to what degree have we been educated to see, analyze, discuss, waste time, drain money, and compalin over problems rather than focus on how to turn challenges into new ideas, opportunities, and benefits?

There is at least one new opportunity behind each challenge equipped with diametrically opposite positive energy. In the new model we are talking about one-to-many and many-to-many possible links. All voids in nature are filled! Our legacy models are no exception.

ADDITIONAL BEM^{HESD}: CONSIDERATIONS, PRINCIPLES, AND TRENDS

The following considerations, principles, and perceived trends need ample elaboration that go beyond the scope of this book. I will, however, provide the brief outline of the important ones below.

The newly forming baseline economic (prosperity) model, BEM^{HESD}, is a reality. It is already trying to form. It is the consequence of the growing innovations and advancements that have been made in the last decades and those that will continue to be developed.

The current legacy/hybrid economic model is not only facing systemic dichotomies but is being affected dramatically by progressions and novelties that substantially block it from being effective as a reference model.

The form of the BEM^{HESD} is growing constantly with greater numbers of variables.

Links with legacy/hybrid models are fading away to the extent that remedies, solutions, interactions, and cause-and-effect relations are creating growing systemic and structural inhibitors and dichotomies. In this scenario, remedies are proving ineffective and will not be able to fully produce desired outcomes in the long run.

Using remedies based on legacy/hybrid models in addressing any aspect of the BEM^{HESD} might ultimately yield a neutral, modest, undesired, or potentially virulent outcomes.

BEM^{HESD} and its successive version, EPM^{HESDX}, are composed of dynamically changing globules that encase a temporary aggregation of elements that join for the time required and can, upon necessity, connect via a virtual network of synapses. These synapses can be activated or deactivated, forming new connections with other elements and or components in other globules or even replicating without having to delete the previous globules.

The prolonged success of the BEM^{HESD} and its successive versions will depend on how close evolved elements introduced into the model will maintain the fundamental value-generating DNA characteristics (^{HESD}: sustainable . . .) of the model.

Elements of legacy/hybrid models that might still be useful must evolve in order to respond to new challenges and enable the development of new opportunities.

Value, evolution, centrality of man, sustainabilty, eco-systems, transformation, change, and adaptation are the only constants of the model. The BEM^{HESD} will continuously change its form and connotations, providing new opportunities focused on value creation providing the possibility to ascend and reach higher plateaus.

As with any element and component, performance yardsticks can be linked via virtual synapses with other globules and elements.

The BEM^{HESD} and EPM^{HESDX} will need an evolved governance framework (i.e., laws, policies, norms, protocols) to enable its proper management and steering.

The success of the BEM[HESD] governance framework will depend on how well it is able to permeate the model's fundamental components and traits, dynamically covering the model as it evolves and reshapes continuously modifying accordingly as requirements evolve.

This virtual membrane also provides a necessary balancing agent not only to the single elements and traits contained within the BEM[HESD] but also the whole, including the connective synapses.

The evolved governance framework will need to be modeled around the BEM[HESD] and will also require out-of-the-box thinking and implementation strategies.

Web inclusivity . . . and Internet consciousness can potentially pose risk and threat factors to long-term prosperity and preventive strategies, and evolved solutions must be developed to steer them beneficially.

Remuneration, money, investments, and financial interests will always move toward ideas, solutions, products, and services that will offer the best possible returns and least resistance to their inception and growth.

Value generation is key to continued future prosperity and development!

At least for the foreseeable future, innovations and advancements will continue to produce a transition from tangible to intangible, physical to virtual.

We are witnessing a new step-level transition to a new plateau of virtualization of uses, requirements (e.g., customer, employer, employee), businesses and business models, processes, modalities, activities, chores, means, techniques, and work routines.

The not-so-distant future will heavily impact, change, transform, and redefine business relations and interactions with

- customers, clients, suppliers, distributors, channels, shareholders, investors, management, employees, and unions;
- time-related matters (e.g., time schedules, shifts, working hours); available free time;
- physical work space needs and requirements, moving away from physical space and moving toward virtual connections;
- plant, equipment, and capital investment requirements; automation of processes, methods, activities, and chores; and
- professions, jobs, and employment; contractual terms; the concept of careers; remuneration and valuation, and measurement yardsticks.

The following might be depictive of a timeline that indicates this shift (the accuracy of the percentages or terminology is not as important as the introduction of the main points, notions and concepts):

Virtualization Timeline and the Adoption of Strategic Evaluative Measures to Assure Migration and Transition Toward BEM^{HESDX} and successive versions EPM^{HESDX}.

	Level of Virtualization (ie. of Jobs, Proccesses, Activities, ...)			
	0-30%	30-60%	Over 60%- 100%	Beyond 100%
1st batch of Migration Modules	Many processes still requiring human intervention	Tipping point as most processes evolve even futher requiring less and less human	Only residual levels requiring human intervention	Possibility for the introduction of new paradigm changing variables such (ie thought controlled atuomation)
Migration and implementations of major Evolved Elements using Alpha-e Protocol assuring adherence to Value Balance and HESD Generation according to	Towards HESD / Mostly HESD / HESD / HESDX			
Public Debt Monetary Policy Investments, Business Banking, Markets Pension and Retirement Employment Personal Knowldege Enhancement Fiscal Policy Etc.	→ → → → → → → → →			

The above table also indicates the first possible modules that might be considered to be migrated into ^{HESD} to create value by the governing bodies and Transition Task Force.

This is why taking on a leadership role is so fundamental in steering events from the onset rather than becoming mere followers and dependents.

A transition in this direction in so many fields requires finding solutions to best fit evolved needs and requirements, as investors, businesses, entrepreneurs, professionals, employees, and individuals in terms of new business opportunities, jobs, remuneration, and transitional periods needed to improve our knowledge and enrich our capabilities, allowing access to continuously evolving opportunities and providing a completely new paradigm for greater challenges in line with our evolving needs and aspirations.

The evolution of businesses, jobs, professions, and remunerated activities, etc., toward a new plateau suggests that solutions to these can be sought and found using the tools, models, and methods natural to that new plateau. Instead forcing legacy or hybrid models to find a lever will induce new structural/systemic complexity and blocks.

An evolved plateau for new investments, businesses, requirements, employment, jobs, etc., suggests the need for evolved types of governance frameworks and the other elements forming the macro- and microeconomic context (e.g., public debt, monetary policy, taxation, pensions, retirement) that generate value and that can truly address evolved needs and requirements of citizenry in a sustainable manner.

There is a need to find solutions that can address an unprecedented number of opportunities to enrich persons' lives, permitting the freedom to move from one personal life project to another based on one's capabilities and aspirations (e.g., from lawyer to tourism pilot, from professor to vintage car developer, from chef to TV producer) while allowing others to specialize even more than what is possible today (e.g., from optometrist to specialized eye nerve surgeon). But these titles will change as tomorrow's life projects take on totally different connotations.

There is already an evolution toward new perspectives whereby, for example, ideas, brands, concepts, human capability, designs, styles, models, processes, knowledge, know-how, talent, inventions, software, hardware, information, data and databases, and all sorts of other intangible assets will become more liquid and transformed into new types of merchandise that can be bought and sold in open markets.

Intangible assets are all those resources that do not have a physical connotation. If they do, it is what they develop virtually in terms of ideas, new ways, and models that these represent and are creating the base for new accounting models. These could form new sources of revenue and growth that could become part of an individual's remuneration, a company's balance sheets, or a state's GDP. Some of these intangible assets might even become resources on par with investments. Having said this many of the shortcomings of the current concepts that include among other things, current patenting processes, need to be addressed and resolved—and an evolved model may help in unleashing hidden potential.

Moreover we still have not addressed the "cost-driven" paradox our legacy/hybrid models are founded on—and which constitutes one the major systemic blocks to prolonged development. In this evolved scenario, it is highly likely that we will need to move away from resources that are accounted for as mere costs toward an evolved view and consideration of these as essential elements that add <u>value</u> and have an intrinsic value not only from an accounting point of view but also conceptually—to be even more exact—fundamentally and substantially beyond this—a true game-paradigm-changing shift. Applied correctly, this evolved perspective might bring a shift of unprecedented proportions in terms of business models, and opportunities and new forms of jobs, job creation, and investment possibilities.

AN EVOLVED CONCEPT OF "VALUE" AND "VALUE BALANCE"

We are already moving toward a scenario whereby resources, activities, processes, and in general intangibles are slowly moving toward new concepts of valuation and accountability. The imminent successive evolutionary step is that they might become more and more assets with real intrinsic value rather than mere costs much more so than we can think today. Far-fetched items, processes, products, services and activities that in the past were considered to drain value from an enterprise could become a value to the business (e.g., maintenance of aircraft, plant, building and machiery, rail, and city critical infrastructure, research and development, strategic national resilience projects).

As this takes place transition toward a new plateau will require a new evolved meaning of "value" together a systemic balancing or equilibrium-generating mechanism that will replace the legacy/hybrid cost concepts and paradox.

Provided the nature of the evolving model, a systemic balancing mechanism for BEM^{HESD} could be summarized by the notion of "value balance," or equilibrium.

This notion is based on the following algorithm: The value of what is contributed (i.e., input, invested) should be ≤ (less than or equal to) the value and quality of what is achieved in terms of real value $^{(HESD)}$. In other words, what we get back in terms of value, quality, and advantages ^(HESD) should be higher or equal to what we contribute.

What we get back in terms of ^{HESD} is expressed as real value, while what we invest in time and resources will be known as "contributed value" (or value and contribution).

In the new reference model, BEM ^{HESD}, the evolved term "value" is seen as benefit, overriding today's concept of "cost." To achieve a balanced outcome, the real value of a project (e.g., a new business venture, service, dam, school, mass transportation project, remodeled or refurbished business facilities) is synonymous with how much benefit it produces.

In an other example, real value ^(HESD) generated for an individual, a business, a community, society or a union of countries in terms of new and future development, investment, and added business opportunities, innovation, employment, job creation, improvement in quality of life and ecosystems, respect for environmental consideration, long-term sustainability, etc., should be greater than or equal to the contribution value for realizing a project.

So long as the equation is met, there should be no "cost," as we know it today, to the concern or community (e.g., through generation of public debt and taxes). Any excess in terms of value achieved becomes a return that can be distributed with evolved yardsticks or simple contribution percentage amongst the various stakeholders to avoid, for example, inflationary phenomena (among many other things).

Should the inverse occur, in an unpredictable scenario whereby ^{HESD} (value) is partially achieved, this could give rise to a sort of levy or penalty that could be called the price for generating damage, for the difference on the community in a proportionate manner (this includes those that designed it, made it, approved it, and were mandated with its supervision).

This theoretically should shift the emphasis of the incentive to becoming more virtuous and sustainable, and to focusing on the true benefits, quality, development of new investment and business opportunities, employment, involvement, sustainability, etc., rather than cutting corners to save on costs. A complete paradigm shift!

Under the new model, the objective is to achieve value comprehensively and holistically.

With all probability, existing/legacy measures of economic success (e.g., sales, turnover, profit, gross margin, return on investment) might no longer be the only yardsticks, or be accounted for in the same way, augmented by focus on what might be more comprehensive measures that bring overall improvement, such as increased future business possibilities, development of new opportunities, quality of life, reduced human footprint, environmental considerations, and the BEM^{HESD} key characteristics (i.e., sustainability, human centricity, development, evolution). Value!

Yet these are mostly things that in the existing models are contemplated as mere costs—unaffordable, unviable, economically unproductive elements or propositions, as mentioned in previous chapters.

Each component of the BEM^{HESD} must bring concrete and pragmatic near-medium- and long-term results, benefits, and returns, and give way to new investment and business opportunities and long-term development and prosperity.

Evolution from a cost- to a value-based model requires equal evolution in terms of aspects dealing with such thing as concurring what defines value in each different sector, profession, industry, process, and in general any sphere of human activity.

This implies deciding and concurring on such things as

> performance measurement yardsticks,
> accounting,
> accountability,
> measure,
> valuation,
> reporting,
> feedback,
> payment,
> reward, remuneration criteria, etc.,

along with the price for generating damage (anything that might produce the inverse of value and damage to an investment, business, community, individual, ecosystem, environment, health, etc.).

This is why and how man (H) becomes central.

If implemented correctly, in theory the incentive of this evolutionary model is centered on doing things right—the investor, the business, and the individual are remunerated for creating value.

No system is foolproof or perfect. As such, a means has to be created to mitigate and remodulate shortcomings or damaging extremes, and one of the primary ways to achieve this is through the Value Balance concept. Lets now see how this might be applied to the real world in the three main domains our current system is made up of i.e.: government (city, state, country); business; the individual.

Government: Value Balance Valuation

In very generic terms, the axiom in use in today's model is that government incurs "costs" to produce benefits for citizens that, in turn, are asked to pay taxes to repay these.

Under BEM^{HESD} the paradigm is evolved. Individuals, businesses, corporations, organizations create value across all sectors of human activity in a country, state, city, etc. The sum total of these becomes total value generated in the system.

Seen from this different perspective, in reality, what a society (e.g.: city, state, union of countries, etc.) produces is value (concretely and substantially different from notions such as GDP or other current emanations of it)!

To provide a brief introduction of how this might translate into government-level valuation (as government accounting evolves), concepts similar to the following ones will need to be factored in to address this paradigm shift.

Government: Value Balance Valuation

Total Real Value Produced $^{(HESD)}$
+ Net Contributions Received (donations, price of general damage,
etc., rather than mere taxes)
– Contribution Provided

= Net Real Value (Excess or Balance or Deficit)

The purpose here is only to introduce the notion/concept, and it only represents a possible starting point from which a Transitional Task Force mandated by their national governing bodies, will formulate an initial formal and concurred version of BEM^{HESD}

(baseline model) from which successive versions will continuously evolve to properly address new opportunities.

In the above example of government (federal, state, and city), total real value produced is the total amount of ^{HESD} citizens, businesses, investors, etc., generate within a certain period. This includes, but is not limited to, things such as business opportunities, investment possibilities, employment (life projects), knowledge enhancement possibilities, sustainability, strategic survival and disaster protection projects, ecosystem enhancement and cleanup, quality-of-life improvement, advanced research opportunities, strategic infrastructure refurbishment, citywide life improvement projects, etc. and of course dams, highways, schools, policing and firefighting and emergency services, hospitals, etc.

In essence, it is the total amount of value a society receives from its citizens, businesses, enterprises, etc., as a result of their value-generating activity. In return for this, a society needs to recognize, reward and provide incentive for this virtuous contribution to prolonged development and well-being.

In itself, this represents a major paradigm-change of significant proportions, yet, it only represents one of the several game-changing elements of the new model.

The role of a government is to provide the right environment, policy, governance frameworks, and regulatory value, acting as a guarantor to allow this. This is a paradigm shift towards value generation-one of exceptional impact and resonance.

In the evolved model, with the exception of natural elements fundamental to life such as air and water and those sectors, each society or country might deem it necessary to be run by a public concern (government, municipality, etc.) in accordance to their preferences and sensitivities around such matters, almost all remaining activities could (ideally should) be run by private concerns to create a continuous virtuous cycle of possibilities and making these available to a larger number of concerns (that is why the new model is ideologically and politically neutral, applicable in any sociopolitical context independent of "ism" preferences, customs, cultural or religious sensitivities).

Ideally, the more a society is open, the more it provides its citizenry the liberty in creating and leveraging new opportunities that generate value, and the more potential for prolonged development, prosperity and well-being.

Under the evolved model, a governing body's (government, state, city . . .) main objective becomes the creation of a context that allows continuous value generation, healthy competition and a level playing ground internally and internationally. Once operational (from the first transition rollout phase of BEM^{HESD} onward), evolved governing bodies together with an adequate representative mix of private concerns and stakeholders will need to act as guarantor of the proper functioning of the process in the:

- Identification of the evaluation criteria for value and its remuneration (quantities, modalities, disbursement, etc.) through a demand/requirement/necessity-driven democratic process and for example, value index commissions or boards for each economic sector;
- Continuous generation of traction for prolonged economic development/prosperity.

There are many ideas that come to mind on the details of how this may organized, achieved, and formalized in the first version of BEM^{HESD} and its operations but this is best achieved through the governing bodies, Transition Treaty Committee and Task Force.

Contribution provided is the value that a government (local, city, state, federal) recognizes for the [HESD] produced in an economy through its interaction with its central bank/Federal Reserve system and an evolved commercial banking system. Among the possible alternatives, one that could be considered to start the process-allowing a smooth transition, could be achieved by applying essentially the same levers used today (see previous chapters)—at least initially, evolving in later stages, as necessary, to fit ever-growing development and prosperity demands.

One of the fundamental differences under the new model is that there will be no free rides! Value achieved has to be demonstrated, vouched, and certified and its effects tangible visible and/or perceivable. This constitutes one of the "missing link" between today's models and the evolving future value based model.

Until today the concepts and means activated through the central banking systems in use by the existing model are relegated to only very limited aspects (i.e., "facilities" and loan generation process through the banking system, and in general monetary policy) and currently with an increasingly limited permeation to the rest of the economy, whereas its true potential is yet to be fully unleashed—through an evolved banking and financial system—putting the capital B back to where it belongs without the need to jettison thousands of other jobs, or hinder the possibilities on leveraging on evolved models and interconnections with other equally evolved elements, paving the way to potentially inconceivable numbers of new possibilities and opportunities.

These limitations, in leveraging of such instruments, have potentially contributed to the many systemic dichotomies and multiple unwanted outcomes that can be witnessed today, and that have been formally reported by a growing number of authoritative government agencies and international organizations (i.e., centralized accumulation, credit crunch, resources seeking virtual investment possibilities, or resources without generalized reinvestment throughout all sectors of the economy), as seen in previous chapters.

Moreover, many economic sectors worldwide growingly have (since World War II) depended upon subsidies, funding, incentives, grants, aid, concessions, rebates, and many "facilities" similar to the ones used for the financial systems stability (being currently enacted)—without desired and/or lasting results.

An evolved approach instead is geared to unleash the true potential of these instruments and unblock this stalemate, putting economic traction, revival and recovery back into the system, endemically and structurally, re-establishing the economic loop currently being by-passed by virtual enhancers while an equally evolved governance framework will allow proper balancing of this mechanism while disincentivizing free rides—remunerating, financing, and incentivizing only those initiatives that will create value provided the incalculable new ways of generating real value.

This could potentially create an unquantifiable number of new opportunities for business, investors, individuals and an evolved financial system that is linked to the economy, creating the need for the involvement of experts from new ever-more specialized and different fields.

Under equilibrium (balance) the evolved model does not produce a deficit or excess in real value produced in an economy. This means all stakeholders have achieved their value-generation goals. In the extraordinary scenario where a deficit occurs, it is a matter of reestablishing an equilibrium, and this will depend on how this will be defined through the Alpha-e Protocol. Ideally it should come from an improvement of total real value produced in terms of development and prosperity in immediately successive periods or before a value-generation year end (ex-fiscal).

A deficit in real value produced means that, for example, damage was produced in a certain activity, project, etc. In this case a penalty will be levied on those responsible to reestablish and ensure value. The sum total of damages produced is netted against voluntary donations from businesses and individuals, and any excess value produced in other areas of the economy, giving "Net Contributions Received." Any eventual/residual leftover shortcoming or excess produced in one period will roll over to the successive value year.

To conclude this section, we must also introduce the notion of "Strategic Value-Generating Initiatives." Examples of these initiatives are such things as the (many more concrete examples involving different economic sectors are covered later):

- Modernization of a national electrical grid, water pipelines, sewage;
- Large scale mass transit projects;
- Natural disaster protection programs for large cities, etc.;
- Mega environmental clean-up programs;
- Enhancement of safety, well-being of citizens and cities;
- Recuperation of abandoned areas and industrial sites.

Based on a nation's or a community's prerogatives, these cyclical programs might need concerted and coordinated steering at the highest levels (government, industry, academia, consumer and stakeholder representatives, etc.) through, for example, localized value generating emanations of organizations to ensure that their combined effect and their rollout sequence also translate into value. Value is not created by taking on the full effort of strategic initiatives in limited time frames creating the paradox of phantom-like useless creations in a desert—these generate damage and go against some of the most fundamental traits of HESD such as sustainability and that of managing inflationary phenomena.

Instead, it is all about comprehensive value generation and careful, modular roll-outs that once evaluated and certified as creating value—their shortcomings will be used as lessons learned in successive phases and roll-out packets.

Value here is also generated through things such as respect of rollout milestones, sustainability, and footprint reduction, and that implementation is achieved according to a concurred action plan with all key players and the involvement of local businesses, workforce, etc., respecting local values and requirements.

The positive implications and interactions of each initiative with other components are potentially incalculable. Just to introduce a couple, these might involve the interaction with the revival of economically depressed areas, abandoned industrial zones, disaster-affected zones, poverty-stricken towns, cities, regions, and nations, together with impacts on such areas as net-positive immigration (rather than an uncontrollable desperation-driven one). Indirect effects might address easing exposure to potential for mass social unrest and extremism.

What it will address will be business and employment, especially with regard to the young and middle-aged that currently are the most affected by the crisis.

Policy and policy makers' rapport with citizens are bound to evolve as a result, and it might bring an evolution in the rapport toward increased involvement, accountability, and a more direct link among commitments, promises, actions, results, achievements, election, and reelection to public posts, for example.

Taxes, Debt, Deficit, etc.

As it is becoming apparent and will become more so as time progresses, it is highly probable that Value, Value Balance, Valuation and Certification processes might progressively replace the current tax and taxation concepts, notions, systems, and modalities. This alone could save immeasurable number of jobs across the world and potentially add many new opportunities through a plethora of new expertise in increasing numbers of new fields that would have otherwise evaporated under Web Inclusivity, innovation, etc.

Increasing number of persons currently working for the ministries of finance or IRS-type organizations, for example, might gradually be refocused in this necessarily human-led (at least for the foreseeable future) valuation and certification processes rather than investigating taxes.

The approach to valuation and certification of value also will need to evolve to a higher form of civilization of the modality—going from the current "inspect to punish" modus operandi to a "service to guide and advise" modality toward investors, businesses, and individuals to refine and remodulate their proposition in helping them to generate and achieve real value. Obviously addressing fraudulent or criminal intent will need to equally evolve towards improving success rate in curbing these.

As government and banking systems (central and commercial) transition to value balance concepts reaching higher levels of evolution and recognition in terms of contribution to value generation, legacy tax concepts will evolve to new less tax-like provisions, conceptually and fundamentally different from today's taxes, toward their theoretical final transformation in voluntary contributions to fund particular areas of interest and programs or generically for the well-being of the societies and economies they operate in.

We need to be reminded that there are many countries today that do not have income tax and in some cases neither sales tax. And many more instead that have relatively very limited tax impositions.

Should a "tax"-like provision or concept still need to continue to exist (in excess of a penalty for damage generation) in an evolved society, this might be used to provide a sense of voluntary contribution from individuals for the general well-being of society (e.g., something to give back to fund a particular interest) that might not need minimums or maximums rates.

As it is becoming evident, to be perfectly clear, in reality in the evolved model (BEM^{HESD}), there is no real reason or justification for the existence of concepts similar to today's notion of taxes and taxation. In theory and in practice, the evolved model does not necessarily require or contemplate the need for such a notion and/or mechanism for its proper functioning. Realistically and reasonably however, the evolution in this direction will most probably be a gradual one—which in itself is already a great achievement. This by no means is to denote a lack of accountability—quite the contrary.

Should there be concurrence among the citizenry, leaders, policy makers and experts (eg.: Transition Task Force) that this anachronistic man-made model and mechanism (that had a reason for being in the past and is a source of major dichotomies and systemic blocks) be transitioned after the Alpha-e Protocol is run, at the very least there might be a possibility that this might be for a limited transition phase or applicable to progressively reduced portions of income and business profits.

Value generation and balance will allow evolution of all other currently blocked legacy elements such as Debt, Deficit, etc. transitioning their elements and components towards value creation through several means each opening new structural and systemic solutions and perspectives to address current dichotomies and blocks and provide resolution in the near-term. The final formal version of concepts such as value balance under BEM^{HESD} for different themes (Taxation, Debt, etc.) and sectors will be achieved through the concurred effort, leadership, onus, responsibility, etc. of the governing bodies and operationally through the Transition Task Force. There are many solutions for each element and module but these will only be my ideas. These solutions include and are not limited to new concepts of Value balance indexing, Value roll-over, Value Excess/Deficit, and Equilibrium strategies, protocol and policies.

Enterprise (Corporation/Business): Value Balance Valuation

Many corporations, businesses, entrepreneurs, and consumers have already taken some steps in the transition process toward the new plateau in terms of their sensitivity and concrete efforts in bringing about positive change in the direction of value generation, be it in their processes, products, services, quality, footprint, sustainability, energy efficiency, giving-back initiatives, eco-environmental systems sensitivity, etc. but these notions are currently being greatly affected and limited by cost centricity. The intent here is to take these notions beyond known thresholds, to unleash their full hidden potential.

Evolution toward the new development and prosperity plateau, both within the context of business models and in the remaining domains (the economic reference model, government, and all the other dimensions covered in previous chapters), will finally be able to free the real potential for new opportunities available on a higher level and increasingly multidimensional model from where we are today.

Seen from a business, corporation, enterprise balance valuation perspective, as financial statements mutate towards evolved P&L and balance sheet statements (eg. Value Generation Notices, Performance and Evolution updates)—these will need to factor in the following introductory high-level notions/concepts (example):

<u>Acme Corporation: Value Balance Valuation</u>

Total Real Value created [HESD]
+ Revenues Realized from Selling Products and/or Services
− Contribution Value Incurred
− Private Contribution to Community or Otherwise

───────────────────────────────

= Net Real Value (Excess or Balance or Deficit)

The purpose here is only to introduce the notion/concept, and it only represents a possible starting point from which governing bodies and a Transitional Task Force will define the initial formal and concurred version of BEM^{HESD} (baseline model) from which successive versions will continuously evolve to properly address new opportunities.

Total real value realized $^{(HESD)}$ for a company or a business concern needs to be valued, accounted for, audited, and certified by much less complex but more qualitatively focused "evolved generally accepted value criteria (EGAVC)," replacing, evolving, and/or enhancing current versions of GAAP, GAAS, IAS, and other quality certification standards, etc.

In itself this will also provide many new and evolved opportunities for independent accounting firms, engineering firms, certification firms, individual certified specialists, etc., in a growing number of fields (from defining and assessing the value model used by a home manager, corner fruit retailer, and a mechanic's business model to the ones used in an investment banking firm, a defense conglomerate, and the one in use by black-hole astrophysicists, and everything in between plus those to come).

These *new* professionals will need to assess and provide guidance in the true actuation in terms of real ^{HESD} generated for the societies and communities where companies operate, for example, in terms of:

- the quality of the products and services they produce and market;
- the value generated and quality of their sales channels and modalities of sales;
- no-nonsense product's longevity and guarantees;
- post-sales support, services, and value these provide;

- CO_2 and hazardous material reduction and footprint reduction, efficiency and energetic consumption;
- health value and eco-environmental considerations;
- increased investment possibilities;
- development of new value-adding products/services;
- research findings;
- inventions and innovations;
- contribution to controlling inflation;
- etc.

and also the value based activation of those sustainable activities that till today where considered financially non-viable or costly:

- refurbishments, improvements, and enhancements to buildings and facilities;
- maintenance of assets, machinery, and tools;
- environmental improvement;
- new opportunity generation;
- new employment (life projects) and their quality;
- the use and involvement of human contribution;
- activities that promote human interaction (business travel, business generating meetings, project/product development and roll-out);
- humanization of workplace and interaction and dignity augmentation (antonym's to mobbing, discrimination, and similar non-productive practices);
- motivation generation;
- professional knowledge augmentation and training, etc.;
- sustainability;
- giving back initiatives, etc.

One should be reminded that there is a substantial paradigm change in place under the new model: the above list no longer represents costs to a company as conceived in today's models!

The focus is value creation! Each of these becomes a potential new revenue stream and source of remuneration for those businesses that create value in these areas.

These new sources of value generation and remuneration will not only be able to compensate / replace loss of revenues derived from, for example, Web inclusivity repercussions but they will be able to open new doors and opportunities that would otherwise remain hidden, just as the many new types of remunerated activities came into being only at each successive step-level evolutionary ascent to a new plateau.

Now can you think of how many new opportunities this might generate in different sectors? How many new jobs (life projects) and revenue streams will this potentially create for a company, investors, and individuals? And how many more will potentially be derived (net of false positives) as these are crisscrossed with other elements of BEM[HESD]?

Moreover, we need to factor in the positive fallout this might have on suppliers, the economy (local, national, and international), and the stock markets that among other things, can finally find it pragmatically convenient to separate a highly speculative market from the real value based markets. Think of the potential positive repercussion on pension funds, on jobs for the young, and on retirement, for example.

Finally, reflect on the effect on sectors such as the travel and hospitality industry (and their supply chain), *as that portion of travel that produces positive outcomes (new contracts, business opportunities, and projects) will be considered value. Augmenting human relations and interaction is value—its virtualization is not necessarily.*

Humans need not (should not) lose the centrality and importance of this very ancestrally humane distinctive trait to a cost-based model.

Contributed value, or contribution value incurred, is what a business (to use today's terminology) pays in salaries and the purchase of products and services from its suppliers with the substantial difference that if done correctly, many of these "costs," in turn, might lead to the creation of potentially additional revenue streams that weigh on a company's P&L and evaporate, as mere dead expenses in today's model.

The focus on an economic concern amplifies, evolving further than it is achieving today. It will no longer be focused on producing a widget or a service but doing it in such a way as to create additional value all around it—putting man, his well-being, the eco-environment, long term prosperity and survival at the center.

Private contributions are voluntary by definition in the new BEM[HESD]. *There is no need to force any concern or anyone to chip in simply because the more value created by giving back to the local communities, the more new revenue streams can potentially be generated from these.*

There are no free rides! Achieving value is not banal and it is one of the preconditions for prolonged development and regeneration of other opportunities.

The same principles of balance, deficit, or excess of value creation, solutions, mechanisms, protocols, and the onus of final detailed definition of these discussed in the previous chapter also apply here. The only difference here is that excess value generation here is synonymous with today's legacy concept of profit but in many ways it will be substantially, qualitatively different especially its reinvestment in value generating business actvities.

Individual: Value Balance Valuation

Could this balance valuation apply to individuals and professionals? In the newly forming BEM^{HESD}, this is already contemplated. Theoretically there is no reason it should not be the case. Moreover, it equally evolves to reap new chances (e.g., valuation, certification, and accounting of an individual's income and those indicated in the previous chapters). How might this work and be applied to a real-life scenario?

Today personal net income is formed basically from two elements: income and taxes. For millennia, existing models did not account for the value an individual brings to society during the course of his life. Why?

In the majority of cases, persons leave a legacy and contribute to an improvement of their loved ones, communities, businesses, or employers throughout their life span. As the existing economy sheds millions of jobs without structural, long-lasting solutions in sight and the introduction of new paradigms under the current model only add complexity and further evaporation of employment, an evolution to a new plateau is as obligatory as migrating away from the barter system was.

This was the same type of jump achieved by migrating from a rural to an industrial economy. This entailed the introduction of new concepts (most of which we take for granted today) such as salary, work hours, holidays, paid vacation and sick leave. Each of these notions was as new to our forefathers as those we will need to face going forward.

An evolved modality will enhance and lever on previously nonvalued contributions in ways incalculable today in terms of development of new opportunities.

Should we look through a different perspective and factor in an individual's real value generation in the equation, this might add new windows to the next plateau of civilization.

Let's consider the following balance valuation model for the individual/professional:

Individual: Value Balance Valuation

Total Real Value Created [HESD]
+ Personal Income Realized
− Contribution Value Incurred
− Private Contribution to Community

_____

= Real Value: Excess or Balance or Deficit

The first thing noticeable is the striking similarity of an individual's valuation with that of a business. This is because the relation between employee versus employer is probably evolving and blurring as we move forward, provided the plethora of new intersections between different elements possible in the BEM[HESD].

It might be that in a not-so-distant future, companies evolve toward a virtual coming-together of professionals that, independent of hierarchical levels and professional seniority they might occupy, seek to achieve a series of common business objectives, each acting in their own capacity, finding it more motivating and economically convenient to remain independent (rather than dependent) in realizing life projects.

Theoretically this might lead to fewer persons wishing to remain mere "employees" as time progresses—at least according to today's notion. To some extent this paradigm shift is already taking place, as evolution might possibly be a step ahead of us.

The problem today is that this paradigm shift does not find resolution or practical convenience (for the majority) under the current model, because it has, among other things (mentioned previously), only translated into precariousness, uncertainty, and devaluation of professionalism, creating the many unresolvable systemic dichotomies we witness today.

Total real value created in ^{HESD} does not only apply to what today is considered remuneration from a job, a professional activity, or investments, etc., but will also enclose value-based remuneration of such things that in the current model are not *valued* (depending on the evolving definitions that it will assume). A few samples might be:

- value creation on the job, professional tutoring, mentoring;
- certified assistance in many spheres: the family and community (e.g., home management, civil service, home/ hospital assistance for the elderly and/or the sick);
- professional child care and sitting;
- personal knowledge and capability enhancement;
- new business opportunity generation;
- new idea formulation and publication and innovations;
- works of artistic value that can enhance a community;
- professional activities providing training and knowledge dissemination of different types;
- remuneration for personal data and information;
- neighborhood enhancement, recycling and enactment of zero miles concepts, etc.

Innovations in many fields provide and facilitate verification of progress, attendance and extent and quality of contribution, for example, through electronic means, and quality review feedbacks from users, while impartial/independent value advisors, auditors, and certifiers (new employment professionals and business possibilities) could certify the validity of declared individual ^{HESD} generation/ improvements or damage.

In this scenario, extremely important contributions of housewives, husbands, grandparents, and a myriad of other persons could finally find appropriate recognition and remuneration. But also create innumerous value adding remunerated new professions in many fields replacing growingly evaporating legacy jobs.

This is about the opportunity for individuals to create value tangibly in many new ways and spheres of activity, that would otherwise not be possible under the current model.

This should create a paradigm shift of substantial impact, and an evolution upwards and away, for example, from cost-based notions of hand-out's and mere welfare.

Contribution value incurred here might be represented by reasonable deductions for amounts incurred in improving ^{HESD} and generating value to be defined and tabulated accordingly, whereas private contributions to the community are exactly that, as described in the previous chapter.

Current mechanisms that assure avoidance of systemic dependence, abuse and or improper/fraudulent use of our current models, will need to evolve to guarantee value generation valuation, recognition and distribution and the proper functioning of the system. Furthermore, the above activities will need to evolve towards professions that will become certified through continuous knowledge enhancement of individuals and the evolved learning system to increase the potential for value generation.

In today's economic model, persons who remain without a job are essentially out of the system. The systemic blocks of the current model are becoming endemic and, in many cases, not only inhibit reentry but will continue reducing possibilities for ever-growing numbers of persons. Based upon one's country of residence, there may or may not be social assistance, and, if there is, it is only for a limited time. After that, there is only uncertainty. Headlines report that as of January 30, 2013, unemployment among the young in the US and Europe reached critical records—an average of 25 percent with peaks of 37 percent in nearly half of the EU countries.

The new model leverages new paradigm shifts to create possibilities that will remain otherwise hidden, bringing the centrality of man back into the equation.

Individuals will be more motivated to achieve life project goals as more and more become professionals and entrepreneurs in a plethora of new fields, seeking to generate value and not only just for themselves!

There will be no free rides though! Value will need to be demonstrated, vouched, and certified here also.

The same principles of balance, deficit, or excess of value creation, and the onus of final detailed definition of these and their criteria and remuneration modalities—together with solutions, etc. discussed in the previous chapter also apply here.

Excess value generation here is synonymous with today's legacy concept of profit but in many ways substantially different. A deficit is an indication that something is wrong and needs to be addressed.

Persons and veterans affected by objective impediments and conditions are obviously addressed under the new model. If voluntarily willing, these fellow citizens will be able to contribute and be involved in different life projects and areas respecting their individual passions and strengths. Independent of this, the evolved model foresees adequate remuneration and assurance of needed facilities to allow a life lived respectfully and in a dignified way through the value balance mechanism.

This also creates value for our societies, taking us forward toward a higher level of civilization.

Retirement and Pension Considerations Under Value Concept

Could this area finally bring benefits to natural generational turnovers, improve motivation and career possibilities, improve new idea generation, and provide added stimulus to the economy? Seen from this new perspective, yes, and there might be many more than we can currently envisage. If properly devised and interconnected with other components it may result in the following:

- value based **pension funds** to finally be able to count on a more stable/balanced economic model and value generation (HESD);
- value based **markets** to be able to create new parallel models more in line with retirement and pension requirements, generating new business opportunities and HESD;
- individuals who choose to do so to retire at a reasonable age (but also not beyond a maximum—which will need to be objectively, substantially lower that the current unrealistic retirement ceilings, to assure and lever natural generational turnover) with reasonable income commensurate to maintaining a standard of living not disparate from the one they created thought a lifetime's worth of challenges;
- a context for facilitations in creating new enterprises and businesses for those who wish to continue their professional lives after retirement leveraging on the wealth of accumulated experience and expertise focused in generating HESD; and
- **governments** and policy makers to be finally freed by one of the many latches that impede them to focus effectively in addressing economic development and future HESD.

In reality, as the model evolves toward the new plateau, many of these aspects might even become of second importance or simply irrelevant, as evolved models may provide opportunities beyond our current perception.

Generational turnover is not an option, it forms the quintessential fundamental building block of any society and its future.

It is at the base of an economies' prolonged success and the fulcrum of the most natural of all events in human evolution and survival—the creation of a family and procreation—our prosperity and survival as a specie.

No man made model should inhibit this nor distort natural processes of generational turnover—as instead our current model are provoking.

These concepts will need to be applied to all currently curtailed and or demonized areas of concern blocked under irresolvable systemic dichotomies that could turn into business opportunities and value, such as health care, public and private hospitals, schools and education, public safety and emergency services, police forces, and so forth.

In evaluating the final initial version of the new model the Transition Task Force mandated through democratically led processes and steered by governing bodies, must constantly remind itself where we stand today and what this might imply if elements are not transitioned and evolved to revive and develop employment, business, investments, the economy, address national debt and the the repercussions on the strategic stance of the nation its, independence, leadership positioning and prolonged success.

THE VIRTUS PROSPERITY MODEL AND THE CONCEPT OF VIRTUATION

The word "virtus" derives its roots from the Greek word "arete" which in its basic sense means "excellence of any kind" that is in addition to what we usually associate it with; moral virtue.

In the search for a name that could most appropriately enclose all the concepts so far covered especially those of BEM^{HESD}, EPM^{HESDX}, Value generation and Value concept and balance, and provide a single, less cryptic name to the next economic model – the word "Virtus" seemed to provide a good match.

Hence, Virtus Prosperity Model could be used to define the dynamically evolving economic model thus far presented, while Virtus Proximus – represents the next (successive) prosperity model(s) as these evolve over time.

Whereas the new word "Virtuation" that includes the essence of words such as virtue and virtualization, encases (but is not limited to) the following concepts:

- Continuous migration towards newer plateaus and value generation levels;

- Evolution of current (legacy) models in the following areas:
  o Central and general banking,

- o Public Debt, GDP, Government Spending, Budgeting (i.e.: towards new forms of Accounting and Accountability for value creation),
- o Government loans, incentives, facilities,
- o Public spending: pensions, health care, education, civil protection, defense
- o Taxation, government revenue recognition,
- o Etc.

- Migration towards new forms of
  - o Accounting, accountability, management of what falls under Public (government owned)
  - o Indexing and recognition of value generation,
  - o Rewarding, payout and distribution of contributions to value creators,
  - o Etc.;

- Planning, phasing and road mapping of strategies that address the phased virtualization of jobs, processes, models; mutating them into opportunities;

- Evolving other fundamental / critical processes in line with needs, such as:
  - o Policy making, and appropriate governance frameworks,
  - o Higher levels of democracy, individual rights and privacy, and civilization,
  - o Regulating and managing justice,
  - o Education,
  - o Free-time leverage, indexing, auditing, certification, assurance of value etc.;

- Planning, coordinated phasing and roll-out of Critical Strategic Initiatives and Projects;

- Evolution of cost concepts towards separation and exploitation of those elements of cost that denote potential for generating value—toward value creation;

- Continuous evolution and implementation of appropriate governance frameworks;

- Fostering virtuous cycles in the development of economic traction.

SIMPLICITY VERSUS COMPLEXITY

To achieve results in BEM^{HESD} simplicity is quintessential to the success. Complexity does not necessarily add value to models, processes, efficacy, efficiency, etc. Paradigm-changing variables and innovations need to be processed via a protocol, such as the ones we saw in previous chapters, for them to produce maximum return in terms of new opportunities and value.

This process can be rendered complex and complicated or vice versa; it depends on our willingness. Many real-life examples teach us that the more systems are open, modular, and scalable, and enhance-able the better their chance of evolving.

This is why the choice was made to create a baseline model that must, be enhanced, and continuously evolve through open, modular, and scalable components, elements, globules, and networks involving the contributions of many experts from all professional fields.

EVOLVED GOVERNANCE FRAMEWORKS

As introduced earlier, BEM^{HESD} requires an equally evolved governance framework to work at all levels of the model to generate value balance at each level.

The development and evolution of such a framework require the involvement of experts from many different fields of expertise and not necessarily limited to those who were mandated with policy formulation and governance and assurance till today.

It will not be an overnight event, but a process. Given the necessity to come out of the recession—it should receive the benefit of a strong commitment and be given the objective to achieve rollouts in reasonable time frames benefiting from modularity, scalability, and a small quick win approach, support of technology (e.g., readily devisable Web-based apps), a natural domino effect, learning curve, repetition, lessons learned, etc.

Their design, implementation, rollout, day-to-day management, and continuous evolution may open many new opportunities in many fields and new ramifications and possibilities that might not be clear today.

These evolved modular governance frameworks need to adhere to certain basic criteria based on a societies preferences (nonexhaustive sample):

- Be balanced (avoid extremes: centralized, overly government-controlled, inflexible, tedious, bureaucratic, complex, boxed in, and un-evolvable);
- For the most part allow privatize-ability, generating new opportunities and virtuous loops;
- Be simple, nimble, and intuitive;
- Be sustainable and evolvable;
- Focus on seeking system equilibrium and value balance;
- Focus on generating ^{HESD} and augmenting value;
- Be open, scalable, modular, and inter-actable with other elements.

EVOLVED VALUE CONCEPT AND VALUE BALANCE FUNDAMENTAL PREMISES

Before work is begun though, a few premises need to be made if we wish the new BEM^{HESD} to produce the *optimal* level of opportunities and results from the new evolved plateau. The following list is just an initial draft of these:

- The context: an open, free, and democratic society where rights prevail (mass social movements around the world demonstrate how evolution is taking many societies at least toward a direction where these fundamental principles are becoming no longer postpone-able);
- Resilience in resolving current issues;
- Strategic vision: a society that wishes to step up to the next plateau;
- Dynamism: be eager to leverage continuously evolving plateaus of development and prosperity;
- Grasp new opportunities, and use evolved modalities, ways, and definitions to bring about continuous new ideas and confront new challenges that add value;
- Be free and willing to venture

    o   beyond dated models and sacred monsters;
    o   away from extreme ideological, political thought processes or contexts;

- o outside of excessively centralized or completely anarchical concepts;
- o away from excessive government control and completely unstructured models;
- o away from highly technocratic and its extreme nemesis; and
- o away from highly bureaucratic and its complete opposite.

The essential objective is seeking to achieve an evolutionary, value-centered balanced paradigm focused around succeeding in value generation [HESDX] and what is best for any society that chooses to leverage it and implement it. It must be poised to reach a new level of civilization and civilized society, and it must be focused on achieving value, both tangibly and virtually.

In this scenario, balance and equilibrium become sought-after objectives not because we need to reach them for dry technocratic, accounting purposes or human-distant concepts such as the national budget, but because the balance or equilibrium points represent the best place to be at any given time in terms of rewards, returns, business, opportunities, investments, employment, and governance over such things as inflation, sustainability, and continuous [HESDX] generation for man and his eco-environment.

It is important to appreciate that, success and transition towards the higher plateau of development entails considering all aspects thus far covered:

- transition away from legacy and hybrid models
- evolution towards a resilient, dynamically adaptive, continuously evolving model
- acknowledgement of a higher plateau, and an upwards evolution towards this

- leverage on new perspectives
- shift away form cost based logics
- transition towards Value generation and Value Balance concepts
- focus on ^{HESDX} development
- transition of legacy elements
- transition of new variables, innovations, etc.
- value focused, adaptive, and evolvable governance framework
- evolution of business models, processes, definitions, etc.
- evolution of strategic sectors such as banking, financial, markets
- successful roll-out and transition strategies
- etc.

Ultimately, the cognizance that we need to start and get on with it.

A FEW EXAMPLES OF
OPPORTUNITY GENERATORS

So as to leave indications to low-hanging, immediate opportunities that can be leveraged and that yield multiplier effects through the utilization and application of BEM[HESD], the following is just a minute list of teasers among a plethora of opportunities that can be activated in jump-starting structural economic recovery and evolution towards new plateaus (these are a subset of the previously mentioned Critical Strategic Value-Generating Initiatives):

Going Beyond a Green Economy Concept

Further potential opportunities lie in programs and projects that, under the current existing legacy models, had little investment appeal for their reduced capability in producing acceptable economic returns.

Under the BEM[HESD] these same projects that have a greater exponential lever and tremendous impact on new and long-term development, investment, business, life projects, sustainability, ecosystems survivability, and environmental recovery finally find investment appeal and viable economic returns, adding opportunities and augmenting long-term prosperity.

Many books have been written on new subject matters, such as green economy, smart cities, zero miles, etc. The emphasis here, however, is beyond these. It is about systemic ecosystem cleanup, revitalization, and renaturalization. It about finally shifting toward the analysis, development and enactment of those projects that might have seemed like economically unviable until yesterday. The fundamental paradigms are changing and, through evolved models, allowing us to reach beyond.

Another example is with reference to the much discussed global climate change issue. For an increasing number of authoritative scientists it is no longer a probability but a certainty. Data and visible facts confirm that de-glaciation, super-fires, and extreme weather conditions are increasing in frequency and intensity. What these hide as secondary effects and unquantifiable consequences are things such as:

- out-gassing and release of noxious gases, such as methane, that were until now imprisoned in large quantities in permafrost all around the Siberian tundra and some other regions of the world affected by this condition;
- potential for exposure to unknown variables e.g.: release of pathogens and viruses that might have been captured in the melting polar ice that could revive and proliferate;
- oxygen reduction and allarming proliferation of certain species such as algea, jelly fish, squids, etc. in our oceans that generate collapse of entire ecosystems in our oceans (currently 150 mega eareas have been identified around the globe) generating billions of dollars of damage to entire economic sectors.
- rising water levels. The quantity of landmasses near or slightly higher than current sea level is incredibly vast. The problem is that most of these areas are occupied by some of the major mega centers of human economic activity, strategic centers of governance, large cities, and human settlements of strategic agricultural importance all around the world; and
- a currently unknown tipping point toward a long-term shift in weather patterns with effects over known ecosystems.

Seen from a new perspective—the amount of project, programs here are enough to generate opportunities for investments, business and employment for many years to come.

Waste

Our miniscule planet is a closed-loop system; theoretically only those objects that have been cast out of the atmosphere have reduced the total available resources.

Extrapolating the same logic, the amount of waste created in each nation in theory is possibly bound to be enormous.

In a time of shortage and scarcity of resources, population growth, growing demands, etc., this might become the first place to look for natural resources.

While a recently extracted steel bar from a torn down building might be recycled immediately, it is true that a dumped washing machine years ago might not hold its original consistency, but nothing is to say that what is left of rusting material might not find viable uses for other ends. Surely it will not find any until we seek ways to transform it into an opportunity. Till today the only issue keeping us away from exploiting waste completely was cost.

The magnitude of the potential resources involved is stratospheric—in the billions, if not trillions, of dollars in the case of developed nations. Theoretically it is equal to all the resources consumed to date, since the beginning of human activity, less the relatively miniscule tonnage of those materials that exited earth's ecosystem transformed into energy or burned (whilst the same is not true for their still-existing gases that might have been reabsorbed by other elements within the ecosystem).

The intrinsic value of each basic element making up each disposed product could even be greater than its value at the moment in which it was first produced. For example, it could be due to a possible increase in the price of the same raw material, growing scarcity, greater extraction and processing costs, greater transportation costs, or commodities market speculations (under the current model). Under ^{HESD} its value-generating capability will be potentially geometrically higher.

Yet waste is, for the most part, still seen as such in many parts of the world. It is something to get rid of. Ironically and paradoxically we are reaching a stage where we have trouble finding places to get rid of it. Maybe also this is an indicator that a tipping point has been reached and evolution is waiting for us to find new ways.

While awareness is growing and new opportunities are being seized in this area, no significant attempts at mass recuperation can be or have been made on old mega dumping sites, for example. The primary reason for this is pragmatic. It is not as remunerating as it potentially could be, seen through today's legacy/hybrid model. The moment the same concept is run through the new model, it assumes totally different connotations.

In addition to waste accumulated on land, think of how much waste covers our riverbeds, lakes, seas, and oceanic floors. This waste includes weapons and military hardware. Overwater instead there are said to be floating islands the size of some states in different oceans and seas across the world that also provoke tremendous direct damage to the oceanic biosphere and to our health.

It would be interesting for example, to understand the amount and the value of different noxious gases (useful to productive processes) that could be recuperated from the atmosphere. How much potential ^{HESD} resides in this is probably not known today. For now these possibilities are perceived only as "costly," economically nonviable cases. Some argue about the economies of scale of such operations and deem them to be disproportionate to their returns. To be fair, they are possibly right—under current circumstances.

Only when this paradigm changes is it possible to transform things such oceanic waste recuperation and recycling into an opportunity of gigantic proportions. Think of the interaction of waste- and food-production elements within BEM, just to provide one teaser among many. Fishermen and/or other hard-hit maritime transportation sector concerns, who today are subsidized to keep them away from the oceans for long periods of time to allow natural rebirth of oceanic life, could produce real value in supporting the waste-collection effort evidently with specifically dedicated assets or ones refurbished for dual use—via value generation—to ensure refitting for both fishing and cleanup uses to address health concerns. This will also allow natural repopulation of species in our oceans and waterways.

Petroleum has existed in nature before the arrival of man and was readily available in many parts of the world, as it spewed out naturally from the ground, forming big pools in some areas (e.g.: Khuzestan region in southwestern Iran). No one saw a true business in it, not until technology and conditions produced a new paradigm by man, generating an economically viable need for it. Once the model changed, the same useless product became an overnight bonanza for many.

A multitude of individuals started seeking petroleum in many parts of the world. These were individuals that drilled wells without any science to back them up and sold petrol in canisters to a market that still had to produce cars in large numbers and build roads, bridges, highways, interstate roads, and fueling stations—anything that would be needed to make the business model work, as we know it today.

With today's technological enablers, nothing is out of reach. Waste, if looked at under a different filter, will provide a wealth of opportunities for a very long time, cyclically, surely adding to [HESD].

The ability to see beyond the obvious is said to be what makes the difference between Steve Jobs, Bill Gates, Rockefeller, and the rest of us. In my humble opinion, though extremely genious individuals, this shortcoming might not necessarily be due to a scarcity of such persons around the world. Rather, they were among the few that made it against the many odds that our current models produce. A new model could allow more and more persons who are seeking the possibility to achieve greater results.

Automated Transportation and Redesign and Modernization of Infrastructure

The technology is said to be already here and ready to be implemented. It could probably benefit from a few more reasonable tweaks, but this evolution has the potential to become another mega opportunity generator.

The current technology allows driving a vehicle with no driver intervention on real roads. In its private vehicle version, it has already been tested in most traffic conditions in northern California. The vehicle will stop when it has to, drive at the recommended speed limits, maintain safe distances, and allow for cars behaving erratically to enter the lane in front of the car, safely making space and keeping distances. It keeps control of the conditions in a 360-degree hemisphere around the car (much more than a human can do, especially with hidden spots and on long, tedious drives).

The number of potential opportunities this creates is enormous. Think of the impact it can have on the physical look of highways in a proximate future. This could mean opportunities derived from the redesign of new cars, or evolved roads potentially cleared of most physical road signs, since they could become visible on head-up displays or directly on the navigators.

It could also mean new types of entertainment stopovers. Each and every element gives rise to yet another set of opportunities that could not have been possible till today. For those professionals that make a living on the road, it might mean a totally different way of pursuing their dreams and improving their quality of life, while for others (travelers, commuters, etc.) this could mean having more rest and entertainment opportunities leading to new business models.

Though ther is never certainty in anything, it is highly probable that the technology will arrive on the roads sooner or later. The question is whether we wish to leverage new opportunities and to which degree and how fast to start a new chapter in economic evolution. Or do we wish to wait until more car manufacturers go out of business, slashing thousands of other jobs in their wake? Do we want to wait for the demise of related industries, reducing our cities to slums?

It is important to understand that value is not created, building bridges and highways all over all at the same time, but producing HESD where value is certified and mostly so with what we already have. Otherwise we are potentially looking at an unsustainable model for a given project.

City Redesign and Evolution

There are a wealth of ideas and opportunities here, and we have not even touched the surface of the iceberg.

Before we get there, we need to clean up our baseline paradigms, philosophy, and pragmatic approach to designing a new evolutionary model based on value generation that will be affected by different things such as the following few nonexhaustive teasers.

Evolved Mass Transit and Traffic Concepts

- evolved next-generation mass and private trasportation programs and projects that can be growlingly personalized
- making cities more human friendly through for example, eradication of urban physical road signs and lighting, substituting them with *virtual* and or smart road signs, smart and energy saving public and traffic lighting, while those that today produce these goods will be able to produce for evolved uses stemming out of interaction between elements in other areas as will become more evident later
- implementation of next generation zero-mile concepts
- less traffic or intelligent traffic management, meaning more possibilities to redesign community areas such as piazzas to improve neighborhood entertainment, shopping, and social interaction possibilities—if done well, this might improve reduction of serious crime typology and rates.

Structural Safety and Maintenance of industrial facilities, office space for business use, and residential housing:

- redevelop, refurbish, and restructure according to safety standards based on exposure to geographical natural events (e.g., hurricanes, earthquakes, inundations, avalanches) affecting each area

- maintenance; enact value-generating concepts in buildings, homes, industrial sites, etc.

The potential immediate windfall on the construction and maintenance industry sectors alone will be unfathomable (note: governance and [HESD] avoid real estate balloons and must mitigate the exposure to speculative bubbles to generate value! The focus is on long-term continued development and prosperity).

Humanization of Urban Setting:

- increased natural settings (i.e., more green areas)
- increased walk-, people-, children-, and bike-friendly neighborhoods whilst allowing for evolved access and traffic reduction strategies
- reconversion of office spaces into evolved uses (e.g., private or individual entrepreneur, small enterprise, leased business services)
- intelligent next-generation alternative energetic sourcing and distribution ever more based on zero-mile and proximity concepts
- alternative next-generation data and communications transmission systems that substantially reduce potential damage from electromagnetic smog and overdose (under a new model all stakeholders are motivated to seek ways to reduce / avert exposure to anything that produces damage to humans, ecosystems . . .)
- Neighbourhood friendly business solutions
- urban quality of life improvement and abandoned area reutilization.

There is a growing move away from preformatted 9-5 job schedules and the need for currently configured physical offices, toward new types of business office concepts. This alone will impact many dimensions of our lives and many business sectors.

For example, effective working hours, the way we interact, potential flexibility, free time, transportation, logistics, augmenting neighborhood and community interactions, and value-based city redesign and replanning (i.e., concepts where persons can meet, congregate, play, shop, and find entertainment, reconverting unused spaces to other creative uses) create a plethora of potential new businesses and value-enhancing opportunities.

The re-humanization of urban settings, increased use of outdoor facilities, healthier life styles might have positive effects on values, violence, crime rates and businesses able to lever on these. Examples of these concepts can be witnessed in certain boroughs of large cities around the world such as Melbourne, Vancouver and London.

As with the preceding chapter, the objective here is to make better use of what we have within our cities, towns, industrial sites, etc.—if done correctly, reasonably with all the projects mentioned thus far and their numerous intersections with other possibilities, this more than what the construction industry (and its entire supply chain) might be able handle for at least many decades to come. Speculation-only-driven additions of billions of cubic square meters of new cement will not create value but damage. [HESD] will need to be certified.

Earthing of Roads and Parking Facilities in Cities

This entails identifying and prioritizing city road systems according to traffic flow and congestion generation capability—in other words, this might (at least in the near future) take an increased number of critical urban roads underground together with parking facilities for both commercial and private uses.

These are not science fiction projects, and they are currently being implemented on relatively important scales in cities around the world, such as Chicago, Sydney, Amsterdam (where the municipality is taking a few roads and their parking spaces below their famous canals), Boston, and Moscow.

The implications for new opportunities would be immeasurable today. If major arteries above ground are liberated from congestion and traffic, some of these areas can become of human aggregation and utility as they have become in many cities around the globe, offering unique hospitality, shopping and entertainment facilities that can potentially increase possibilities geometrically across different sectors!

People, for example, may wish to move back into redeveloped neighborhoods or remodel unused office space for living purposes, adding to the revitalization back in the real estate and construction industry, but also in high tech, defense and aerospace, telecommunications, and a plethora of others that would be affected in a domino-style positive economic revitalization.

Enactment of Next Generation Pollution-Free Concepts

Not long ago, smog was assimilated with air pollution. Today this concept is evolving with advancements in many areas. Hence, this concept includes pollution from electromagnetic waves—from different sources to that of vehicle braking systems to animal farming gases and agricultural pesticides, chemical, radioactive, expired medicines, food and biological sources.

Electromagnetic pollution alone is growing exponentially in terms of its sources (e.g., digital and satellite, radio, cellular, electrical wiring and machinery), all of which have been deemed damaging to human health to different degrees based upon different studies.

Being able to confront these opportunities from a different perspective will allow us to undertake very big projects in areas such as earthing and safe insulation of literally thousands of kilometers of electrical grids, for instance. Since human centricity and value become central—industry has all the incentive to produce health and environment conscious products and services

Evolved Agriculture and Food Production

Our current agricultural/food models rely mostly on automation that has taken the human element considerably out of the equation, but it still uses a legacy model in running the rest. It is the same underlying model that man has used for centuries—namely, the exploitation of increasingly larger parcels of land.

Many reports from the UN suggest that the amount of land being used for agricultural purposes has increased exponentially in the last decades, taking away valuable woodlands and rain forest. The public, and a growing number of agriculture concerns and farmers are becoming very sensitive with regards to practices negatively affecting soil quality and its availability.

In the fishing industry, data suggests that natural balances in fish stock renewal capabilities in streams, rivers, lakes, seas, and oceans are being negatively affected at alarming rates (UN Food and Agriculture Organization).

In other areas of the world, vast fish farming techniques are being implemented with varying degrees of success; however, some business entities have become the center of attention due to the type of food they use to feed the fish in captivity (that might produce mad cow-like consequences or pose yet-unknown effects).

Others question the damage to both local ecosystems and the fish themselves in amassing extremely large numbers of the same type of specie in fixed geographical areas for extended periods.

In the animal stock industry, living conditions for some animals are improving in some areas. The vast majority of cattle, sheep, and chickens still are brought up in many areas of the world in extremely stressful and unhealthy conditions that could create health hazards to humans directly via food or indirectly, as carriers for the development of new viral forms that could lead to epidemics.

Recently studies also indicate a growing concern over things such as gas production of large herds and exceptional food consumption requirements that, in some cases, outweigh the benefit they produce.

There is much controversy around GMO's (genetically modified organisms) products and strategies—the development of new alternatives that will address these concerns bringing the potential for better solutions business propositions and returns for all stakeholders could now be a viable possibility.

There are, on the other hand, numerous successful business models (e.g., Israel, Italy, France, Spain) that can testify to many evolved, qualitatively higher capabilities that can provide a baseline for even more improvement in each of the above areas.

Recent evolved concepts and ideas include:

- Protection of the qualities intrinsic with localized denomination of origin and uniqueness of natural characteristics—specific to geographical areas;
- naturally fed, regenerated, and grown;
- next-generation intelligent right-size farming, breeding, and stress reduction solutions;
- next-generation fishing moratoriums; and next generation natural fish farming solutions that do not require physical boundaries;
- next generation agricultural and bio-friendly solutions.

These add value to all stakeholders and, hence, will need to be remunerated. These new strategies are all going in the right direction but need to be developed even further. Through a new perspective we might be able to render currently economically unattractive models finally viable and remunerative whilst adding further development opportunities. Every contemplation potentially produces a myriad of new ideas.

Much more can be done to augment value generation for these sectors, rendering them even more attractive and remunerative.

Natural Disaster Protection and Mitigation

The word "mitigation" is used here because we currently cannot prevent natural disasters from happening, but we might be able to mitigate their effects and improve survivability and possibly reduce damage. The number of projects and the titanic efforts required might need years just to design and start roll out and be continuously updated and maintained—the most providing new opportunities cyclically.

Value and opportunities here are generated by addressing the full spectrum of dynamics and issues that occur prior to, during and after an event.

- In pre-event: the emphasis of value generation could be on things such as advanced warning, protection and mitigation projects.
- During the event the emphasis shifts towards emergency services, activating casualty and damage reduction mechanisms
- In post-event: the emphasis of value generation mutates towards reconstruction of not only individual lives but that of business and infrastructure

Generating value against the effects of cataclysmic or devastating consequences of natural events such as: drastic rainfalls, snowfalls, flashfloods, forest fires, inundations, tsunamis, earthquakes, tornados, hurricanes, soil erosion, massive sand movements etc. means being able to design, undertake, develop, implement and maintain numerous very large projects in just about every country around the world.

Some of these projects are already underway in some countries but face the restrictions posed on them by current models.

Concrete examples could be:

- Environmentally friendly disaster protection systems for:
  o New York
  o Venice
  o Holland
  o Southern Louisiana
- Flash flood mitigation systems in
  o Italy, Bangaladesh, China, Central Europe . . .
  o Urban areas such as Las Vegas and Toronto
  o Along the Mississippi and other major river systems around the world
- Pre, during and Post-earthquake projects in
  o Italy, California, British Columbia, Chile, China, Iran Turkey, Japan, Indonesia, . . .
- Reforestation in Brazil, Australia, the Congo basin, . . .
- Drinking water protection and smart distribution projects in many parts of the world
- Soil erosion and desertification mitigation projects
- Etc.

Life as we know it exists within a well-balanced mix and range of parameters such as temperature, sea water salinity, exposure to ultra-violet rays, breathing gas composition, CO2 and chemical release in ecosystems, rainfall, . . . and earth crust pressures that may start to be effected by century long, oil and gas extractions, etc.; we have enough telltale signs to begin a process of addressing these issues with the benefit of developing many opportunities in terms of business, jobs, investments and value generation.

Research, Development, and Innovation

A plethora of programs and projects need to be revitalized, especially those out in left field—blue-sky projects and beyond the immediate horizon—as they are the ones that will continue creating vital lymph and a virtuous cycle for near-term innovations. In other words, this is not limited to low-hanging next-generation products and services (e.g., the next version of a tablet), but things that today might appear on the outer margins of innovation radar in all sectors.

- advanced technology, aerospace and defense. Many useful programs here have been frozen for the cost consideration
- pharmaceuticals: projects that ended in the valley of death (not enough patients to justify an investment, or those requiring considerable investments)—*going beyond curing the symptoms toward the root causes*
- construction: next-generation concepts, buildings, etc.
- energy and propulsion: *going beyond the hot water or spin paradigm*. We still rely, for the most part, on millennia old legacy concepts such as the production of hot water to generate steam to run a turbine that finally produces energy or other sources to spin a magnet. It is time we sought another axiom to produce energy.

If we looked beyond these legacy boxes, we might find a world that has been hidden from our eyes, just as the vast pools of naturally gushing petroleum pits had no apparent value to our ancestors.

The sun and the moon create enough energy to run most all biological, meteorological, tidal, atmospheric and marine current systems and to some unknown extent influence even geological and natural electro-magnetic systems, of our entire planet yet we are convinced that they (or the energy they generate in nature) cannot growlingly replace fossil fuels(?). Additional areas for example where we can start working with through a different non cost focused perspective are:

- breaking the cold fusion barrier—harnessing power form cold fusion;
- leverage hydrogen based solutions.

- space exploration and exploitation. The potential opportunities here are as vast. Freedom from the cost paradigm could unleash a potential for opportunities truly unfathomable;
- eco and bio system and other natural sciences research;
- advanced studies and investment in actions and systems to protect against unwanted effects of strategic experiments in advanced physics (eg.: un-controlled propagation and chain reactions, mini black holes, etc.), biology, nanotechnology, cyber-science and artificial intelligence, Web awareness and control, etc. Recent data suggests that when the atomic bomb was first detonated, it might have been done without adequate knowledge/proof of the possibilities of an uncontrolled chain reaction that could propagate;
- Development and research in the arts (all sciences and fields of art).
- Address poverty and famine structurally across the globe through systemic programs such as the one's being adopted by various non-government organizations;
- Combat and reduction of diseases across the globe.
- Structural eradication of underdevelopment and poverty;
- Next generation reforestation projects respecting bio-diversity and diversification strategies;
- Massive intelligent, eco-friendly and sustainable, next generation; water management and distribution projects desperately needed in many nations (Israel, Jordan, Egypt, but also places such as Las Vegas and Los Angeles).

Leverage on "Uniqueness" concepts

Have we asked ourselves why we dream of going to places such as Paris, London, Rome, Venice, Madrid, Tokyo, to Egypt? How about Yellowstone National Park, Rio de Janeiro, the Grand Canyon, Crater Lake, Monument Valley, or the Amazon River? Or the Caribbean, Thailand, Mauritius, or the Seychelles? Dive in the Maldives or Sharm el-Sheikh?

It is because they carry uniqueness. They are one-of-a-kind places that naturally attract us. Tourism and adjacent industries are among the many sectors suffering from the effects of reduced economic traction, yet they provide business and investment opportunities and development potential for millions of persons around the world.

Should we choose to think of rendering the places and habitats in which we live, including curing our rainforests, seashores, etc., in sustainable and unique ways [HESD]—just as our ancestors did with a fraction of our capabilities in the past, leaving an incalculable wealth in terms of legacy—we might find tremendous new opportunities in many fields.

Uniqueness is not a concept strictly connected only to the travel sector but it has applications in just about all economic sectors, products and services and even to an evolved financial market. It is all about creating value propositions that generate value in particular ways.

"Web Uniqueness"

Web uniqueness is the positive response to Web inclusivity. The amount of information to be elaborated here is so extensive it will necessarily need to be the focus of a specific paper. Anything that generates Web uniqueness will be able to counter-act the effects of Web inclusivity at least for a determined period of time. There are several ways this can be achieved but for the purposes of this book it important to convey the fact that different business propositions and models are possible.

Health Care and Medicine

Many public and private hospitals and, in general, many in the field of medicine and health care have the opportunity to change their paradigm 180 degrees. The cost vortex should no longer impede going beyond the boxes what is economically viable today.

Evolving the paradigm further—in the unfortunate case of sickness or malady a person (no longer a patient) becomes the focus of greater value to doctors or a hospital (not just sources of income or cost).

The resolution of a malady no matter how rare is value! The efficiency of emergency rooms and availability of adequate levels of staffing, state of the art machinery and beds is value! An environmental ambiance that provides courtesy, privacy and natural settings (beyond todays levels) is value. The doctor to patient ratio and their availability is value. Family support facilities for those who need to watch over their loved ones is value. Finding a diagnosis through a network of expertise without having the individual need to waste years in searching for the right doctor in different geographical areas from the comfort of home or the closest hospital is value. Not prematurely discharging individuals for cost purposes is value. Pristine, clean, sanitized settings and systems (air conditioning, life control, food production and distribution, waste management, rooms, wash rooms, etc.) create value.

Obliviously taking advantage of the system or its abuse produces the nemesis of value.

In advanced research for cures value is derived from shifting the paradigm to finding root causes and focused cures that do not have bad side effects. Rather than curing symptoms—opening also to holistic approaches rather than a predominantly chemical one.

Great strides and advancements have been made in recent decades, but much more can be realistically done. The hospital-doctor-individual rapport must be allowed to evolve to new heights. All of these examples form the premises for areas where value can be generated indefinably and, with them, new sources of revenue streams for this sector, its immediate supply chain and adjacent and/or inter-connectable economic sectors.

Other Examples

The list of opportunities lying ahead of us on the new plateau is immesurable.

Sooner or later, mankind will face the need to seek an alternative place it can call home, be it for economic motives (depletion of or new source of natural resources), to mitigate sociodemographic and sustainability issues, extinction risks, mitigate currently unknown mutations to earths eco-systems or catastrophic natural disasters, or simply space exploration exploitation and even colonization.

There is objectively no feasible way these feats to be achieved through the current model, as it is stratospherically cost prohibitive. The only way to address and accomplish these kind of challenges is through an evolved model.

Evolved financial services and banking, pension funds and investment banking, stock market and commodities markets, media, education and universities, other strategic long-term survivability mega programs and initiatives—these are but a miniscule fraction of the ideas that emerge through this perspective.

Many other examples can be added and elaborated in the aforementioned and many other sectors—airlines, transportation, aerospace, retail, logistics, travel and hospitality, real estate, energy, utilities, etc. but as mentioned this is only an introductory book to a new concept.

Imagine how many more there could be through other perspectives (i.e., yours)!

Only our will, imagination and true value generation might pose the limits.

CONCLUSION

We are at possibly one of the greatest crossroads in the evolution of mankind—at least for our living generations, it is. The evolution is already taking place and will continue to do so as our legacy model becomes less and less usable and responsive to our changing needs. As awareness around the newly forming evolutionary economic model, BEM^{HESD}, increases, momentum will build up the desire to change and evolve.

In finding a solution, we should avoid wasting time focusing and or demonizing the current state of affairs; after all, it is of our own making. Additionally, our current economic model was the fantastic creation of genius minds. In many ways, we owe the living standards we enjoyed till today in part to them.

Many scholars based their findings on the discoveries of those who preceded them, building upon their contributions and harmonizing them to the times in which they lived.

We should welcome constructive disagreement on views, as they will continue providing needed corrections and rebalancing the models from time to time. Who knows how many times we were saved by these corrections that stemmed from conflicting points of view?

Fundamentally, however, we need to come to grips with the brutal facts of the current, prolonged global economic recession. The model of the economy we have in front of us can no longer be objectively managed through the same mechanisms, rules, assumptions, etc.

New paradigm-changing variables are pushing the limits of our existing legacy/hybrid models and have changed our ways of interacting, doing business, and providing for our loved ones. We face the need for an evolved set of baseline assumptions, paradigms, modalities, and approaches to match these new variables if we wish to reap the benefits of the new opportunities.

We have reached a step-level evolutionary moment. On one hand, the complexity of the legacy/hybrid models and their limits impede us in mastering a new model and reaping the opportunities it offers. On the other hand, we are not moving in the right direction because we either fail to see the evolution in action or we wait till someone else starts.

We can, as a generation, decide to postpone inevitable evolution and continue the strife we live in today and masochistically continue paying the consequences or decide to embrace it and benefit from it, letting us to put back faith in the future and provide for the sustainable well-being of ourselves and our future generations.

Systemic dichotomies and structural blocks in our existing models (e.g., public debt, retirement, taxes), Web inclusivity, innovation, and virtualization force us to address a reality that is already here. We must face new challenges with equally evolved concepts.

Should we wish to achieve real economic recovery, open a new chapter, and migrate to a new plateau of long-term development and prosperity, we must be able to embrace and leverage new concepts, ways, and modalities as our forefathers did centuries ago with much less knowledge and capability than we have today and not be afraid to let go of old "sacred monsters," allowing these to finally join their parent reference models in an honorable and well-deserved retirement and remembrance in history books before any additional damage is unnecessarily created through current models.

As one steps back, one starts to form a broader and more evolved perspective, a sense of whole, not only with regard to the myriad of possible new opportunities. One understands now how and why no matter what the most goodwilled policy maker does or might wish to do in total good faith, so long as she or he works within the boundaries of existing economic models and their relative cause-and-effect theories, any remedy legacy or hybrid model might produce, be short-lived, have little or no effects, or worse yet have drastically negative impact on the economy with unknown virulent effects—failing in their positive intent in providing valid answers.

To each person reading these lines, this book was made to reach out to as many as possible, as this is about our lives, families, professions, investments, businesses, life endeavors, dreams, living generations, and posterity—be you living in Los Angeles; Beijing; New York; Shanghai; Paris; London; Munich; Frankfurt; Amsterdam; New Delhi; Mumbai; Rio de Janeiro; San Francisco; New Jersey; Washington, DC; Boston; Mexico City; Vancouver; Seattle; Miami; Orlando; Phoenix; Raleigh, North Carolina; Arlington, Virginia; Austin, Texas; Seattle; Vienna, Virginia; Omaha, Nebraska; Plano, Texas; Scottsdale, Arizona; Irvine, California; Newport, Rhode Island; Lucca, Siena, Urbino, Spoleto, Arezzo, San Giminiano, Portoveseme, Taranto, Milano, Torino, Ancona, Livorno, and Genova in Italy; Marseilles, Lyon, and Grenoble in France; and Cordoba, Alicante, Bilbao, Valencia, Toledo, Granada, and Barcelona in Spain.

To those who live in Auckland, New Zealand; Perth, Melbourne, and Adelaide, Australia; Toronto, Calgary, and Quebec city in Canada; Dubai and Abu Dhabi in the UAE; Kuwait City; Seoul; Dammam; Jeddah; Montreal; Riyadh; Muscat; Saana; Cairo;

Amman; Beirut; Khartoum; Granada; Haiti; Dominican Republic; New Caledonia; Jakarta; Kuala Lumpur; and Singapore.

To those living in Yerevan; Baku; Almaty; Bishkek; Liverpool; Fukuoka; Nagoya; Manchester; Birmingham; Bradford; Jaywick Sands in Essex; Camden, Croydon, and Ealing in the greater London area; Christchurch; Baghdad; Geneva; Basra; Guyana; Islamabad; Tehran; Jerusalem; Isfahan; Tel Aviv; Abadan; Stutgart, Haifa; Zurich; La Paz; Shiraz; Osaka; Bogota; Managua; Odessa, Havana; Salzburg; Yazd; Caracas; Istanbul; Neishapur; Helsinki; Oslo; Asuncion, Reykjavik; Kagoshima; Stockholm; Agadir; Athens; Thessaloniki; Budapest; Prague; Leipzig; Innsbruck; Basel Johannesburg; Strasbourgh; Kiev; Asmara; Addis Ababa; Dar es Salaam; Zanzibar; Kinshasa; Lusaka; Windhoek; Sendai; Smirne; Ankara; Montevideo; Aleppo; Buenos Aires; Santiango; Lima; Zhiuhataneho; El Paso; Houston; San Antonio; Santo Domingo; Tangiers; Rabat; Tahiti; Samoa; Honolulu; Kiribati; Tunis; Casablanca; Marrakesh; Santos; Manila; Moscow; Yalta; Cyprus; Santorini; Kabul; N'Djamena, St. Petersburg, Rome; and those living everywhere else.

Should we wish to proceed, the question that emerges is: how can we, as individuals, do anything?

Whatever the evolutionary path one might wish to choose, the first simple step is up to each one of us; increasing awareness around the possibility of a solution, sharing information and disseminating knowledge among social networks. It starts by asking our policy makers to spearhead and lead evolution toward a higher plateau of civilization—fortunately technology allows us to do this even in ways unthinkable till today even from the comfort of our own home.

Nothing should ever be imposed. The America's, Switzerland's or Sweden's of the world are achieved though the will and dreams of their people.

Whatever evolved model you might prefer, it needs to be shared, evaluated, improved, completed, tested, verified, concurred, accepted and ratified through a democratic process and only then rolled out systemically in phases.

This is one way any model, including this one, can transition safely from being a concept, a notion and a theory towards its successful roll-out and continuous evolution.

Extreme, haphazard approaches produce equally similar results and revolutions only lead to horrendous unjustified fraticide and bloodshed and economic degradations that last many decades.

Peaceful and reasoned democratically led transition and evolution is a much better strategy one with the greatest potential for success.

But any initiative requires a sense of directional movement towards its achievement and this requires a will and an appreciation for the essence of time.

If you think Fonluce's "Virtus Properity Model", holistic or "Value Based Evolutiornary Prosperity Model (BEM^{HESD} or EPM^{HESD})" or any other model of your choosing might help, you may wish to consider to tweet it, text it, mail it, post it, share it with the persons you wish. Those in your neighborhoods or the towns and cities that make up your world. Ultimately though, it might need to be shared with key decision and policy makers.

This is a way you may contribute in making a difference to yourself your family, business, employment, investments, retirement, generation in realizing your endeavours and dreams.

The motion of a single water molecule interacting with another creates a momentum that generates waves in the largest of oceans. The interaction of the smallest particles of matter is what created the big bang, our planet, our solar system and the vast universe that surrounds our miniscule spacecraft we call earth.

It is up to each one of us to decide when and if we might wish to start this process. We have the necessary knowledge and technology required to allow us to reach the next plateau of development, and progress.

Yet, it can't be just about our individual return/benefit. Should it not also be about leaving a testament of ourselves towards our prosperity? How, given one of the most unique challenges our living generations faced; we came through, achieving, potentially the biggest step level ascent in human evolution to date?

Do you wish to be a part of this exceptional opportunity?

The uniqueness of our lives, the people we encounter, this opportunity to be alive—to breathe, to witness, to hear, to sense—and this exceptional chance we have to marvel at the magnificence and wonders of the universe, as humans, are a miracle of a statistically infinitesimal probability. We have the option to turn this occasion into an era of enlightenment, prosperity, fulfillment, and realization.

It's about being able to look in the eyes of our sons, daughters and loved ones and feel we've chipped-in our share, just as our forefathers did before us, leaving a legacy of themselves in a humble recognition for a gift called life.

It is time we brought back hope, optimism, can do attitude, positiveness, resilience, the right to realize dreams, a sense of perspective and relativity, happiness and smiles back in our lives—be you young, middle-aged or young at heart.

Someone once said, "Today is the first day in the rest of your life." Another added, "As your children wake up tomorrow, hand them drawing paper, and whisper to them, today you begin your life. Paint it as you wish and dream it to be."

Today is what we wish it to be. We have the irreplaceable chance to fill the magnificently empty pages we have _each_ been granted in this uniquely valuable moment, and ephemeral mystery called life—our moment in life. It may be that we have reached a unique stage in evolution as a specie, society and civilization. A stage where individuals can begin a process of focusing on what their positive natural, innate abilities, gifts or essence would otherwise indicate them to do in realizing their aspiration, dreams; in generating value all around us; in reaching new levels of awareness, in developing solutions for the less fortunate and protecting life and the natural habitats we have been granted to explore and enjoy; not only resolving the immediate problems we face but also initiate the long search towards new frontiers and places beyond our planet that one day we may call home as it evolves towards new cycles in its sustainability of life.

A new era where economic models, priorities and necessities growingly foster and complement human needs, priorities and requirements in a virtous cycle of developing opportunities, sustainability and protection of our eco-habitats.

A time where a new level of civilization is reached in addressing challenges we face in a holistic way centered around value creation in all domains and assuring prosperity for current and future generations.

Reasonably, we however cannot do this with our current models.

We could decide to continue as is or—decide it is time to move on!

BIBLIOGRAPHY

Bilal, Sanoussi, Isabelle Ramdoo, and Quentin De Roquefeuil. *Economic Policy Papers.* ECDPM, 2011.

Bloomberg. "http://www.bloomberg.com/quote/CCMP:IND/chart." n.d. (accessed July 3, 2012).

Bremmer, I. "State Capitalism and the Crisis." *McKinsey Qarterly*, July 2009.

Carmen M. Reinhart and Kenneth S. Rogoff. *The Forgotten History of Domestic Debt.* NBER, p.41ff:, 17. April 2008, NBER, p.41ff:.

CIA World Fact Book 2011. *www.cia.gov.* n.d. (accessed April 30, 2012).

Colvin, Geoff, CNN Money. "Senior Editor ant large money.cnn.com/2010/07/29/news/international/china_engineering_grads.fortune/index extracted April 27 2012." n.d.

Congressional Oversight Panel. *://cybercemetery.unt.edu/archive/cop/20110401223133/http://cop.senate.gov/reports/library/report-031611-cop.cfm.* March 16, 2011.

Cooper Ramo et al, Joshua. "The Foreign Policy Centre." *http://fpc.org.uk/fsblob/244.pdf.* n.d. (accessed 2012).

David Epstein; Vivek Wadhwa: Duke University. *soc.duke.edu/globalEngineering/pdfs/media/framingEngineering/insedeHigherEd_QualvsQuan.pdf.* n.d. (accessed April 27, 2012).

Ed Brunette ZDnet.com. "zdnet.com/blog/brunette/us-vs-china-vs-indiain engineering 125." Extracted April 27 2012.

Foreign Policy Centre; Joshua Cooper Ramo. n.d.

Frontier Advisory Analysis; The World Bank, IMF, CIA World Fact Book. n.d.

Greer, Thomas H, and et al. *A Brief History of Western Man.* HBJ, n.d.

IHS Janes International News Briefs. "www.janes.com." *www.janes. com.* n.d. (accessed Oct 17, 2012).

IMF—World Economic Outlook Update. "www.imf.org/external/ pubs/ft/weo/2012/update/02." 7 16, 2012.

International Monetary Fund. "www.imf.org." n.d.

Investopedia; Reem Heakal; et al. *www.investopedia.com.* n.d. (accessed Aug 8, 2012).

John Williamson; Peterson Institute for International Economics. *www.iie.com/pubblicaiton/papers/paper.cfm?researchid=486.* n.d. (accessed April 10, 2012).

Maddison, Angus, UN, and The Economist. "http://www.economist. com/blogs/graphicdetail/2012/06/mis-charting-economic-history." *The Economist.* n.d. (accessed 7 3, 2012).

McKenzie, R, Gordon Tullok, and et al. *Modern Political Economy.* Mc Graw-Hill, n.d.

McKenzie. R; Tullok Gordon. *Modern Political Economy.* McGraw-Hill, n.d.

McLamb, Eric. "ecology.com/2011/09/day-seven-billion." n.d. (accessed April 12, 2012).

OECD, Martin Davis, and et al. "www.oecd.org/dev/pgd/45068325." *www.oecd.org.* n.d.

PriceWaterhouseCoopers. "Junior Mine Survey." Feb 2009.

Reinhart, Carmen, and Kenneth S Rogoff. "This time is diferent: Eight Centuries of Financial Folly." *Princeton University Press ISBN 0-691-14216-5,* 2009: 23, 87, 91, 95, 96.

Schiere, Richard, and Alex Rugamba. *Chinese Infrastructure Investments and African Integration.* African Development Bank Group—Working Paper Series n.27—May, 2011.

The Economist—Economist Intelligence Unit. "http://www. economist.com/content/global_debt_clock." n.d. (accessed Feb 18, 2013).

The Economist; Stefan Halper. "The China Model The Beijing Consensus is to keep quiet." n.d.

The Federal Reserve System. "www.federalreserve.gov/monetarypolicy/files/20120717_mprfullreport.pdf." 7 12, 2012.

—. "www.federalreserve.gov/newsevents/files/bernanke-lecture-four-20120329." n.d. (accessed Aug 6, 2012).

The Federal Reseve System. "www.federalreseve.gov/pf/pdf/pf_2.pdf." *www.federalreserve.gov.* n.d. (accessed Aug 7, 2012).

The White House. "www.whitehouse.gov/infographics/us-national-debt." *www.whitehouse.gov.* n.d. (accessed June 20, 2012).

The White House, Macon Philips. *www.whitehouse.gov/infographics/us-national-debt.* n.d. (accessed Aug 7, 2012).

The World Bank DataBank. n.d. (accessed April 30, 2012).

Treasury, US Department of. "www.treasury.gov/about." *www.treasury.gov.* n.d. (accessed October 15, 2012).

UN Department of Economic and Social Affairs Population Division. "www.esa.un.org/undp/wpp/Excel-data/population." n.d. (accessed Sep 14, 2012).

UN University; UNEP. "www.un.org/en/sustainablefuture/pdf/New%20balance%20sheet%20PR%20%20FINAL.pdf." *www.un.org.* n.d.

US CBO. "www.cbo.gov/publication/41486." n.d. (accessed Feb 15, 2013).

US Congressional Budget Office Understanding and Responding to Persistently High Unemployment. "www.cbo.gov/sites/default/files/cbofiles/attachements/02-16-unempployment.pdf." Feb 2012. (accessed Aug 7, 2012).

US Congressional Budget Office. *www.cbo.gov/sites/default/files/cbofiles/ftpdocs/117xx/doc11766/2010_08_05_federaldebt.pdf.* n.d. (accessed May 15, 2012).

US Congressional Budget Office: The Budget and Economic Outlook Fiscal Years 2012 to 2022. "http://www.cbo.gov/sites/default/files/cbofiles/attachments/01-31-2012_Outlook.pdf." *www.cbo.gov.* Jan 2012. (accessed Aug 7, 2012).

US Department of the Treasury. "http://www.treasurydirect.gov." *http://www.treasurydirect.gov.* n.d. (accessed July 3, 2012).

—. *www.treasury.gov/connect/blog/documents/20120719_dfa_final5.pdf.* 07 19, 2012. (accessed 08 02, 2012).

US Department of Treasury website. *www.treasury.gov.* n.d.

US Department of Treasury. "www.treasury.gov/about/history." n.d. (accessed July 8, 2012).

—. "www.treasury.gov/about/history." n.d.

—. "www.treasury.gov/resource-center/data-chart-center/tic/ documents." *www.treasury.gov.* n.d. (accessed feb 15, 2013).

US Department of Treasury; The White House. *http://www.treasury. gov/resource-center/international/g7-g20/Documents/G-20%20 Seoul%20Fact%20Sheet%20-%20Sustainable%20External%20 Imbalances%20and%20Orderly%20Global%20Adjustment.pdf.* n.d. (accessed 8 7, 2012).

US Federal Reserve—Flow of Funds Accounts of tjhe US—Etimate Ownership of Debt Held by Public. n.d. (accessed May 2012).

US Federal Reserve; European Central Bank; US Treasury. n.d.

US GAO. "http://www.gao.gov/assets/310/304648.pdf." *www.gao. gov.* n.d. (accessed Aug 10, 2012).

—. *www.gao.gov/special.pubs/longterm/debt/ownership.html.* n.d. (accessed Feb 15, 2103).

US Government Accountability Office. *www.goa.gov/special.pubs/ longterm/debt/debtbasics.html.* n.d. (accessed Aug 6, 2012).

US Treasury Department. May 12, 2012.

US Treasury Direct. *www.fms.treas.gov/bulletin/b2012_1fd.doc.* n.d. (accessed May 31, 2012).

World Bank. June 2012.

ADDITIONAL BIBLIOGRAPHY, AND RECOMMENDED READING

The following is a very brief list of resources (Web-based or otherwise), a bibliography that can be consulted for a more detailed analysis, additional reading, complementary and alternative views, and continuously updated information:

1. OECD
2. United Nations
3. FAO
4. UNHCR,
5. International Monetary Fund
6. World Bank
7. US Government
8. The White House
9. US Congress
10. US Department of State
11. US Senate
12. US Department of Treasury
13. IRS
14. GAO
15. Federal Reserve System
16. European Central Bank
17. European Union websites
18. CIA World Fact Book
19. International Red Cross websites
20. Dodd-Frank Wall Street Reform and Consumer Protection Act
21. Glass-Stendall Act, Economic Stimulus Act of 2008

22. American Recovery and Reinvestment Act of 2009
23. Emergency Economic Stabilization Act of 2008
24. Troubled Assets Relief Program (TARP)
25. Keynesian Economics
26. Austrian Economics
27. SEC
28. CNN
29. BBC
30. *The Economist*
31. *Harvard Business Review*
32. CNBC
33. Bloomberg
34. Il Sole 24 ore
35. *Wall Street Journal*
36. *The Population Explosion: Causes and Consequences*. Yale New Haven Teachers Institute. Caroline Kinder.
37. World Bank. *Consequences of Rapid Population Growth: An Overview and Assessment* by Geoffrey McNicoll.
38. blogs.worldbank.org
39. oecd.org/dataoecd/34/39/45068325.pdf
40. African Development Bank Group. Working Paper Series. "Chinese Infrastructure Investments and African Integration." May 27, 2011. Richard Schiere and Alex Rugamba.
41. Reuters. "China Woos Caribbean With Offer of $1Billion In Loans by Linda Hutchinson-Jafar." September 13, 2011.
42. "Year 2020, Consequences of Population Growth and Development on Deposition of Oxidized Nitrogen" by James N. Galloway, Hiram Levy II, and Prasad Kasibhatla
43. US Department of Treasury. "Tax Policy General Explanations of the Administration's Fiscal Year 2013: Revenue Proposals."
44. US Federal Reserve System websites and documentation

45. The White House. "G-20: Fact Sheet on Sustainable External Imbalances and Orderly Global Adjustments." November 12, 2010.

46. International Monetary Fund

47. "European Central Bank: The Macroeconomic Effects of Fiscal Policy" by Antonio Afonso and Ricardo Sousa

48. Heyne, P. T., P. J. Boettke, and D. L. Prychitko. (2002). *The Economic Way of Thinking* (10th ed.). Prentice Hall.

49. Larch, M., and J. Nogueira Martins (2009). *Fiscal Policy Making in the European Union: An Assessment of Current Practice and Challenges*. Routledge.

Additional Recommended Rading of Published Works by:

50. Paul Krugman

51. Ben Bernanke

52. Murray Rothbard

53. Warren Buffet

54. David Epstein

55. Vivek Wadhwa

56. Paul Volker

57. Timothy Geithner

58. Mark Zandi

59. Michael Spence

60. Alan Greenspan

61. Nouriel Roubini

62. Joseph Stiglitz

63. Randall Kroszner

64. Bill Mitchell

65. Milton Freidman

66. Anna Schwartz

67. Roger Malcolm

68. Francis Fukuyama

69. Robert Murphy

70. Fareed Zakaria
71. Robert Altman
72. Michael Lewis
73. Warren Mosler
74. David Laidler
75. Randall Wray
76. Richard McKenzie
77. Gordon Tullock
78. Joshua Cooper Ramo
79. Zhao Qizheng
80. John Nesbitt
81. Stefan Halper
82. Joseph Nye

ABOUT THE AUTHOR

Albert B. Fonluce is currently an executive with a global top ten aerospace multinational. His diversified international experience has been acquired in top three consulting firms, Fortune 100 conglomerates, top ten defense corporations, leading investment banking and tier one financial services through twenty seven expatriate assignments and relocations in different continents around the world. He has matured several years of experience providing top level advisory for governments, public and private concerns. He complements his curriculum with an international education that includes an MBA in International Business and the Naval Academy. Well versed in several languages has gained expertise in different functional areas especially in corporate strategy and nurtures passion for economics and international policy and government affairs.

During his lifetime he has experienced several exceptional, life-changing scenarios such as revolutions, disruptive regime changes, and collapse of socio-economic models. He is married and has a son and enjoys travelling, sports and the company of friends and family.

INDEX

286, 294, 300, 345, 372, 384,
387, 407, 416
Money   7, 11, 13, 27, 48, 53, 60,
63, 86, 106-16, 118-19, 123-4,
126, 128, 131, 133, 137,
139-40, 142-5, 164-6, 223-4,
252, 254-5, 377-8, 387-8
Monopoly   11
Murray Rothbard   483

N

Nanomaterial   92-3, 96
Nanotechnology   48, 59, 90-4, 96,
103, 309, 316, 348, 369, 462
Neoclassical   254, 273
Net Real Value   413, 422
Nixon   9, 108, 237, 252-3
Nouriel Roubini   483

O

OECD   200-1, 478, 481
Opportunity   xi, ix, xii, 2, 400, 444
Orderly Global Adjustment   279
organizations' post-cure survivability
ratio   169
Ouroboros   143

P

Paradigm   iii, 7, 27, 29, 31, 35,
42-3, 62, 65-7, 89-90, 100-2,

118-19, 153-4, 254-5, 310-11,
313-15, 320, 330, 339, 347-8,
413, 428-9, 448, 461-2, 465
Paul Volker   483
Pension Funds   38, 118-20, 123,
396-8, 425, 467
Pensions   13, 21, 29, 38, 105,
118-21, 186, 372, 374, 384,
396, 398, 407
Performance and Evolution updates
422
Persians   45, 150
Peterson Institute for International
Economics   277, 478
Plateau   iii, 2, 4, 29-30, 148, 218,
254, 256, 323, 336-9, 350-1,
360, 365, 367-8, 370-3, 390,
392-3, 396, 404, 407, 409,
422, 425, 427-8, 433
Policy   4, 17, 22, 29, 37, 71-3,
105, 111, 113-14, 118, 140-2,
221-2, 249-51, 253-6, 258,
269, 271-2, 276-7, 285-6,
288-90, 294-301, 387, 419,
471-2, 482-3
Pollution   95, 185, 456
Population Growth   3, 266, 268,
309, 446, 482
Prasad Kasibhatla   482
PRC   194, 196-8, 201, 204
Private Contributions   426, 430

U

UN xiii, 49, 101, 192-3, 199-200, 202, 214, 267, 283, 332, 390, 440, 457, 462, 478

Unemployment 3, 13, 52, 88, 144, 154, 189-90, 208, 216, 226, 241-2, 245, 250, 252, 260, 275, 287-91, 297, 301, 309, 345, 385, 431

UNHCR 481

Uniqueness 62, 206, 458, 463-4, 474

US 2, 4, 9-10, 21-2, 24-8, 30, 35, 125-7, 133-5, 160-1, 180-1, 222, 224-5, 227-34, 241-2, 244-6, 252-3, 262, 275, 285-7, 305-7, 359-60, 375-7, 445-7, 469-70

US Congress 233, 242, 246, 479, 481

US Department of Treasury 9, 222, 229, 234, 253, 270, 277, 279, 285, 480-2

US government xiii, 92, 224-5, 229, 233, 241, 253

US Government Accountability Office 92, 224-5, 241, 480

V

Value Balance Concept 412
value balance indexing 421

Value Balance Valuation 413, 422, 427-8

Value Concept 433, 441

Value creation 149, 282, 335, 337, 357, 374, 397, 403, 421, 425-6, 431

Value Excess/ Deficit 421

Value-Generating 418, 444

Value generation 387, 391, 404, 415, 420-2, 425-6, 428, 430-1, 433, 442, 448, 452, 458-9, 467

Value Generation Notices 422

Value roll-over 421

Value year 418

Virtual 8, 47, 50, 60-1, 64, 75, 83, 86, 103, 107-8, 114, 123, 125, 141-4, 213, 216, 253, 256, 316, 342, 344, 356-7, 393, 403-5, 416-17

Virtuality 115

Virtualization Timeline 406

Virtuation 435

Virtus iii, 351, 435, 473

Virtus Proximus 435

Vivek Wadhwa 262-3, 477, 483

W

Wall Street 129, 137, 278, 280, 282, 285-6, 481

Warren Buffet 483

Warren Mosler 484

Washington Consensus 276